汉 语 教 学 名 家 讲 坛

汉语教与学必备：教什么？怎么教？ 简体

（下）怎么篇：组织教学

Chinese Essentials: What and How (Volume Two)

How: Designing Teaching (Simplified Chinese Edition)

傅海燕 著

U0952334

北京语言大学出版社
BEIJING LANGUAGE AND CULTURE UNIVERSITY PRESS

图书在版编目（CIP）数据

汉语教与学必备：教什么？怎么教？下，怎么篇：
组织教学/傅海燕著. –北京：北京语言大学出版社，2007.5（2016.7 重印）
ISBN 978-7-5619-1868-5
Ⅰ.汉…
Ⅱ.傅…
Ⅲ.汉语-对外汉语教学-教学研究
Ⅳ.H195

中国版本图书馆CIP数据核字（2007）第068229号

北美地区售书独家代理：美国希望教育基金会
Executive Agency in North America: Hope Education Foundation
www.hope-edu.org Tel:1-800-341-7983

书　　名：汉语教与学必备：教什么？怎么教？（下）
　　　　　怎么篇：组织教学（简体）
责任印制：陈　辉

出版发行：北京语言大学出版社 BEIJING LANGUAGE AND CULTURE UNIVERSITY PRESS
社　　址：北京市海淀区学院路 15 号　　邮政编码：100083
网　　址：www.blcup.com
电　　话：发行部　(86－10)82303650/3591/3648
　　　　　海外部　(86－10)82303080
　　　　　编辑部　(86－10)82303647
　　　　　读者服务部　(86－10)82303653
　　　　　网上订购电话　(86－10)82303908
　　　　　客户服务信箱　service@blcup.com
印　　刷：北京中科印刷有限公司
经　　销：全国新华书店

版　　次：2007 年 5 月第 1 版　2016 年 7 月第 7 次印刷
开　　本：787 毫米×1092 毫米　1/16　印张：21.25
字　　数：383 千字
书　　号：ISBN 978－7－5619－1868－5/H·07087
　　　　　05200

目 录
Contents

作者
Author

Haiyan Fu has been teaching Chinese to speakers of other languages at postsecondary institutions since 1982 and teaching high school for the last eight years. She is currently teaching all levels of Mandarin Chinese at Northside College Preparatory High School in Chicago. In 2003, she was selected to appear in the Annenburg Foundation production "Teaching Foreign Languages K-12: Putting the Standards to Practice." Fu is a trainer in the U. S. Department of Education's Teacher-to-Teacher Training Corp; a writer for Chicago Public Schools' Project MAJIC, a U. S. Department of Education-funded effort to develop K-12 curricula for Chinese and Japanese; an AP Chinese textbook reviewer for the College Board, and has been president of the Midwest Chinese Teachers Alliance since 2000. In 2006 she was elected as a board member of Chinese Language Association of Secondary-Elementary Schools.

Fu has a Master's Degree in education from Smith College, and an Ed. D. from the University of Massachusetts at Amherst, specializing in second language acquisition, instructional leadership and curriculum development. She is certified in Chinese, English, ESL, Language Arts and Bilingual Education in the State of Illinois.

傅海燕自 1982 年开始在中国及北美大学从事对外汉语教学。1999 年开始在芝加哥高中教授汉语。2003 年傅老师的课堂教学被选入 Annenburg 基金会与美国外语教学协会委托波士顿电视台录制的课堂教学示范系列，作为培训中小学外语教学师资的样板。2004 年加入美国教育部资助的芝加哥公立学校汉语日语教学大纲编写小组。2004 至 2005 年审阅伊州中文教师资格考试框架设计、内容与评分；2005 年开始为全美大学委员会审阅中文教材。自 2000 年起担任美国中西部中文教师联盟主席。2006 年被选为美国教育部教师对教师培训计划的培训员、美国中小学教师协会理事会理事。

1989 年获史密斯学院教育硕士，1996 年获麻州大学教育学院教育博士。主要研究课堂教学教法及课程设计与发展。持有美国伊州初高中的中文、英文、英文为第二外语、双语教学及语言艺术等科目执教证书。

致 谢
Acknowledgements

After 26 years of teaching Chinese to non-Chinese language speakers, I have accumulated some classroom experience that I wish to share with other teachers. However, I would never have thought about writing anything down if it was not for the encouragement and support of the following people.

My husband, Kenneth Kocanda, urged me to take on this project and helped to edit the book. Without his continuous support and countless hours of work, this book would not have been possible.

Several people gave me feedback and suggestions. The contribution of these three friends, colleagues, and partners on many projects was instrumental in this particular book. Their generosity in sharing their experiences and opinions as well as the encouragement to make this book a reality is a testimonial to their friendship and professionalism and will always be cherished.

Dr. Yu, Hongwei translated the segment of Questions and Answers and compiled the List of Measure Words and the Usage of "duo."

Jane Lu contributed to the early idea of this book and cooperated with me to begin this project.

Dr. Yvonne Lau, who has worked with me on many projects, and given me suggestions on styles of writing and discussed concrete examples of classroom practice with me.

Special gratitude goes to Golden Yuan for believing in me and giving me technical support to publish this book.

I dedicate this book to all my students and their parents, especially those who granted me permission to use their work in this book.

Acknowledgement of Permission:

Student Work (1999 to 2006 Northside College Preparatory High School)

前言
Preface

"What" and "How"
"教什么"与"怎么教"

In Chinese we call teaching — "教书," which literally means "teaching book." Traditionally, a language teacher comes to class with a textbook and student workbooks. The teacher teaches according to the book and students learn from their books. This kind of practice would be convenient if there were books fit for all classroom situations. The reality is that in the United States, Chinese as a world language in the K-12 classroom is an emerging, fast-growing and ever-changing phenomenon. Students of Chinese language are a very diverse population with regard to age, grade levels, needs, language backgrounds and learning styles. Instructional conditions vary in terms of class size, contact hours, intensity of instruction and the availability of equipment and materials, etc. Professional development for teacher preparation and training is inadequate. There is no teaching material that is one-size-fits-all. An effective classroom teacher must have an effective teaching practice to cope with these challenges. Many teachers have organized teaching and learning materials based on the needs and characteristics of students with the goal of making classroom practice more practical than just "teaching books." This is a good practice. This is true teaching: 教学 vs. 教书. This kind of practice should not be used out of desperation but out of necessity.

"Teaching"译成中文常常成了"教书"。按照字面的意思译成英文"教书"就成了"teaching book"。传统的教学方式就是老师照本宣科，学生在练习本上做功课。这样的做法本可方便课堂教学，前提是有一本教科书能满足所有课堂教学的需求。在美国，目前汉语在中小学课堂作为外国语教学虽起步不久，但发展迅速。学生的来源及情况十分复杂。学生的年龄、年级、需要、语言文化背景、学习方式方法都不同；班级人数、授课时间、教学强度、教具和教材的装备不一。教师的培训不足。没有一部教材是万金油。要想教得好，就得找出好的教学办法迎刃而上。很多老师早就开始根据学生情况，针对教学的需求，自己组织上课用的材料。这才是对路的教学：是“教学”而不是“教书”。这样的教学不应是出于不得已，而应是必需。

This series is designed to facilitate true teaching. It aims at reflecting and encouraging a break from traditional practice by combining language materials, teaching references, and instructional design into a single series for easy, quick and solid practical use.

编这套书的目的就是要辅助这样的教学。反映并鼓励这种打破传统的教学办法，把教学的素材、教学参考资料和教案设计集中在一起。使教与学的索引，参考、运用简便，省时，实际。

This series endeavors to face two essential questions for a teacher of K-12 world language:

What do I teach in a K-12 world language classroom?

How do I teach in a K-12 world language classroom?

这套书试图面对中小学（幼儿园至12年级）汉语作为外国语教学课堂教学的两个根本问题：教什么？怎么教?

Let's consider these two questions in simple and realistic terms.

我们一起用简单而现实的语言来探讨这两个问题。

"What"
“教什么”

We expect young learners of Chinese to become world citizens and lifelong learners.

作为教师，我们期望我们的学生能成为世界公民和终身学者。

Language is a tool of communication, and thus, we teach learners a new communication tool. We teach interaction and good manners. We teach to develop high proficiency in Chinese.

语言是交际的工具。我们教我们的学生新的交际工具。教他们与人交流和交流的方式方法。教他们发展交际的技能。

Language is part of culture, and represents and reflects the world views and customs held by the people of a culture. Therefore, as language teachers, we teach learners a new perspective on life experience that is different in many ways from their own. We provoke curiosity and nurture respect and love through achieving understanding in another language.

语言是文化不可分割的部分。语言代表并反映不同文化中人们的世界观和风俗习惯。在教语言的同时，我们介绍给我们的学生新的、与他们自己不同的对待人生的看法和角度。我们通过了解另一种语言引发好奇，培养尊重和爱。

Learning a foreign language is something with which most young learners have no experience. In addition to teaching a language, we teach learners how to learn something that is challenging and unfamiliar. We impart knowledge and skills so that at a young age, learners can discover a new world through studying a world language and discover their own strength in learning. We foster diligence and work ethic, and teach them develop knowledge and learning skills.

在课堂上学习外国语是学习一个对大多数幼小学生来说完全陌生的知识领域。我们教给他们怎么学具有挑战性的科目。我们传授知识和方法。让孩子们通过学习一种新的语言去学着探索新的世界，发现自己的能力和长处。我们培养勤奋和上进。我们教他们学会知识及学习方法并锻炼学习能力。

"How"
"怎么教"

A language teacher's job is to make the learning process easy, fun, and to make learning make sense to learners. We try to engage learners in this long-term, effective and fruitful endeavor.

教师的职责是将学习的过程和学习的内容化难为易，做到寓教于乐，使学习触类旁通。通过这样的教学理念与实践让学生致力于长期、有效的努力中。

Making learning easy, making it fun, and making it make sense are correlated. If something does not make sense, then it won't be fun, thus it won't be easy. If something is too hard, then it is not fun. If something is interesting, it must make sense one way or another and because it is fun it will be enjoyable and it won't feel too hard. If it feels easy the learner will be more inclined to continue.

化难为易、寓教于乐、触类旁通是相关的。不懂就没意思，就不会容易；太难就不会有趣；有意思一定是理解了妙趣所在；而有趣使你更投入从而不感到太辛苦。感觉容易就不会因畏惧而退缩。

Make it Easy. Nothing is easy. Learning a language is not an easy endeavor. But this does not mean there is no way to make the learning process easier for learners. Making learning easy by no means implies a lowering of standards. It simply means finding sensible ways to set up learners for success instead of failure.

化难为易。世上无易事。学习一门外国语绝非一件容易的事。但是这并不是说不能找出办法简化学习的过程。化难为易也不是要降低标准。化难为易是找出办法帮助学生成功。

Make it Fun. Making it fun eases the anxiety, sustains interest, and lets learners enjoy the process. It promotes the active participation of learners.

寓教于乐是为了消除紧张，保持学习兴趣，让学生在学习上感到满足与愉快。鼓励学生的积极参与。

Make it Make Sense. Making it understandable makes learning meaningful to learners. It requires the instructor to understand learners. What makes sense and what does not to these learners?

触类旁通指的是学生的理解。一方面，学习的内容要在学生理解程度以内，并能加强学生对目的语言和文化的理解，达到举一反三；另一方面，学生觉得学习的内容有意义，即与他们的生活有联系，学习的内容可以用来表达自己的思想感情。这需要教师了解学生。

Being able to speak in a foreign language is a rewarding experience, especially for a language like Chinese. Regardless of any scientific evidence, most of people have the notion that Chinese is a harder language to learn than most others. So, if a young learner speaks Chinese successfully, the sense of pride and achievement will be tremendous. This enthusiasm can translate into a passion and a motivation for more learning, even for other subject areas.

学会一门外国语是一个有回报的经历，特别是学会说汉语。不管有否科学依据，多数人觉得汉语是种很难学的语言。要是一个小孩子会说汉语，就会感到自豪，会有很大的成就感。这样的热情鼓励学习，不光是汉语还可以派生对其他学科的学习热忱。

How does a teacher achieve the above objectives? The answer is: Know your students, know your subject, and know your methodologies.

教师怎么才能做到"化难为易、寓教于乐、触类旁通"呢？答案是：懂得并了解你的学生，懂得并了解你要教什么，懂得并了解你怎么教。

This series will help you with the latter two areas.

这套书帮助你弄明白这后两项。

Integration of "What" and "How"
"教什么"与"怎么教"的结合

The "What" part of the book provides a series of building blocks. Each block is structured with a topic and connects functional language use with linguistic structures. Grammatical patterns are grouped according to functional use, and vocabulary is ordered by category and topic.

这套书的"什么篇"介绍一系列的集装板块。每一个板块都围绕一个话题将语言材料与语言功用串联在一起。也就是说，语言的语法结构是按语言的功用挑选组装在一起的。词汇是按话题和类别排列的。

The "How" part presents a progression and sequence of teaching and learning for Chinese in grades 6 ~ 12 classrooms. It demonstrates sampled thematic unit and lesson design variables and related instructional strategies, activities, and assessments to provide users with concrete "how" tips for good classroom practices and guides the user to connect "what" and "how." The unit design intends to be pragmatic, yet flexible and helpful to the users. At the same time, it respects the users' choice of methods and texts.

这套书的"怎么篇"建议中小学、主要是6~12年级的汉语课堂教与学的进程和步骤。建议并示范以主题贯连的教学单元、教案设计，包括变量的设计；有关的教学指导建议、课堂活动和测试。并给使用者一些具体的课堂教学的小诀窍。引导使用者把"教什么"和"怎么教"——教学内容和教学方法联系起来。教学单元的设计力求具实用性、灵活性和支持性，同时尊重使用者对教材和教法的选择。

The design comes from this analogy:

这套书的设计来自这样一个比喻：

Building a house is a constructive process. When building a house, we must have basic building materials, such as bricks, a framework, a blueprint, etc. The process is initiated with a purpose, proceeds with a blueprint, and involves an architect and the work, skills, and creativity of builders.

盖一座房子是一个建造过程。盖房子要有基本的建造原料，如砖瓦泥沙等；要搭起架子来，还要有蓝图。这个全过程的展开首先需要一个明确目的，然后要图纸设计，要有建筑设计师和建筑工人的参与，贡献他们的智慧与劳动，他们的技术和创造精神。

In a language class, a teacher facilitates a creative, constructive process for learners engaging the target language. This resembles the process of building a house. The learners are builders. The teacher is an architect. The purpose of the tasks is to build learners' proficiency in the target language; the blueprints are unit designs and lesson plans — a carefully structured road map to success; the bricks are the vocabulary; the frameworks for connecting basic structures are sentence patterns.

在语言课堂上，老师协助学生参与学习目的语这样一个创造性的、建设性的过程。就像盖房子的过程一样。学生是建筑工人，老师是建筑设计师；教学的目的是发展目的语的语言能力和水平；蓝图就是精心设计的教学大纲和教案，建筑材料是词汇及使用知识，框架是语法句型和运用。

However, the construction that takes place in a language classroom requires more when compared to constructing a building. 1) The classroom construction process is a hands-on experience using more experimentation. It is an interactive and on-going process with goals of long-term progress, requiring recycling and spiraling language materials. 2) The teacher is more than an architect. A teacher is a provider, a facilitator, a tutor, a motivator, and a mentor. A teacher must provide the learners with building materials, to help to develop the skills, and to give room and opportunity for the learners' creativity. More importantly, a teacher must demonstrate, model, and nurture love for learning and ways to achieve learning. 3) The learners are special builders. The learners are in different developmental stages in terms of physical, mental, and emotional maturity. They have specific characteristics and needs in terms of cognition, motivation, learning styles, and cultural and linguistic diversity. More importantly, the learners must feel ownership in this constructive process. They are decision-makers and critical thinkers in learning as well as active and creative users of the language. The new language should become a conduit for expressing their true feelings.

然而，课堂中的建设过程比盖房更复杂。1）这个过程不仅需要第一手参与的经历，而且是一个不断尝试的过程；是一个有长远目标的、互动的、进行的过程；需要不断复习、重复，螺旋式上升性地运用语言材料。2）老师不仅仅是一个建筑工程师，还是一个供应师，不断地提供建筑的材料，帮助提高建筑的技巧，并给予机会让学生有创造发展的空间；同时老师还得展示、示范，培养学生对学习的热爱和学习的技能。3）学生是特别的建筑工人。他们处于身、心、情感发育的不同成熟阶段。他们在认知、学习动机、学习风格、语言文化背景方面的特点和需求不一。更重要的是，他们要在学习过程中有主人翁的态度和权益。他们是学习和语言运用的决策人、思考者。目的语将成为他们表达真实情感的又一渠道。

This series is an endeavor to bring "What" and "How" together in an organic way by providing "what" as building materials with basic frameworks and demonstrating "how" as blueprints. It is written with a sincere hope to provide a service to K-12 Chinese language teachers and learners everywhere.

这套书以"什么篇"提供建筑材料和框架，"怎么篇"做蓝图，两部分所反映的教学理念和思路，探索的教学设计和框架，分享的教学经验和技巧，力图将"教什么"和"怎么教"有机地结合起来。这不是一套语法理论的书，也不是一套教学法研究的书。而是为中小学汉语教学课堂提供的具体服务，是中小学汉语作为外国语教与学的参考、辅助与必备。

Fu, Haiyan, Ed. D.

傅海燕

使用说明
Users' Guide

Volume Two concentrates on teaching design. It has two parts.

下册集中讨论教与学的设计。本册两篇。

Part I, Teaching Tips — Best Practices, focuses on practical teaching techniques and provides examples of effective experience in grades 6 ~ 12 middle and high school Chinese classrooms. It presents instructional strategies in question and answer format and demonstrates some learning activities by categories.

上篇：教学小诀窍——好经验。以两种形式介绍6～12年级中学汉语课堂教学行之有效的教学技巧与经验：课堂教学问与答，课堂教学活动案例。

Part II, Thematic Unit Design, provides users with an introduction to the rationales behind the thematic unit designs introduced in this book, a step-by-step unit design template and directions, a list of suggested units and 10 actual unit designs with possible variations. The content of teaching and learning in each unit links to Volume One of this series, *Functional and Grammatical Walk Through*, for easy, quick, and practical guidance.

下篇：主题教学单元的设计。包括主题教学单元的设计原理，教学单元设计步骤、模式与指导意见。并附有主题教学单元系列表，十个主题教学单元的具体设计，每一单元设计均包括三个等级教学的变量建议。每一教学单元的教学内容均与上册《什么篇：语用与语法走廊》的有关章节紧密相连，便于查阅。

Intended Objectives　目标：

- To promote effective teaching and learning by sharing some instructional strategies and techniques applied in the classroom.
- 分享教学课堂策略与技巧以提高教与学的质量。
- To assist curriculum design and lesson planning by providing suggestions, step-by-step instructions and concrete examples.
- 提供具体教学建议、教学步骤和教学实例以辅助课程设计和教学安排。

Format　编排：

Part I　上篇：Teaching Tips — Best Practices　教学小诀窍——好经验

Introduction　简介

20 Questions and Answers on Effective Language Teaching and Learning 有效教学问与答

Suggested Activities and Assignments　对课堂教学活动和作业的建议

Part II　下篇：Thematic Unit Design　主题教学单元的设计

Introduction　简介

Mapping of Themes and Topics　教学单元主题题目规划

List of Suggested Units　教学单元表

Unit Design　教学单元设计

Application　使用：

Users, teachers, administrators, or parents may use this book to become familiar with the general picture of Chinese curriculum and the content of teaching and learning.

教师、教学行政管理人员或家长用这本书可以全面熟悉了解中小学汉语教学教程的覆盖面和系统性。

- Teachers may get quick references and assistance for instructional design and lesson planning.
- 任课教师可以快速查阅对课堂教学及备课有用的资料。
- Teachers may model or employ some of these strategies and techniques to enrich their classrooms.
- 任课教师可以示范和运用书中介绍的教学策略与技巧。
- Teachers may follow the principles advocated in this book and modify the given examples to create their own teaching techniques.
- 任课教师还可以遵照书中介绍的教学理念，按照课堂实际，模仿改变书中介绍的例子，创造出自己的教学手段。

Part I

上篇 Teaching Tips — Best Practices

教学小诀窍

——好经验

Introduction
简介

K-12 Chinese classroom practice presents a great challenge. The challenge has stemmed from different aspects of classroom teaching and learning, from the practice, or rather, the lack of practice of Chinese as a world language in the K-12 curriculum, and most of all, it comes from learners.

中小学（幼儿园至 12 年级 K-12）课堂教学具有十分强的挑战性。挑战来自于课堂教学的多方面；来自中小学汉语教学在整个 K-12 课程设置中的教学实际，或更确切地说是教学实际的匮乏；最重要的是来自教学对象——学生。

K-12 learners in North America are a very diverse group of young people. Young learners have specific learning needs and characteristics. Learning a language is a long and time consuming process. It requires the learners' long term commitment, devotion, and diligence. A teacher's job is to inspire enthusiasm to learn and make the initial enthusiasm last and to create opportunities that allow the growth of all learners individually and together.

中小学学生的学习需求和学习特点很独特，情况不同。而学习语言是一个长期费时的过程。需要学生的长期投入、精力和勤奋。老师的工作是要鼓励学生的学习热情并尽量使之延续；让学生集中精力地学习并保持这样的势头；提供和创造各种机会使每个学生和大家一起学有所成。

How are we going to achieve these goals? This section explores some directions. "How" is the question we ask throughout the book, and "how to" is the answer we search for every step of the way.

如何达到上述目的？本书这部分试图探索途径。“怎么教”是我们在这一部分中从头至尾地不断地发问，而“怎么去做”也是我们一步一步地探索找寻的答案。

Principle：Three “Makes”
教学理念：化难为易、寓教于乐、触类旁通

To make a long story short, we summarize our instructional principles into three “Makes”: Make teaching and learning easy, make it fun, and make it make sense.

我们强调的教学理念是：化难为易、寓教于乐、触类旁通。

Making learning easy, fun, and understandable are correlated. If something does not make sense then it won't be fun, thus it won't be easy. If something is too hard, then it is not fun. If something is interesting, it must make sense one way or another and because it is fun you will enjoy it more and you won't feel that it is too hard.

化难为易、寓教于乐、触类旁通是相关的。不懂就没意思，就不会容易；太难就不会有趣；有意思一定是理解了妙趣所在；而有趣使你更投入，从而不感到太辛苦。

Make it Easy　化难为易

How do we make it easy? Not by lowering standards, not by dismissing high expectations, but by seeking sensible ways to set up learners for success instead of failure.

化难为易并不是要降低标准、放弃期望。化难为易是要寻求明智的途径与办法让学生取得成功的经验。

Make it Fun　寓教于乐

How do we make it fun? Not by fooling round, but by arousing curiosity, flaring up passions, encouraging good work, and creatively promoting the active and creative participation of learners.

寓教于乐不是玩玩闹闹，而是引发好奇心、煽动学习热情、鼓励勤奋的精神、辅助学习技能的发展及调动学习上积极的参与和发挥。

Make it Make Sense　触类旁通

In order to answer "How do we make it make sense?" we need to ask "of what" and "of whose sense?" Making sense is to make meaning, to make both the target language and the classroom instruction understandable and thus, meaningful to learners.

触类旁通的"通"就是懂，就是理解，理解建于"通"，引至更深更高一层的"通"，就是举一反三，融会贯通。这样的理解，强调学生的理解能力是建立于学生的生活经验与学习经验上的理解，是反映学生用目的语表达和创意的理解。

At the root of all these answers are the students — the learners. The three "Makes" are of the learners, to the learners, and for the learners. The three "Makes" should be the beginning objectives as well as the end products of classroom instruction and activities.

化难为易、寓教于乐、触类旁通的精髓是从学生出发，是课堂教学授课和活动的出发点与终结点、目的与产品。

In order to achieve making a Chinese language class easy, fun and understandable, carefully designing a well structured, student-centered and task-based course is the best option.

要使汉语课堂的教与学达到化难为易、寓教于乐、触类旁通，精心设计以学生为中心的、以语用实践为基础的、教学指导明晰、结构严谨的教学不失为一个好的选择。

Student-Centered Learning
以学生为中心的教与学

What is student-centered learning? It is not student-decided learning. It is to keep the student's characteristics and needs in mind and design learning and teaching accordingly.

以学生为中心的教与学并不是学生自主的教学——学生想学什么就学什么。以学生为中心的教与学是从学生的特点和需求出发设计课堂教与学。

Younger learners are individuals. A world language is a tool for communicating with a broader audience. Learning a world language in the classroom develops a tool of self-expression through interaction. In a K-12 Chinese classroom, teaching and learning begins with new expression of oneself by sharing personal information and feelings and building the understanding, appreciation and respect of others, and recognizing one's individual identity and roles within the community: the class, the community at large and of culture of the target language. A teacher's job is to make learning happen: to help young learners achieve comprehension and communication of meaning — their own and others.

中学学生也是独立的学习个体。一门世界他国语言是与更广泛的听众交流的工具。学习一门世界他国语言就是要发展一种能力和水平，是一种用另一个互动自我表达的工具的能力和水平。在 K-12 的课堂上，用新的表达自我的方式的教与学是通过如下方式来取得的：分享个人的情况与情感、建立相互信任、敬佩和尊重他人、承认个人的自我及个人在社区中的位置。这个社区的概念由小及大，从班级至所学的语言和文化。老师的职责是使学习开展起来：帮助年少的学生用自己的理解，通过他们自己之间的交流，在他们自己与别人之间的交流中懂得别人的意思并表达自己的想法。

A popular assumption is that in a Chinese language class, we are teaching the Chinese language and culture, and in order to model the use of Chinese and create an authentic Chinese learning atmosphere, every language material has to be Chinese, in Chinese and of Chinese. I am not against this general belief in practice, but I have reservations in K-12 classroom teaching and learning practice. I strongly believe that the K-12 Chinese language teacher's conviction should be, even though not limited to, to impart knowledge of and about the Chinese language and culture to our learners. Nevertheless, effective execution and delivery goes beyond Chinese language and culture. To make the teaching and learning of Chinese language and culture easy, fun, and sensible to learners demands that Chinese teachers adopt a multicultural and multilingual perspective. They must have knowledge and understanding of the diversity of the class and yield to variations in terms of language materials and teaching methodologies.

一种流行的理念是教中文就是教中国的文化和语言，就要示范中文的用法和创造真实的中文学习的气氛。用的语言素材都要是中国的、中文的和有关中国和中文的。我本人在原则上并不反对这一理念。但就K-12课堂教学具体实践，我有保留的想法。我认为，向我们的学生传授中国的语言文化是中小学的汉语教师的神圣教职之一。但是只靠中国文化和语言并不能有效地达到目的。要想让汉语教与学化难为易、寓教于乐、触类旁通需要教师在语言教材和教学方法的挑选和使用上具有多元文化和多元语言的观点、知识和理解，创造出综合的具包容性的灵活多样的形式和内容。

Classroom practice should reflect this sensitivity to the characteristics and needs of students and emphasize the following:

- Encourage the use of the Chinese language to express oneself and one's feelings through language experiences that are closer and familiar to learners.
- Foster and nurture motivation and active participation in the learning process and the learning community.
- Respect the individuality and diversity of learners, recognize the talent and creativity of individual learners and provide opportunities for individual growth.
- Support the connection and transfer the learning of Chinese language and culture to other areas of study.

课堂教学要反映出对学生特点和需求的敏感并强调如下的方面：

- 鼓励学生用汉语表达自我和情感，这种表达通过学生熟悉的、与学生的生活相关的语言经历来完成。
- 培养和精心爱护学生的学习动力和学生在学习过程中及在学习集体里的积极参与。
- 尊重学生的个性和不同，承认个人的才能和创造性，为个人的发展提供条件。
- 支持学生把中国语言和文化的学习与其他的学科的学习联系起来，并把学习的热情与经验转让和传递到其他的学习中。

Task-Based Learning
以语用实践为基础的教与学

Currently, many foreign language teaching and learning guides or standards, such as the ACTFL recommended Foreign Language National Standards① (www. actfl. org), the College Board's AP (Advance Placement) Chinese Teaching Guides and the AP Chinese Course Description (www. apcentural. org), just to name a few, use performance indicators to rate language proficiency in order to account for teaching and learning.

现在很多外国语教学的指导与标准，如美国外语教学协会（ACTFL）提倡的全美外语教学标准和美国大学董事会推出的 AP 中文教师指导课程说明等，使用表现迹象（performance indicator）来划分语言能力水平的级别。

The main objective of learning a world language is to be able to perform real life communication in the target language. Task-based learning, if designed prop-

---

① 注：*ACTFL Performance Guidelines for K-12 Learners.* Yonkers, NY: The American Council on the Teaching of Foreign Languages, 1998.

erly, supports this goal with strength.

这一做法的基本目标是要推动语言学习的结果向提高在实际生活中运用目的语能力的方向发展。以语用实践为基础的教与学（task-based learning）如运用得当，将有力地支持这一教学目的。

K-12 learners are at developmental stages physically, mentally, and psychologically. Their understanding is based on what they already know and what they are able to comprehend. They understand and learn new concepts and language after repeated instruction and demonstration through concrete examples and practical application. Task-based learning is especially supportive to younger learners.

中小学的学生处于身、心、智的发育期。他们的理解是建于已知和能力基础上的。理解并学习新的概念和语言要经过明确的和反复的指导和示范，要通过具体的范例和实际的练习。以语用实践为基础的教与学对年幼的学生更具有支持性。

The unit designs and sample activities provided in this book aim at embodying task-based learning with emphasis on supporting functional use of language performance through:

- thematic units, projects, and portfolios;
- use of authentic materials; and
- engaging in three modes of communication: interpretational, interpersonal, and presentational.

本书中教学单元涉及列举的教学活动力图通过强调以下的方面使以语用实践为基础的教与学具体化。支持表现具体语言运用的能力：

- 主题贯连的教学单元，综合教学项目，作业集锦的形式；
- 使用真实语言素材为教材；
- 积极参与三方面语言交际活动：人际交流，理解诠释，报告展示。

Structured Learning
教学指导明晰、结构严谨的教与学

We strongly believe, as with learning in general, younger learners look for patterns, guidance, and opportunities to identify themselves.

我们认为，与其他普遍意义上的学习一样，年少的学生找寻规律，依据指导，探求机会自我认同。

The design of the Chinese classroom practice in this book accommodates the characteristics and needs of young K-12 learners with focus on scaffolding learning with progressively designed content and process, providing clearly and systematically structured instructions, and integrating authentic and cumulative assessments for evaluation. The younger the students, the more important this becomes.

这本书中设计的课堂教学兼容中小学年少学生的学习特点和需求，强调通过循序渐进的过程，清晰明确、结构严谨的教学指导及真实和累计的评估来支助汉语的学习。学生的年龄越小，就越需要这样的教学。

Scaffolding learning refers to the following:

- The content of teaching and learning being carefully thought through and being closely related to the cognitive abilities and subject knowledge of the students: moving from simple language tasks to more comprehensive and sophisticated ones, following gradual steps to develop depth, working from general situations to specific situations.
- The teaching and learning process stresses consistent but gradual development of proficiency through constant reviewing, recycling and spiralling of language materials and usages.

支助学习指的是：

- 学习的内容是精心设计的：充分考虑学生的认知能力反映学生的基本知识——语用任务由易入难，由浅入深，从普遍到特殊。
- 教与学习的过程强调依靠不断地复习、重复和螺旋式上升使用语言从而连贯但渐进地发展语言能力。

Clear instructions strike for easy to understand, succinct language, easy to follow step-by-step directions, easy to include detailed requirements, and easy to adapt sample works.

清晰明确、结构严谨的教学指导力争使用简洁易懂的语言，简单易行的、层层递进的指令，容易包罗的细节要求和容易照仿的范例。

Authentic and cumulative assessment provides relatively fair and true evaluation of the performance and progress of learners. It encourages life-like language use and development of proficiency in all areas. It allows creative use of the target language and leaves rooms for different learning styles.

真实和累计的评估为学生的表现和进步提供相对公平和真实的评价，从而鼓励生活化的语言运用和语言能力水平的提高。允许创造性地使用目的语并给出空间有利于发挥不同的学习风格，因人施教。

20 Questions and Answers on Effective Language Teaching and Learning
有效教学问与答

Index of 20 Questions and Answers
问答总表

Question 1：How do I teach pronunciation and tones effectively？
问　　题1：怎么有效地教发音和声调？

Question 2：How do I help learners to remember characters？
问　　题2：怎么帮助学生记忆汉字？

Question 3：How do I conduct dictation effectively？
问　　题3：怎么使听写更有效？

Question 4：How do I teach on the first day？
问　　题4：怎么上好第一堂课？

Question 5：How do I incorporate games into classroom instruction？
问　　题5：怎么在课堂教学中运用游戏？

Question 6：How do I encourage development of learning skills？
问　　题6：怎么鼓励学生提高学习技能？

Question 7：How do I use questions to engage learners？
问　　题7：怎么利用提问让学生积极参与课堂教学？

Question 8：How do I draw audience's attention to individual presentations？
问　　题8：怎么让其他学生注意听个人口头报告讲演？

Question 9：How do I design a productive homework assignment？
问　　题 9：怎么设计高效的家庭作业？

Question 10：How do I teach grammar？
问　　题 10：怎么教语法？

Question 11：How do I help learners to increase their vocabulary？
问　　题 11：怎么帮助学生扩大词汇量？

Question 12：How do I encourage different learning styles？
问　　题 12：怎么鼓励学生发挥不同的学习方式与风格？

Question 13：How do I design a good project？
问　　题 13：怎么设计一个好的综合性的学习项目？

Question 14：How do I teach cultural behaviors？
问　　题 14：怎么教授文化行为？

Question 15：How do I use class time efficiently？
问　　题 15：怎么有效使用课堂教学时间？

Question 16：How do I use songs in language teaching？
问　　题 16：怎么用歌曲教语言？

Question 17：How do I incorporate computer use in the Chinese classroom？
问　　题 17：怎么在汉语课堂教学中综合运用电脑？

Question 18：How do I enhance reading comprehension？
问　　题 18：怎么加深阅读理解？

Question 19：How do I encourage cooperative learning activities？
问　　题 19：怎么鼓励提高集体合作学习活动的质量？

Question 20：How do I encourage and sustain good language behaviors of learners？
问　　题 20：怎么鼓励和保持学生优良的语言行为？

20 Questions and Answers
20 个问与答

These tips come directly from everyday K-12 Chinese language classroom practice. They work for us. Hopefully these tips will provide support to you in some way.

这些教与学的小窍门来自每天中小学课堂的实践，都是课堂教学的经验之谈。希望能抛砖引玉对其他老师有启发。

Question 1: How do I teach pronunciation and tones effectively?
问　题 1：怎么有效地教发音和声调？

Rationale 基本原则：

> Motivate learners by setting them up for success
> Assist new learning by making connections to what is already familiar
> 用成功经验激发更大的学习兴趣
> 用已知带动对不知的学习

Pronunciation is the first thing to teach in a foreign language classroom. It literally and figuratively sets the tone for the whole course. Literally: Chinese is a tonal language. Tones of each word differentiate meaning and are thus important in language use. Figuratively: The first impression is ever the last impression. The first lesson lays the ground for building the classroom culture. How we teach at the beginning impacts greatly the days to follow. It is extremely essential that we begin Chinese teaching and learning with the right tone. The strategies and techniques we use are:

发音是外语教学的第一课，其重要性不言而喻。首先，汉语是一种有声调的语言，声调区别语义。其次，第一节课会决定以后课堂学习环境，所以学好语音声调为汉语课以后的教学“一音定调”，学好语音声调至关重要。以下是几个小技巧：

1. Prioritize it: Phonetic learning will be a main focus throughout the first

phrase of teaching and learning. Phonetics includes sound, tones, and spelling.

- Repeatedly make the learner aware of correct sounds, tones and rules of use during the course of instruction.
- Create various opportunities for learners to listen, pronounce, spell, and use correctly.

1. 强调语音的重要性：语音和声调教学是第一阶段教和学的重点。
   - 老师应强化学生对正确语音、声调和其使用规则的意识。
   - 创造机会让学生听、说和正确使用。

2. Make it real: Teach tones and sounds with real words, meaningful utterances, and tone changes in short sentences.
   - Teach meaningful sounds that relate to daily life, e.g. 饿-hungry, 渴-thirsty. (Aren't these two words essential for physical survival in China?)
   - Select short phrases or sentences that have tone changes, e.g. 我很渴。(I am thirsty.)

Learners will gain some immediate gratification in learning.

2. 强调语音和声调的实际应用：用真词和句子来教语音、声调和声调变化。
   - 用与日常生活相关的词“饿-hungry”“渴-thirsty”来教发音。
   - 用有声调变化的短句“我很渴”教声调变化。

这样会立竿见影。

3. Dramatize it: Emphasize the importance of tones in Chinese language by dramatizing the effects of different tones.

3. 将语音和声调戏剧化：通过将声调戏剧化来强调语音声调的重要性。

4. Get it right the first time and get it right with confidence: Find ways to help students pronounce Chinese sounds and tones correctly by identifying sounds and tones that students are familiar with in their mother tongue and comparing with Chinese sounds and tones. For example, “e” is one of the most difficult vowels for English speakers. Instead of pronouncing it directly, we teach the “ge” sound first while instructing how

to pronounce it properly.

4. 将语音和声调与学生母语联系起来：比如说，“e”对母语是英语的学生来说是很难的，“ge”相对容易发音。教学时可先教此音并告诉学生发音要领，再扩展到“e”。

Question 2: How do I help learners to remember characters?

问　　题 2：怎么帮助学生记忆汉字？

Rationale　基本原则：

Stimulate long term memory by making connections
Reinforce memory by encouraging use of self-reference and imagery
Strengthen memory with constant exposure
Encourage learning by making character learning more interesting
通过触类旁通
通过鼓励学生使用个人参考和想象巩固记忆
通过不断练习加强记忆
通过趣味化教学提高学习积极性

Character writing, if not the most difficult task in learning Chinese, is considered as one of the most difficult. It is an area of teaching and learning that demands constant attention, assistance and motivation. The hardest part is not really the writing itself. It is remembering the writing and holding on to the memory long term that can be frustrating for students. Memory is about making connections. Memory will not to happen effectively in isolation. We usually experience sudden memory of something because we are "reminded of", that is, one memory triggers another. We all know that characters were originally pictographic: the earlier ones were created from images. Most textbooks provide drawings of a few characters to start with. They are helpful, but are far from adequate.

写汉字，若不是最难的，也是学汉语的一个较难的方面。这一方面教学需要精心辅导和鼓励。写并不难，难的是记住字。记忆是将事物联系起来。有效的记忆不可能孤立产生。它通常在提示下产生，一个记忆触发另一个。我们知道汉字最初是象形的。虽然有些教科书开头提供一些字的图画，但往往不足。特别是对年幼的孩子，太抽象的形象常难以理解，对学习汉字适得其反。

For classroom learning, our tips for young learners are:

对青少年，我们使用以下技巧：

1. Make connections: When teaching character writing, besides teaching the stroke order and radicals, try also to provide hints on how to remember the shapes of the characters: take the whole character or dissect it into parts to either compare with other learned characters or some images the learners familiar with. Make the memory more vivid to learners.

1. 不孤立地教汉字：除了笔划、笔顺和偏旁，教汉字时应注重提示学生如何记住字形。我们可以将字分解成不同部分，与其他已学过的字或学生熟悉的形象比较。这样会印象生动。

2. Learner-controlled learning: If we want the characters to make sense to learners, the images had better come from them. Encourage learners to make their own memories "I think this character (or part of a character) looks like this, what is to you?" (Remember student comments and references, and remind them who has said what. This action prompts memory, too.)

2. 学生灵活掌握：如果我们想让学生理解汉字，学生应使用他们自己的图像并通过自己的方式记忆。比如说，某个字或部分字像什么等等。

3. Constant comprehensible exposure: Use learned characters in reading and writing. Post them on the wall, write on the board, use them in reading materials, etc. However, the exposure, though constant, should be just a little beyond the progression of instruction in order to avoid overwhelming and, thus, intimidating the learners.

3. 创造学习环境：在读写中使用已学过的字，并将它们挂在墙上、写在黑板上等等。但是，特别是对初学汉字的学生来说，汉字出现的难度和数量都应有一定的控制，以免不必要地造成学生对汉字学习缺乏自信。

4. Make it fun: It is important to associate character writing with interesting experiences and successful memories. Play games with characters associate writing characters with fun activities. Reward learners who take the initiative to learn characters. Give public praise to those who do homework with more characters, or who have improved in dictation, etc.

4. 寓教于乐：将写汉字与有趣和成功的记忆联系起来。比如，做汉字游戏、创造有趣的写字活动、奖励主动学汉字的学生、表扬使用汉字多或有进步的作业。

5. Use any opportunity to expose students to learned characters and encourage use of characters in different contexts.

5. 利用各种机会让学生接触汉字，鼓励学生尽可能地在各种情况下和不同的上下文中使用汉字。

Question 3: How do I conduct dictation effectively?

问　题3：怎么使听写更有效?

Rationale　基本原则：

Set learners up for success not for failure
Reinforce attention and memory
Give students control in the learning process
建立良好开端
强化注意力和记忆
学生灵活掌握

We conduct dictation almost daily to reinforce memorizing characters. There are several little tricks to make this routine more student-centered and engaging to achieve better results:

我们通过听写来加强汉字记忆。可通过以下技巧使学生主动参与：

- Encourage students to rehearse before the dictation to increase their confidence. Just a couple of minutes work wonders.
- 鼓励学生听写前练习来加强信心，几分钟即可。

- Ask the students what they want to write first, so they feel more involved.
- 让学生决定写什么来加强他们的参与感。

- Always ask for all three elements associated with characters: sound (*pinyin*), meaning (English), and shape (character) so they develop the habit to associate the three aspects as a whole.
- 始终要求学生将声、意和形结合起来并养成这种习惯。

- After dictation, ask the students to check each other's work for mistakes, grade the dictation, and have the grader sign his or her name. The purpose is to reinforce memory of the characters, but it will be done in two ways: when checking another's work for mistakes, the student will have one more chance to look at the characters; and when checking another's work, the student will be more critical. They will look at the characters more carefully and more responsibly. (The teacher must recheck and regrade afterwards.)
- 写完毕后，要学生互相检查错误、打分并签名。这样做的目的是为了加强记忆和责任感。在修改别人作业的时候，学生可以有机会再看一遍刚听写的汉字；同时，在看的过程中他们会更仔细、更负责。(教师应该在学生互改后再次修改和评分。)

Question 4: How do I teach on the first day?
问　题4: 怎么上好第一堂课?

Rationale　基本原则:

Motivation in learning is the key factor in yielding good results in learning
调动积极性是学习的关键

The first day of any class is an important day for a simple reason — the first day of the class sets the tone for the course, especially if it is the first time that the teacher has ever met with the class. This is the showdown situation. It is the beginning of a new relationship and the start of the conquest of unfamiliar knowledge. The learners come to class with uncertainties and anxieties. The first impression is crucial.

第一天的课，尤其是老师第一次和学生见面至关重要。它不仅是师生间关系的开始，也是探索新知识的开始。学生对课程不了解并感到紧张，第一印象非常重要。

A good beginning will lead to a good year. How are we going to do it? A smart teacher will definitely come to class well prepared to achieve two things to assure learners:

一个聪明的老师肯定会事先作好充分准备以达到以下两个目的：

1. Set firm rules and high expectations.
2. Produce immediate results and, thus, gratification.

1. 强调要求和期望。
2. 争取立竿见影的效果。

Setting firm rules and high expectations are the first steps to motivate and engage learners. High expectations give confirmation and encouragement to the students. They demonstrate the teacher's respect for learners, their maturity and their intelligence as well as teacher's confidence in them. Firm rules set boundaries for behavior. They help to maintain class order and give guidance to academic performance. The learners will be given the impression that this is going to be a safe learning environment and they are set up for success, not for failure. They will, in turn, respect the teacher and respect the teacher's authority.

强调要求和期望是激励学生的第一步。高标准是老师对学生的肯定和鼓励，表明了老师对学生、对他们的成熟和才能的尊重和信心。严要求是行为规范，有助于维持课堂秩序并引导学习；学生也会因此得到安定和自信的感觉，会因此更尊重老师和老师的威信。

Another little effort that goes a long way to help to establish classroom culture is the teacher modeling learning by showing interest to remember all the students' names. It demonstrates the teacher's respect for the students, the teacher's willingness for learning new things, and the teacher's enthusiasm in welcoming and including all the students into the new class.

有件事虽小但意义重大：老师应努力尽快记住所有学生的名字。这小小的努力向学生表明老师尊重每个学生、老师示范学习新事物的精神、老师对新学生欢迎的态度。这些都为建立一个新的课堂文化奠定基础。

The second essential step on the first day of class is that successful learning must happen. The learners will find out with first-hand experience, even if it is just a little, that the Chinese language should not intimidate to them. Learners become excited about learning the new language, and gain satisfaction in learning it, and, as a result, look forward to coming back for more.

第一天关键的第二步是争取立竿见影的效果。学生应通过亲身体会感到中文并不可怕。学生也会对学习新语言感到兴奋、满足和期待。

Question 5: How do I incorporate games in classroom instruction?
问　题5：怎么在课堂教学中运用游戏？

Rationale　基本原则：

> Engage learning through intense but entertaining activities
> Stimulate the interest of learners with competition and teamwork
> 通过强化但有趣的活动吸引学生
> 通过竞争与合作激发学生兴趣

Young learners often appreciate playfulness more than adult learners. Games are activities young learners are familiar with in daily life. To integrate games into classroom instruction is certainly a fun way to go. When learners are playing with the language, they learn with enthusiasm and the effort they put into learning is painless. The most effective games that support language learning are the games that:

青少年学生比成人更喜欢游戏。课堂教学中使用游戏当然是一种有趣的方法，学生们有热情并轻松。对学习语言最有效的游戏有以下特点：

- Are most relevant to the content of teaching and learning;
- Mobilize a variety of intelligence and learning styles;

- Involve all four language skills (speaking, listening, reading and writing);
- Are competitive and interactive in nature;
- Interest learners;
- Inspire active participation, especially the equal participation of all learners; and
- Require clear, precise, and short instructions.
- 与教学内容相关；
- 利用学生的智慧；
- 包括听、说、读、写四种技能；
- 有竞争性和互动性；
- 有趣；
- 鼓励学生参与；
- 指令清晰、准确、简短。

Avoid games in language classrooms that have complicated rules, require sophisticated equipment, are too time consuming, do not provide equal opportunity for all players, or are irrelevant to learning.

语言课堂应避免需要烦琐程序和工具、费时和不鼓励人人参与的游戏。

Question 6: How do I encourage development of learning skills?

问　　题6：怎么鼓励学生提高学习技能？

Rationale　基本原则：

Learn how to learn through language learning
Learn how to learn through critical thinking
通过学习语言学习如何学习
通过积极思考学习如何学习

In addition to gaining subject knowledge, young learners are learning how to learn everyday. In a language classroom, not only do we teach new communication mannerisms and tools through teaching the language, we also give them new perspectives and life experiences that are in many ways different from their own. We provoke curiosity, nurture respect and love through achieving understanding and meaning in another language. We should encourage the development of their learning skills according to their cognitive capacity, one step at a time, through language learning and critical thinking.

青少年学生除了主课的学习外每天都在学习如何学习。我们不仅通过教语言教他们如何使用一种新的交流工具和言谈举止，而且向他们展示了一种与他们本身的有很多不同的新生活视角。我们激发学生的好奇心并通过让他们理解另一种语言来培养对他人的尊重和爱心。我们应按照他们的认知能力来鼓励他们逐步学习学习技巧。

Effective learning skills are gained through good learning habits. A teacher should guide learners to foster good habits in learning. Here are a few tips that help young students succeed in learning:

有效的学习技巧是通过好的学习习惯来培养的。所以在课堂教学中，老师应引导学生培养好的学习习惯。以下是几个技巧：

1. Remind students to keep things in good order:
   - Organize study materials.
   - Organize notes.
   - Organize study time.

   (Make it routine or a requirement for students to do so.)

1. 提醒学生做事有条理：
   - 按学习需要整理学习用具。
   - 整理笔记。
   - 安排学习时间。

   (将这些程序化或要求学生这样做。)

2. Ask students to pay attention to details:
   - When getting back homework, pay attention to the teacher's corrections, and try not to make the same mistake twice.
   - Provide opportunities for learners to discover patterns and rules, and define rules through summary.
   - Encourage students to compare points of difference and similarity.
   - Guide students to make connections between new learning, previous learning, and personal experiences.

2. 要求学生注意细节：
   - 要求学生认真对待作业中老师的修改，以免重复相同的错误。
   - 通过总结为学生提供发现规律和规则的机会。
   - 鼓励学生比较语言的相似和不同之处。
   - 引导学生将新知识与已学到知识或自身经历联系起来。

3. Invite students to ask questions about：
   - something they are not sure or clear about，
   - something they are curious about，and
   - something that seems odd to them.

   （You never know，other students may benefit from the answers to your questions.）

3. 鼓励学生对以下问题问为什么：
   - 感到吃不准的问题，
   - 感到好奇的问题，
   - 感到奇怪的问题。

   （你想象不到，其他学生会从对你问题的回答中收获匪浅。）

Question 7：How do I use questions to engage learners?
问　　题 7：怎么利用提问让学生积极参与课堂教学?

Rationale　基本原则：

Engage learners to promote effective learning
保持学生注意力以提高学习效果

Younger learners have shorter attention spans than older learners. In order to assure effective learning，a teacher needs to engage learners. One effective way to call on their attention is by posing questions to them. The type of questions a teacher asks for this purpose must trigger critical thinking. In other words，a teacher provokes critical thinking and comparative learning by asking questions that draw attention，curiosity and help learners to summarize what they learned. We have three little tips on this issue：

青少年较成年学生注意力时间短。为确保学习效果，老师应保持学生注意力。提问是一有效方法。为此而问的问题应激发学生思考，也就是说提适当的、吸引学生注意力的问题可以激发他们的思考能力。以下是三个技巧：

1. Ask open-ended questions from "What? When? Where?" to "Why?" and "How?" to encourage critical thinking. Give hints, provide examples, use humour, and encourage guessing. Lead them to the right answers.
1. 提可随意回答的问题，比如用“什么”“什么时间”“什么地点”“为什么”和“怎么样”一类的问题来激发学生思考。给学生暗示、举例、幽默来鼓励他们思考并得出正确答案。

2. Get everyone involved. Do not confirm the correct answer until several people answer.
2. 让人人参与。等到数人都回答后再给正确答案。

3. Do not forget to reward good answers (not necessarily correct answers) with encouragement and, more importantly, some "bonus points." Positive reinforcement brings more active participation.
3. 奖励好答案。好答案不一定是对的，给好答案鼓励或加分可以让学生更积极地参与。

Question 8: How do I draw audience's attention to individual presentations?
问　题 8：怎么让其他学生注意听个人口头报告讲演？

Rationale　基本原则：

Encourage other learners to actively participate in presentations
Expand learning opportunities
鼓励学生积极参与他人的口头报告讲演
增加学习机会

Individual classroom presentation is usually an indispensable part of a task-based project. Individual presenters use the occasion to brush up on their presentational mode of communication. Moreover, the audience has an opportunity to improve listening comprehension. In order to achieve the best result, the audience must take an active role in the process. Here are two suggestions to encourage active audience participation:

课堂个人口头报告讲演是以实践活动为本的语言运用综合项目。报告讲演者由此提高讲演技巧，观众可提高听力。观众必须积极参与才能达到最好的效果。以下是如何保证观众积极参与的技巧：

1. Make audience participants more than just recipients of the presentation:
   - The presenter raises three questions related to the content of the presentation before presenting, and checks the audiences' answers. This requires close attention to details.

1. 让观众参与而不是只做听众：
   - 报告讲演前给观众提三个相关问题并与观众核对答案。要注意细节。

2. Make audience become graders rather than listeners:
   - The audience grades each presentation according to rubrics.
   - The grade sheets are collected at the end. Make sure graders sign their names. Obligation demands a sense of responsibility.

2. 让观众打分而不是只做听众：
   - 观众按评分标准给每一个报告讲演打分。
   - 书面评分要收上来。因为义务意味责任，确保打分人签名。

Question 9: How do I design a productive homework assignment?
问　题 9：怎么设计高效的家庭作业？

Rationales　基本原则：

Reinforce learning through follow-up work
Scaffold learning with progression and consistency
High expectations yield good performance
通过各种活动巩固所学内容
为学习内容持续渐进提供辅助
高期望促进产生优质表现

Homework assignments for younger learners give the value of sustaining classroom learning, especially for 6 ~ 12 graders. However, for this age group, the complication is that students take at least 6 ~ 7 courses a week, plus many extra-curricular activities. The language class assignment happens to be one among the millions of things they do. In order to give assignments that are more productive, we prefer meaningful work to busy work. Our ideas of designing meaningful work are:

青少年的，尤其是6 ~ 12 年级学生的家庭作业有巩固课堂学习的作用。但是，这一年龄组的学生每周至少有6 ~ 7 门课，外加其他课外活动。外语作业只是他们万件要做的事情中的一件。作业要精而不是多才会更有效。我们认为：

- Scaffold new learning with older materials.
- Support development of proficiency through activities involving multiple skills.
- Deliver instructions one step at a time.
- Reinforce learning with pre-activity for warm up, activity to engage, and post-activity to follow-up.
- 可用旧材料（学过的语言材料）来教新内容。
- 通过发挥多种技能的活动来巩固提高语言能力教学。
- 要循序渐进。
- 通过预先准备，吸引学生和补充练习来加强学习效果。

When giving assignments:
- Make work meaningful by leaving room for creativity.
- Allow and encourage work beyond the required minimum.

布置作业时应注意：
- 允许学生发挥。
- 允许并鼓励额外作业。

The homework assignment framework　家庭作业的框架

Content　内容

1. The homework assignment should include development of all four skills: Listening, Speaking, Reading, and Writing.
1. 家庭作业应含括听、说、读、写四种技能。

2. Homework should be a task-based activity: Create something meaningful.
2. 家庭作业应有的放矢：应有针对性。

Procedure　程序

1. Homework should cover content that has already been practiced during class and should be an extension of classwork.
1. 家庭作业应与课堂教学联系，作为课堂教学的延伸。

2. Homework assignments should give minimum requirements but expect maximum effort.
2. 家庭作业应注重所含内容而不是数量。

3. Give clear instructions.
3. 家庭作业应要求清楚。

4. Provide samples.
4. 家庭作业应有范例。

Most importantly: As a routine, ask students to repeat what their homework assignments are, and record the specific requirements and due dates in their agenda books. Otherwise, there will always be excuses for incomplete work.

可能最重要的是：至少让学生重复两遍所布置作业的内容和具体的要求，并让每个学生记录，写在自己的日程安排表上。不然总会有学生不完成或没按要求完成作业。

Question 10: How do I teach grammar?
问　　题 10：怎么教语法？

Rationale　基本原则：

Human brains constantly look for patterns
Grammatical patterns are related to functional language use
人的大脑不断地寻找规律
语法规律应与语言使用联系起来

Do we teach grammar? To answer this question, first, we need to define what grammar is in K-12 classroom practice, how much and to whom should it be taught, and more importantly, how it should be taught.

在中小学的汉语课堂教学中，我们教不教语法？要回答这个问题首先要给“语法”定义：要明确我们教什么？对多大的学生教？怎么教？

We don't teach grammatical jargon to students. We do teach sentence patterns, related functions and usage of patterns.

在中小学的课堂上，我们基本不教抽象的语法术语和理论。我们所涉及的语法概念是句型、句型的语用功能和使用。

We would not teach grammar to elementary school learners. But high school students do learn English grammar in their English classes. Many students have experience learning other foreign languages. If a teacher wants to take advantage of conscious learning to make connections and comparisons to the dominant language or other foreign language experience of high school students, why not?

对小学生，我们基本不教语法。而对中学生，我们可以介绍常用的语法知识，即句型及使用。很多中学生都有学习外语的经验。教师可以充分利用这一点，通过和他们的母语或所学外语进行联系和比较来教授语法。

Grammatical structures are frameworks for functional language use. Linguistic knowledge is part of proficiency. Grammatical patterns should not be the starting point or the focal point of teaching but should be identified to assist and expand functional use of the language.

语法结构是语言应用的框架。语言知识是精通语言的一部分。句型结构和语法规则不应是教学的起点或重点，但对辅助和促进语言使用有很大作用。

During classroom instruction, we point out grammatical structures for functional use and through functional use. We also help students to summarize grammatical structures for and through comparative study. We also purposely select and group necessary grammatical structure to help students to develop functional coherent discourses. When teaching visual images (characters), concepts and sentence structures alike, teach most effectively by creating contexts that are meaningful to learners. Offer constant opportunity for learners to discover patterns of language and in language use (you design it, but make it seem incidental.) In these cases, the teacher does not have to explain much about grammar. But is it being taught? Yes.

句型结构应以语用为目的，为组织语言搭架子，通过语言应用和比较来教。因此，应在教学中创造语言环境和机会，让学生发现语言规律和如何应用。在这种情况下，老师不必过多地解释语法，但的确是在教语法。

Question 11: How do I help learners to increase their vocabulary?
问　　题 11: 怎么帮助学生扩大词汇量?

Rationale　基本原则:

Learning through understanding
Learning through use
通过理解学习
通过使用学习

One way to develop their language proficiency is to help learners to enlarge Chinese vocabulary. We suggest three ways that we use in our classes:

- Take advantage of lexical characteristics
- Give choices
- Encourage correct use in context

帮助学生扩大词汇是扩大他们语言技能的一种方法。有三种方法可用:

- 利用词汇特点
- 给予多种选择
- 鼓励不同环境中语言的正确使用

1. Take advantage of lexical characteristics　利用词汇特点以扩大词汇量

For example, many Chinese phrases are interpretive. Words derive from other words. This kind of expansion of vocabulary is effortless. Don't avoid it.

许多中文词通过组合形成新的词，这种词语扩展的方式简单明了，可多加以介绍。

Verb to Noun　动词变为名词：

学：

大学　大学生

中学　中学生

小学　小学生

Verb to Adjective　动词变为形容词：

看：好看，不好看，难看

听：好听，不好听，难听

2. Give choices　给予多种选择以扩大词汇量

K-12 learners don't always like to repeat what other people are saying. Give them choices. Give them a list of vocabulary, let them select as many as they want to learn and use.

中小学学生不喜欢重复别人。要允许他们选择，可以给他们一些词并让他们选择。

There are only minimum requirements, never maximum limits in language use. Students remember more solidly what they want to learn and ask for more when learning successfully.

只有最低要求，没有最高要求。学生们只有在愿意学习的时候才会记得牢固，在有成就感的时候才会要求学习更多。

3. Encourage correct use in context　鼓励不同环境中语言的正确使用以扩大词汇量

Encourage correct use in context by providing situations and language tasks in order to make leaning and vocabulary use meaningful. Encourage the use of words to express their personal feelings and stories. Connect teaching to their real-life situations. Through personal functional use, the words lead to their own self-expression.

通过提供情景和任务鼓励不同环境中语言的正确使用。鼓励学生将语言学习与他们的实际生活联系起来，表达个人情感、叙述故事。学生通过个人语言使用把语言变成自己的东西。

Question 12: How do I encourage different learning styles?
问　　题 12：怎么鼓励学生发挥不同的学习方式与风格？

Rationale 基本原则：

Different learners have different learning styles
Effective learning occurs in different ways
学生有不同的学习方式
不同学习方式将使学习更有效

First, a teacher needs to recognize the different learning styles of individual students. Second, create opportunities for learning differently. Third, give encouragement with positive reinforcement. It is just that simple!

第一，一个教师首先应接受学生的不同学习方式②。第二，为不同学习方式创造机会。第三，正面鼓励。

Once, we gave an assignment: Write Characters with Images. The students were asked to self-select six verbal phrases they really wanted to remember, draw pictures of them and write characters next to the pictures.

比如，有一次给学生机会选择六个动词词组来写汉字的作业。学生可选择他们要记住的词并先给字配画然后给画配字。

---

② For more details on different learning styles, please see Silver, Strong, & Perini. *So Each May Learn*. Alexandria, VA: Association for Supervision and Curriculum Development, 2000.

有关不同学习风格的论述，请参阅 Silver, Strong, & Perini. *So Each May Learn*. Alexandria, VA: Association for Supervision and Curriculum Development, 2000.

The assignment came back with four different kinds of artwork:

- Abstract graphics
- Computer generated art
- Self-created drawings
- Drawings of images resembling the shapes of the characters

学生们在作业里使用了四种艺术形式:

- 抽象图案
- 电脑图画
- 个人作画
- 据字形而设计的图画

When learners are given choices in learning and they have more control of the learning process and the content. They feel more comfortable and have more confidence in learning, and they perform with more enthusiasm and creativity, making them learn better.

学生有机会选择适合自己的学习风格时，对学习内容和过程就更有把握，由此产生良好的感觉和建立起信心，继而发挥主动性和创造性。

Question 13: How do I design a good project?

问　题 13: 怎么设计一个好的综合性的学习项目?

Rationale　基本原则:

> **Make learning meaningful and purposeful and therefore, more real**
> **Scaffold learning with progression, modeling, and clear instruction**
> 通过有意义、有目的的活动让学习有真实性
> 通过循序渐进、示范和有组织的教学让学生学习如何学习

Project-based learning is a form of comprehensive learning. It is effective for engaging in all three modes of communication.

综合性的学习项目对三种交流方式都有效。

A good project must bear the following characteristics:

1. It is task oriented to provide meaningful and purposeful language use.

2. It is flexible in topic and uses a variety of formats to allow choices, room for creativity and different learning styles.
3. The learning process progresses to achieve cumulative results.
4. It has clear requirements.
5. It has writing samples.
6. It has rubrics.

它有以下特点：

1. 有意义并目的明确。
2. 课题灵活并形式多样，便于学生选择和发挥。
3. 循序渐进。
4. 要求明确。
5. 要有范例 。
6. 要有评估标准 。

This is to say a task-based project should be developed around a real life situation. It usually has a communicative purpose. It requires use of language to gather information and present information. It can be used at the beginning levels of learning the target language.

例子和评估标准清晰，也就是说综合性的学习项目围绕现实生活并有交流的目的。这种活动需要通过使用语言来搜集和提供信息。

The product of a task-based project can be an artistic display such as a picture book, journal, a display board, a power point presentation, a video, a performance, etc. to accommodate different learning styles.

综合性的学习项目可包括艺术展示，比如画册、日记、板报、电脑投影展示 、录像、表演等等，以适应不同学习风格。

A project is a process. The language learned and the proficiency of language use is developed during a period of time and step by step. New learning is generated from the need to perform newer tasks and expands upon reviewing, recycling and spiraling of previously learned language material. A task-based project for young learners must be clearly structured. Basic instructions consist of:

- Be clear about the topic and format.
- Lay out detailed content, specifics on sentence patterns, vocabulary, and other required elements.
- Provide examples of writing presentation and rubrics.

年龄小的学生使用此种方法必须步骤明了，包括：

- 明确话题和形式。
- 规定内容、句型、词汇及其他必要成分的使用。
- 提供范文、评估标准等。

Question 14: How do I teach cultural behaviors?

问　题 14：怎么教授文化行为?

Rationale　基本原则：

Modeling
Respect cultural differences
老师以身作则
尊重文化间差异

In a Chinese language classroom, we teach the culture as well as the language. There are many things we cover in our lesson plans. One of the most effective ways of teaching cultural behaviors is through teacher modeling. If we think about it carefully, we are not trying to make our learners into Chinese persons. Our goal in teaching the Chinese culture or introducing cultural behaviors is to impart knowledge and foster the appreciation and understanding of the Chinese language and culture. In order to do so, we, as teachers, must first demonstrate through our own behaviors our acceptance, appreciation, and understanding of all cultures and languages to say the least. We must be the role model of what we advocate.

课堂上我们既教语言，也教文化。教学内容也很广。其中一种有效的教文化行为方法是老师身教。我们并不想将学生变成中国人。我们教中国文化的目的是传授知识，培养学生对中国语言和文化的修养和理解。为此，老师应首先通过自身的行为，接受、欣赏、理解其他文化和语言，来以身作则。

Chinese teachers, especially those who are originally from Chinese speaking areas and are not very familiar with K-12 classroom cultures in the U. S. , need to be aware of the following. Some behaviors are classroom management taboos. Here are a few important tips:

中文老师，特别是来自对美国中小学文化不了解的地区的老师，应了解课堂管理的禁忌。应注意以下几点：

Some Chinese Classroom "Dos and Don'ts"

中文课堂中的一些行为准则

- Do respect learners regardless of their age, gender, race, religion, socio-economical status, physical ability, and sexual orientation.
- 尊重任何年龄、性别、种族、宗教、社会及经济背景、身体状况和性取向的学生。
- Do be fair and constructive with your comments to students.
- 对学生评论公正并有建设性。
- Invite students to talk or to participate with the whole or open hand "invitation" gesture. Do not use a finger to point at a student when referring to a student or asking a student to answer a question.
- 要学生参与时，使用手势邀请学生，而不是用手指学生。
- Never humiliate or make fun of a student.
- 不要羞辱或嘲笑学生。
- Do not physically touch a student.
- 不要与学生有身体接触。
- Do not show your concern for a student's appearance by making personal remarks. High school students would not appreciate it.
- 不要对学生外表作个人评论，中学生不欢迎这种做法。
- Do not try to be a friend or a parental figure to students.
- 不要试图扮演学生的朋友或父母角色。

Question 15: How do I use class time efficiently?

问　　题 15：怎么有效使用课堂教学时间？

Rationale　基本原则：

Order in class produces efficiency
Engaged learning guarantees effective learning
课堂秩序保证效率
学生注意力保证效果

Classroom instructional time is precious. It is a challenge encouraging learners to be on task all the time. One effective way is to set a routine for repeated classroom activity. Once a class activity becomes a routine, it saves time repeating directions.

课堂教学时间宝贵，让学生跟上教学有一定的挑战性。一种行之有效的方法是将课堂活动程序化，一个课堂活动一旦成为规律就会节省时间。

For example, our class has three routine activities for dictation:

1. Dictation is always the first activity of the day.
2. Practice on the board is allowed for about two minutes before the actual test.
3. Student's name and date in Chinese characters is included on the test.

Once students understand these expectations and are used to the routines, they will go to the board to practise as soon as they walk into the classroom, and they automatically write their names and the date without further reminder or instruction.

比如，我们的课堂听写有三个固定的活动：

1. 听写总是课堂第一个活动。
2. 听写前在黑板上练习两分钟 。
3. 姓名和日期要求用中文写。

学生们一旦了解老师要求并习惯了规律，他们将会主动去做。

Setting up routines is crucial for young K-12 learners, especially for beginning language classes. The earlier that learning habits are established, the more ordered the class will become, and the available time will be used more efficiently.

对中小学学生来说，养成习惯很重要。习惯养成得越早，课堂就会越有秩序，时间也就会利用得越有效。

Question 16: How do I use songs in language teaching?
问　　题 16：怎么用歌曲教语言？

Rationale　基本原则：

Learning through music promotes interests in learning
Songs are vocal expressions of language
通过音乐学习有助于提高学习兴趣
音乐是语言的声乐表现形式

We have been asked repeatedly by other teachers: Do you use songs in teaching? How do you do it? The answer is yes, but with some considerations.

经常有老师问是否在教学中使用歌曲，怎么教。答案是肯定的，但要慎重考虑。

Among young learners, many like to sing. Teaching songs in the target language definitely has the benefit of promoting interest in learning the language and the culture. Also when singing, language is used with music, and words are voiced with rhythms and tones. Music helps to interpret meanings and emotions expressed by the song. It is a fun way of learning the language. Nevertheless, Chinese is a tonal language. Often the tones of words in Chinese songs become unrecognizable when sung. We would not recommend teaching listening comprehension using songs. For beginning learners, we would suggest that nursery rhymes or rhythms and poems be sung or read aloud as songs. Use Chinese songs with previously learned words. Do some pre-singing activities, such as explaining the emotions or ideas in the song, or learn the words before singing to achieve better results.

许多年少学生喜欢唱歌。学歌可提高学习语言和文化的兴趣。唱歌时，语言通过韵律和声调表示出来。音乐有助于释义和表达情感，是一种学习语言的有趣的方法。但是，中文是一种声调语言。许多情况下，词的声调在歌中不易辨别，使用歌曲教听力不合适。对初学者，用儿歌、韵文或诗歌代替歌曲更合适。选择有学生学过的词的歌曲，或预先作一些准备活动，比如解释歌中意义和情感或先学歌词等。

Question 17: How do I incorporate computer use in the Chinese classroom?
问　　题 17: 怎么在汉语课堂教学中综合运用电脑?

Rationale　基本原则:

Learning through multiple intelligence
Learning through use of technology
调动多种智能参与学习过程
运用科学技术学习

Computer use in a language classroom has advantages and disadvantages. One of the worst disadvantages is that it can be a distraction: if the class has too many students, like our current Chinese II class, which has 36 students, some students may not be on task while sitting in front of a computer — the temptation of online surfing is too big. It is hard to supervise. Moreover, not all computer facilities have mechanisms that block sites unsuitable for young learners. Also, some educators argue that typing on a computer weakens the skill of hand writing characters. Still, there are many ways to effectively incorporate computer use in Chinese language classroom. Here are some positive uses of Chinese computing:

语言课堂使用计算机有利也有弊。其中一弊是分散学生注意力，尤其是学生人数过多时更是如此。上网比做功课更有诱惑力，所以很难管理。还有人认为用计算机打字不利于手书汉字。尽管如此，有许多方法在语言课堂里使用计算机：

- Enhance phonetics and spelling: Since most Chinese word processors use phonetic input methods, learners can use a Chinese processor as soon as they know a phonetic system.
- Practise listening comprehension: Ask students to type dictated words. They learn words through listening comprehension. Authentic listening materials can be found online for class use.
- Help identify characters: When students write with a Chinese word processor, they need to continually check if the typed characters are correct.
- Create texts: Using a Chinese word processor makes writing easier.

Students can use a Chinese word processor to write, revise and edit. They can also create power point presentations with Chinese texts. Their work can be permanently saved.

- Research and use authentic materials online.
- Since the trend of language tests is to use computer technology for all areas of learning, the earlier the learners are trained on computers, the more skilled they will become.
- 加强语音拼写：许多中文处理软件使用拼音输入，学生学了拼音后即可使用中文处理软件。
- 协助听力练习：老师说时让学生写。网上也有许多听力材料可用。
- 帮助认字：学生用中文打字时需不断检查汉字输入得是否正确。
- 写作：用电脑写作容易。学生可随时修改、编辑并可存档。
- 网上收集信息和材料。
- 语言测试趋向于使用电脑技术、学生越早训练，就越熟练。

To avoid the above mentioned drawbacks, do two things in class:

- In order to keep students on the intended task, limit the time available for each computing or word-processing task, and demand specific results.
- In order to encourage writing and memorizing characters through handwriting, make dictation of characters, phrases and sentences a daily assessment, and require handwritten drafts for essays.

Another tip for using computers correctly is that a teacher must emphasize the ethical issues related to computer use. Students must learn to cite sources properly and have the habit to do so when researching information online.

有两种做法可以避免前面提过的问题：

- 规定时间和要求，以保证学生**集中精力**于课堂活动。
- 听写或文章要求手写或手稿，以保证学生通过书写记汉字。

另外，强调正确使用电脑及网上信息的相关原则与事宜，如引用他人资料要作脚注等。

Question 18: How do I enhance reading comprehension?

问　　题 18：怎么加深阅读理解？

Rationale　基本原则：

Reading is a meaning creating process
阅读过程是创造语义的过程

Chinese characters are always a headache for learners because they are most challenging. But a teacher should explain that students do not need to know every character to begin reading. Contextual clues and common knowledge about the subject matter will help readers to achieve comprehension of the main ideas of the text.

汉字学习是学生的难点，最具挑战性。但是老师应让学生知道阅读理解并不需要认识所有的汉字。对一篇文章背景知识的了解，加上上下文的提示，能帮助读者对文章的大意、梗概作出大致的猜测和判断。

The key here is to practise guessing and creating meaning in context. In a classroom teaching and learning situation, the class may concentrate on pre-reading, reading, and deep reading, and after-reading processes③ to develop reading strategies and vocabularies. In a situation without any instructor or references, reading comprehension can still be practiced. Students should be given reading tasks with increasing difficulty on various topics to explore the guessing game themselves. Of course, the use of in-class reading activities and texts with increasing difficulty is a means to scaffold the development of reading comprehension.

关键是练习据上下文猜测意思。在课堂教学中，全班可以做阅读前活动、阅读和深入阅读活动和阅后活动等系列的阅读技巧训练。加强对阅读的策略和词汇的学习。课外，在没有老师和参考资料的情况下也可以练习阅读理解。学生应该常用不断加深难度、不同题目的阅读材料练习猜测语义，提高阅读能力。

---

③ For more details and references on reading, see Yu-Lan Lin's *Reading and Writing Analytically*. US Department of Education — Teacher to Teacher Initiative Workshops on Chinese Language Teaching. (2006). Retrieved from http：//www. t2tweb. us/Workshops/Sessions. asp

有关阅读理论和教法，请参阅林游兰，*Reading and Writing Analytically*. US Department of Education — Teacher to Teacher Initiative Workshops on Chinese Language Teaching. (2006). Retrieved from http：//www. t2tweb. us/Workshops/Sessions. asp

What is equally important is to reinforce reading through writing. Use reading materials as examples for writing at the same time. Use writing to review and expand the use of vocabulary and sentence structures. This will enhance future reading comprehension.

阅后写作可以帮助提高阅读能力。用阅读材料当写作范文，同时通过写作复习延伸扩展对词汇和句型的学习，提高阅读理解能力。

Question 19: How do I encourage cooperative learning activities?
问　　题 19：怎么鼓励提高集体合作学习活动的质量？

Rationale　基本原则：

Student-centered learning that requires learners take control of learning
Cooperative learning requires sharing responsibilities and sharing learning
以学生为中心，最大限度地调动学生的主动性
集体合作学习活动是分享责任、共同提高

6 ~ 12 grade learners are not strangers to cooperative learning. In English, they do peer-editing, and in social studies they have group projects, etc. It can be argued that foreign language classes need interpersonal communication more than other subject areas. Cooperative learning activities are beneficial to language learning. However, a cooperative learning activity must include the following rules to guarantee its effectiveness④.

6 ~ 12 年级的学生对集体合作学习活动不陌生。在英文课上、社会学课上，甚至数学课上都有小组学习活动。外语课更是经常进行人际交流活动。集体合作学习活动对学语言更有效。当然，为了保证集体合作学习活动的效率，有几条规定要遵守：

---

④ For more details, please see Silver, Strong, & Perini. *So Each May Learn.* Alexandria, VA: Association for Supervision and Curriculum Development, 2000.

请参阅 Silver, Strong, & Perini. *So Each May Learn.* Alexandria, VA: Association for Supervision and Curriculum Development, 2000.

1. Work with a purpose:
   - The cooperative learning activity needs to have a purpose, such as performing some real-life tasks to make it meaningful.

1. 活动要有目的性：
   - 与真实生活类似的活动具有意义。

2. Provide clear instructions:
   - The activity needs to have a schedule, a time limit, a defined procedure, and step-by-step instructions.

2. 活动要有明晰的指令：
   - 活动的时间安排、时间限制，活动的步骤，每一部的指令都要简明清晰。

3. Work with individual roles and shared responsibilities:
   - The group has to be small.
   - Each learner must have an indispensable role in the group.
   - Each member of the group must be given a share of the work that contributes to group success.

3. 个人的角色和责任：
   - 分组要小，三人一组最合适。
   - 每个成员都要有一个不可缺少的角色。
   - 每个成员对小组活动的贡献都将影响全组活动的成败。

4. Work with pressure or competition:
   - There has to be a built-in mechanism to stimulate competition between groups as motivation for high quality performances.

4. 压力和竞争：
   - 建立某种机制使小组间有一定的压力和竞争，这是激发高水准表现的条件之一。

Question 20: How do I encourage and sustain good language behaviors of learners?

问　题 20：怎么鼓励和保持学生优良的语言行为？

Rationale 基本原则：

Use positive reinforcement to motivate learning
正面鼓励

- Be fair.
- Apply rules consistently.
- Generously reward the success of expected behaviors.
- 公平。
- 执行规则时保持一致性。
- 奖励好行为。

Suggested Activities and Assignments
对课堂活动和作业的建议

"Integration" is a good word. When designing an activity, an assignment, or an assessment, the instructor must consider this word. That is to say a K-12 Chinese instructor must connect the content of teaching and learning not only vertically and horizontally, but also inclusively.

"综合性"是个好主意。涉及课堂活动、课上课下作业和评估手段时要想到这一点。K-12 的老师应该把教与学的内容上下左右联系包罗汇总在一起。

A traditional homework assignment consists of doing exercises in student workbooks. This kind of work includes, but is not limited to copying text, filling in blanks, finishing sentences, questions and answers, etc. This type of work definitely has its value. However, for high school and younger learners, we suggest:

传统的家庭作业一般是学生做练习册里面的作业。这样的作业包括抄写汉字和生词、填空、完成句子、回答问题等。这样的作业有用。但是，对中学生，我们还建议一些其他作业形式：

1. Instructors incorporate more meaningful and fun ways of engagement in classroom activities and homework assignments. The purpose is to foster active involvement and creativity in language use and also to develop proficiency from the first day.

1. 给学生有意义并有意思的作业。让学生从学汉语的第一天起就用汉语做积极和创造性的事，提高用汉语的水平为作业的目的。

2. Instructors use homework assignments as an extension of in-class activities. The benefits here are also twofold: to reinforce the results of classroom learning; and to prepare learners with the background knowledge and skills to create better work leading to more effective learning.
2. 把家庭作业作为课堂作业的延伸。好处是两方面的：强化课上所学的知识和技巧；为学生的家庭作业打下基础，帮助学生做出更好的作业。

3. Instructors should give benchmarks for expected performance, but also give direction to reach results of high standards, and also leave room for different learning styles.
3. 给出作业的要求底线，但明确高期望作业的指导意见，创造可发挥的余地。

4. Instructional requirements must be clearly defined. Especially when assigning homework, make sure the students all have a clear understanding and record the specifics of the homework assignment in their notebooks.
4. 作业的指令和要求一定要扼要、清晰、明确、具体。特别是家庭作业，下课前一定要反复强调，让每个学生记录下来。

Index of Sample Activities and Assignments
课堂活动和作业案例总表

Activities to Develop Oral Skills　提高口语技巧的活动

Example 5	Teaching with Rhymes — A Class Song	例 5　韵律——班歌
Example 6	Tongue Twister	例 6　绕口令
Example 7	Snowball Rolling	例 7　滚雪球
Example 8	Timed Speeches	例 8　计时快说

Learning with Actions　边做边说

Example 9	Where Are We Going?	例 9　上哪儿去?
Example 10	Fashion Show	例 10　时装表演
Example 11	Drama	例 11　演戏

Comprehensive Language Tasks and Projects　综合项目

Example 12	Task-based Projects	例 12　实现具体目的的综合项目
Example 13	Parody of a Popular TV Show	例 13　模仿流行电视节目的滑稽剧
Example 14	A Movie Story Line	例 14　电影故事
Example 15	Cooperative Learning — Group Project	例 15　合作学习——集体项目
Example 16	Writing to a Pen Pal	例 16　笔友活动
Example 17	Interview	例 17　访谈
Example 18	Make a Book	例 18　编书
Example 19	Make a Video Production	例 19　制作电视片
Example 20	My Journal	例 20　我的日记/周记

More Samples and Variations in Use　更多实例与变换使用

More samples and variations in use are introduced in subsequent unit designs.

更多实例与变换使用在下面介绍的教学单元中可看到。请老师们根据课堂的需要挑选使用自由发挥，创造出更多自己的活动来。

20 Sample Activities and Assignments
20 个课堂活动和作业案例

Games　游戏

Integrating games into classroom instruction is certainly a fun way to go. The most effective games that support language learning are games that mobilize and use a variety of intelligence, involve all four language skills (speaking, listening, reading and writing) are competitive and interactive in nature and interest learners as well as inspire their active participation.

课堂游戏是有意思的活动。对语言教学有益的游戏一定有以下的特点：调动多种的智慧，全面运用听、说、读、写的技巧，有竞争性，互动，让学生感兴趣，由此激发他们积极参与。

Games that should be avoided in language classrooms have complicated procedures, require sophisticated equipment, and do not provide equal opportunity for all players to participate.

应该避免玩的、不适宜的游戏常常是因为程序太复杂，需要太多太复杂的设备，或不能让学生有公平参与的机会。

Example 1 Win-Lose-or Draw　输赢在此一画

The name of this game comes from an old TV game show from the late 1980s because the game models the show's format.

这个游戏模仿 20 世纪 80 年代一个有名的电视游戏节目的形式，因此借用了游戏的名字。

One player draws pictures on the board, while the others guess the meaning out loud. This game prompts writing, reading, speaking and listening of Chinese.

It involves competing teams of three to four players. The goal of game is to earn the most points and win the game. Points are earned by drawing pictures, and guessing the words or sentences written on a card. Cards are created by students.

这个游戏就是画画儿猜字，要求学生听、说、读、写汉语。玩这个游戏可以有数个队参加，每队 3 ~4 个队员，得分高的队是赢家。

游戏的玩法：

- 分队。每个队员做五张卡片，卡片上写一个中文词或中文句子。
- 检查卡片是否正确。收齐卡片，按组分放。
- 轮流以队为单位玩。一队一次派一个队员上前抽他队一张卡片（给老师看卡片上的句子和字数，由老师在黑板上画出表示字数的横线）。见卡后，按卡片上的汉语在黑板上画画儿，其他队员猜意思，直到每个字都被猜出为止。时间限制：一分钟。

游戏规则：

- 轮流玩，直到每队每人都玩过才可进第二轮。
- 画的人不能说话，不可用数字，不能用手势。
- 如卡片上有错字，被抽卡人发现，抽卡人自动得分。

游戏的使用：

- 复习词汇和句型。
- 听、说、读、写全面练习。
- 需要老师的辅助，课上使用。

窍门：

一队只有一分钟可以得胜。如该队队员画画儿，其他队员大声和快速说出所有跟图画有关的、可能的词，老师听见就会写在黑板上了。

Requirements：

- Teams of three to four players
- Instructor
- A time keeper

Materials：

- Index cards or small pieces of paper

Procedure:

Step 1: Form teams

- Three to four players form a team. There must be at least two teams to play.

Step 2: Preparation

- Each player creates 5 cards, each card bears a sentence or several words using previously learned characters and sentences.
- Each team must brainstorm sentences as a team to avoid duplication.
- Then each individual writes words or sentences.
- Each team checks its cards to ensure that each card is written correctly.

Step 3: Play

- The cards are gathered and piled face down according to team.
- Teams take turns to send one player at a time to draw the meaning of a different team's card. (Team 1 draws from Team 2's pile, Team 2 from Team 3's, and so on.)
- The player **silently** reads the sentence on the card and shows the contents only to the teacher. (The instructor makes sure that the player understands the sentence.)
- The instructor draws dotted lines on board indicating the number of characters in the sentence.
- The player goes to the board to draw pictures while the rest of the team shouts out possible answers.
- The time keeper starts the clock as soon as the player begins drawing.
- The instructor, upon hearing any word in the sentence, writes it down over the appropriate line.
- The team wins a point if all the blanks are filled within one minute.
- The instructor cleans the board quickly and keeps score on board.

Rules:

- Teams take turns to play.
- Each player plays once until everyone on the team gets a chance to play.
- The player who draws is not to utter a sound at any time (except when

confirming the meaning with the instructor aside before drawing).

- Each round must be completed in one minute. A team that is unsuccessful loses the point to the team that produces the card.
- The team that discovers a card bearing a sentence with incorrect characters or grammatical errors automatically wins a point.
- Only drawings are accepted. No numbers. No gestures.

Use:

- This game is good for reviewing sentence patterns and vocabularies.
- It can be used periodically.
- It is an in-class activity because it requires an instructor's facilitation.

Tip:

- The team must try to shout out all possible answers in order to score in time. For example, if the player draws a person, the rest of the team should quickly say all possible vocabulary related to a person.

Example 2 Jeopardy　危急关头

The game adopts its name and format from the longtime popular TV game show.

这个游戏模仿有名的电视智力竞赛节目而来。

游戏的玩法:

- 预备

  a. 确定五个类别。$ 100, $ 200, $ 300, $ 400, $ 500（根据语言的难度定类）。

  b. 分两队。每个队员做 25 张卡片，每类 5 张。卡上写一个中文词或中文句子。

  c. 检查卡片是否正确。收齐卡片，按组分放。

- 竞赛开始

  a. 轮流以队为单位玩。一队一次派一个队员参赛。

  b. 选手选择一个难度的题目。要求对方给一张卡片。

  c. 见卡后，大声念出卡片上的汉字或句子，念对得分。时间限制：一分钟。

- 计分：各队累积计分，多者为胜。

游戏规则：

- 轮流玩，直到每队每人都玩过才可进第二轮。
- 除选手外，其他人不能说话，不可给暗示，不能用手势。
- 如卡片上有错字，被抽卡人发现，抽卡人自动得分。

游戏的使用：

- 需要一个计时员。
- 复习词汇和句型。
- 听、说、读、写全面练习。
- 预备活动可作为家庭作业。
- 需要老师的辅助，课上使用。

Requirements:

- Two teams
- An instructor
- A time keeper

Materials:

- Large paper (8.5cm × 11cm or 8.5cm × 14cm)
- Dark and thick markers

Preparation:

Write phrases or sentences on paper clearly in order for people to see over a short distance.

Procedure:

Step 1: Form teams

- Divide the class into two teams.

Step 2: Preparation for game time (as homework assignment)

- Make five categories of questions ranking them by levels of difficulty ($100/$200/$300/$400/$500).
- Each player must create 25 cards, 5 cards per category.

Step 3: Pre-game

- The team checks the cards to ensure that each card is written correctly.

- Sort cards by category.
- Designate five people on the team and each manages one category.
- Designate a time keeper for each team.

Step 4: Play

- Arrange the classroom seating so that the two teams sit facing each other.
- Flip a coin to decide the order of play.
- A player asks for a question by choosing a category.
- The person who is in charge of that category picks a question and holds it up for the player to read.
- The player must accomplish the task (read or translate) within one minute.
- The winner selects a player from the other team to play. (No one is to be selected a second time until everyone on the team gets a chance to play.)
- The time keeper starts the clock as soon as the player is shown the question.
- The team earning the most money wins.

Rules:

- Teams take turns to play.
- Each player plays in turn until everyone on the team gets a chance to play.
- Each round must be completed in one minute.
- The team that discovers a card bearing a sentence with incorrect characters or grammatical errors automatically wins the points.

Use:

- This game is good for reviewing sentence patterns and phrases.
- It is an in-class activity because it requires facilitation by an instructor.
- It can be used partially as a homework assignment and partially classroom activity.
- It utilizes writing, reading, listening, speaking and translation.

Tip:

We usually use this game when teaching time expressions. Occasionally we use it for vocabulary.

Notes:

- The five categories for time expressions:
  - $ 100: Simple single time expressions (in characters), such as 二零零七年，下午，几点
  - $ 200: Simple combined time expressions (in characters), such as 二零零七年二月三日，下午三点
  - $ 300: Time expressions refer to present, last and next (in characters), such as 今天晚上，上星期日，下午三点
  - $ 400: Time expressions use verbs to indicate time (in characters), such as 上课以前，吃饭以后，打球的时候
  - $ 500: Sentences include $ 400 expressions (in English), such as, "I often do my homework before dinner."
- For people who are not familiar with the game show Jeopardy: There is no real money involved in this game. The dollar amount is only used as a way to keep score.

Analysis of the activity:

1. For learning language:
   - It employs all four language skills.
   - It supports review of vocabulary.
   - It makes a connection between spoken and written languages.
2. For engaging learning:
   - It invites and motivates the active participation of all players.
   - It gives a chance for learners to challenge themselves by providing questions of different levels of questions.
   - It shares learning through competition as well as accommodation and cooperation.

Example 3 Charades 打哑谜

This game derives from a traditional game for guessing movie titles. In the Chinese classroom, it can be played with different levels of sophistication.

这个游戏常用来猜电影名。在汉语课堂上可以用来做各种语言学习的活动。

Simple version: Verbs are actions

A person or two people go to the front of the class and use body language to demonstrate a concept. The class guesses the meaning in Chinese.

Note:

As the topic suggests, we usually use this for learning verbal phrases.

Materials:

A list of verbal phrases to be learned will be helpful.

简单玩法:

顾名思义，学生到教室前边，做一个动作，请全班猜意思。

若学习动词，最好事先给一词汇表。

Complex version: Guess what they are trying to tell us?

You may have teams plot a sentence or a scenario and act it out for others to guess.

Note:

It is not recommended to make the game too complicated.

复杂玩法:

分队用肢体语言表演一句话或一个故事情景，请对方猜。

情节不宜太复杂。

Analysis of the game:

- It inspires connecting mental images and physical movements with language to reinforce language learning.
- It keeps preparation to a minimum.
- It is age appropriate for grades 6 ~ 12 learners. They are mature enough to act out concepts and, more importantly, usually not too self-conscious acting front of the class.
- It is learning with laughter. This game can be entertaining.

Example 4 Quiz Show　智力竞赛

This game can use many topics for language learning. The example here uses weather conditions and locations of cities. Participants ask and answer on the spot questions, quizzing each other on the knowledge and vocabulary.

这个游戏可以用来辅助各种话题的语言学习。下面的例案是有关城市地理和天气的。参赛者当场发问或回答，测试有关的词汇与地理等方面的知识。

This game consists of preparation and execution stages. It is recommended that preparation and execution are done during separate class periods.

这个游戏分两部分。建议用不同的课堂时间来进行。

准备：

- 分成3~4个队。
- 每队准备有关若干城市的测试问题，写在卡片上（用所学句型和词汇）。
- 讨论后可分头回家准备卡片。

执行：

- 集中本队卡片，检查是否正确。
- 比赛开始：各队轮流参赛提问，其余队接受挑战。每次有一个选手回答问题。
- 答对得分。

得分：

一轮三分钟。得分多的队得胜。

Preparation:

- Index cards.
- Reference may also include *Functional and Grammatical Walk Through* (4): List of Countries, Languages and Continents.

Procedure:

Step 1: Team up

- Divide the class into teams of three to four.
- Specify rules and expectations.

Step 2: Prepare for a quiz show (can be a part of a homework assignment)

- Each group is given a number of cities.
- Teams brainstorm questions related to these cities using learned patterns and words.
- Teams write questions on index cards.

Step 3: Double check questions

- Teams meet to ensure that all questions are correct.

Step 4: Quiz begins

- Each team goes on stage in turn as hosts.
- Hosts take turn asking questions.
- Select other teams to answer questions.
- One player answers one question at a time.

Scoring:

- Each round is three minutes.
- The team that answers the most questions within the time frame wins.

Analysis of the activity:

- It is interactive and competitive.
- It builds proficiency with support.
- It integrates various communicative skills.
- It is connected to cultural learning.

Activities to Develop Oral Skills　提高口语技巧的活动

Pronunciation, tones, fluency and speaking speed are all important elements of oral proficiency. Here are some tricks aimed at exercising these aspects of speaking.

这都是练嘴的活动。说得标准、说得清楚、说得快都是口语水平的一部分。需要练习，才能提高。

Example 5 Teaching with Rhymes — A Class Song　韵律——班歌

The activity is to create a simple rhyme and sing it. It practices sounds, tones, tone changes and adjective as predicate. It requires use of all language skills, and can be used as a class activity, homework assignment, or even assessment. Students may create their own versions in writing and speaking.

这个活动是全班编个歌谣，念熟背会。用于语音阶段的发音与声调及形容词谓语句的练习。可以扩充成听、说、读、写的全面学习。可以让学生继续创造自己的歌词。课上、课下都能用，也可作测试。

Preparation for the activity:

- Know *pinyin*.
- Know positive and negative patterns of description.
- Know tone changes.

Procedure:

Step 1: Create a class song

As the class progresses, a rhyme comes into being sentence by sentence:

傅老师不饿。
傅老师不渴。
傅老师很忙。
傅老师很好。

Step 2: Rehearse

- The whole class says or sings it aloud (with attitude!).
- Small groups repeat until memorized.

Step 3: Write from memory

- A volunteer goes to the board to write it down.
- Others write it out in *pinyin*, too.

Step 4: Peer editing

- Check each other's work in pairs.

Step 5: Create another verse

- Go home and write another verse using other subjects and adjectives.

Follow-up:

Come back with a new verse memorized and perform it.

Analysis of the activity:

- It makes learning easier but fruitful, boosting the confidence of learners.
- It helps to expand simple words into sentences using both positive and negative patterns.
- It employs tone changes and fluency of speech.

Example 6 Tongue Twister 绕口令

Pronunciation and fluency are related to the physical aspect of speech. This activity intends to exercise the "speaking muscles" of your class.

这是一个练嘴的活动。强调的是发音与声调的准确和说话的流利程度。

做法：

- 发一个词汇、词组或短句的单子。
- 练习：默念，听老师读，跟老师读，加快语速。
- 背诵：集体与个人。
- 挑一条或两条计时背诵，有错重来。

Preparation for the activity:

Handouts: Practice rhyme sheet

Procedure:

Step 1: Create a list of items: words, phrases, sentences

Step 2: Pre-speaking practice

- Read the list of rhymes to review vocabulary.

Step 3: Read aloud

- Teacher leads reading rhymes aloud in class with increasing speed.

Step 4: Class memorization

- The class tries to say one rhyme from memory.

Step 5: Individual experiment

- Select individuals to perform from memory.

Step 6: Time your speech

- Ask the students to time the teacher reciting one rhyme to see how fast it can be done.
- Have students set individual speed records.

Follow-up 1: Homework

Select two or three rhymes to practice: memorize and time.

Follow-up 2: In class competition

- Students select one best-practiced rhyme to perform.
- Time the performance.

Analysis of the activity:

- It supports review and lays ground for further learning.

- It makes mechanical exercises exciting.
- It connects class work with home work.
- It makes assessment natural.

Example 7 Snowball Rolling 滚雪球

This game is a practice for speaking in sentences. A narration is built up sentence by sentence until it becomes a paragraph. It has some natural competition. This game can be used for any topic. The example below identifies the locations of cities. The title can be "Where do your relatives and friends live?" It requires use of all language skills and can be used as a class activity, a homework assignment, or even for assessment. It can also serve as the foundation of creative language use and cooperative learning.

这个活动是说句子，一句一句地加长叙述，直到完整地说出一段话。有一定竞争性，可用于任何话题。下面例子是有关城市方位的，题目是“你的亲朋好友住在哪儿”。这个活动可以从听说扩展到读写。从个人、机械地练习到合作、创造性地运用语言。

做法：

老师说一句话，学生模仿。老师不断加句子，学生跟上。一次可以有数个学生跟着做，学生会抢着先说，因为句子会越来越多。

Preparation for the activity:

Prepare a list of cities and states.

Procedure:

Step 1: Start a snowball

- The teacher makes a statement about a city.
- Select students to imitate in order.

Step 2: Get rolling

- The teacher keeps adding sentences one at a time.
- Select students one by one to repeat the expanding statement.

Step 3: Reading sample

- Read all the recited sentences.

Step 4: Work in class

- Jot down the location where relatives or friends live.
- Model the sample to describe one orally (to a partner or to the class depending on available time).

Step 5: Homework time

- Write several similar passages about different cities.

Follow-up:

- Peer editing
- Report to class

Analysis of the activity:

- It develops speaking fluency with intense repetition.
- It creates a competitive yet comfortable situation to practice speaking.
- It builds proficiency with scaffolding.
- It is open-ended and leaves room for expansion and variation in learning.

Example 8 Timed Speechs　计时快说

This game emphasizes oral proficiency. Student gives a speech for two full minutes. See how much and how well students can say something. It can be used as a class activity, a homework assignment, or even for assessment.

这个活动强化口语能力。每个学生给两分钟的时间，看能说多少、说多流利。讲话是有准备的。但两分钟内说完、不能停，还要接着自由发挥。叙述要求完整，逻辑清楚。

班级人数多时，分四人一组。指定一个计时员。老师走动听取每人的讲演。

Preparation for the activity:

- Develop a speech prototype in class.
- Prepare a written draft based on the classroom development.
- Memorize the speech before class.
- Take two minutes warm-up before presenting.

Analysis of the activity:

- It supports speaking improvement.
- It makes mechanical exercises purposeful and exciting.

- It creates a listening opportunity for other learners.
- It gives continuity and progression to learning.
- It makes assessment natural and cumulative.
- It provides a cooperative learning experience.

Tips:

- It is important to followup on homework assignments. We regularly assign oral practice as homework. If students are asked to write a passage, they will be asked to present it memorized in the next class. However due to two considerations, we prefer the presentation to be timed.
  a. The number of students in class and availability of class time; and
  b. Training fluency of speaking and the natural and logical development of a speech.
- The requirement is to speak as much as possible for two minutes on a given topic. Of course, at early stages of learning, the speech will have to be developed in class, edited, prepared and memorized at home.
- It is not advisable to let students memorize a wrong sentence. Practice certainly will not lead to perfection if practice is done wrongly.
- Also, two minutes of warm up in class before presentations will help to relax the nerves and yield better performances.
- If a student finishes the prepared story less than two minutes, then he or she should try to add more relevant language. This is an opportunity to develop proficiency and flexibility when speaking naturally.

Note:

If the class is too large (our Chinese II class one year had 36 students!), divide it into groups of four. Designate one person as a time keeper.

However, the teacher must walk around the room and try to listen to some of every speech.

Learning with Actions 边做边说

Young learners of grades 6 ~ 12 appreciate and learn better with physical movement and actions. Learning with actions not only stimulates more parts of the brain, but also motivates learners to be engaged, entertained and relaxed, and it also rescues them from boredom. Sitting on a chair for 45 ~ 100 minutes per class is not a way to learn.

要是语言学习伴随或通过肢体活动进行，6～12年级的学生的学习兴趣会更高，表现会更好。因为边做边学不仅调动多方面脑力活动，而且通过娱乐和轻松的方式让学生投入。在椅子上坐上45～100分钟不是愉快的学习方式。

Example 9 Where Are We Going?　上哪儿去?

这个活动对学习指路比较有效。

每个学生写出十个指令。分组。按一人的指令行动。轮流给指令。

预备部分可以作为家庭作业事先准备。

还可让学生把单句的指令连起来，说成或写成对一个活动的描述。

Language task: Giving directions: Tell us where to go
Functions: Using vocabulary and patterns to give directions.
Use: Class activity, homework assignment, assessment

Preparation for the activity:

Study vocabulary and sentence patterns related to given directions.

Procedure:

Step 1: Create a list of ten commands, such as

往前走两步。

从这儿下楼。

Step 2: Walk out the door

- A commander is chosen.
- The whole class acts according to given directions.

Step 3: New command

- After the first move is completed, a second commander is chosen to give a new order.

Step 4: Continuation

- The game continues until the whole class returns to the classroom.

Follow-up 1: Homework

Give directions to a place: Chinatown?

(Class may search online to help get directions.)

Follow-up 2：For a later project

How do we get to your house from here?

Example 10 Fashion Show　时装表演

In this game, students describe what a model is wearing. The description and presentation can be based on interpersonal interactions. The content of the game and activities are expandable.

一学生做模特状，其他学生从头到脚描述他/她的穿戴。

可先对话问答以熟悉句型和词汇。

还可加衣物的价钱、颜色等描述。

在这一活动的基础上还可以布置说、写、扩展使用等家庭作业。

Preparation for the activity：

- Vocabulary：Clothing/Colors/Money
- Grammar：Measure words/ "是……的" structure/Exchange rates

Procedure：

Step 1：Warm-up activity

- Describe what you are wearing today by using：

今天我穿了一件（一条/一双）……

我的……是……（颜色）的。

Step 2：Have a student go before the class (or do a cat walk if the model so desires).

Step 3：Have another student describe what the model is wearing by using the same patterns above.

Follow-up：Homework

Go home and write the description down.

Elaboration：

- If you know how to say the price of the piece of clothing, add the price to the description.
- Go to your closet and do a rough count：How many pieces of clothing are there?
- How much are your possessions worth in total?
- If you know the exchange rate and can do the math, how much is that in

RMB? (Possible byproducts: Gratefulness to your parents? Is it time to clean up your closet or your room?)

- The activity may start with an interpersonal element, such as asking each other the price of their clothes before the fashion show begins.

Analysis of the activity:

- It helps learners to identify Chinese words with their own lives.
- It reinforces use of different measure words for different objects.
- It creates situations to differentiate and identify items and give descriptive comments about thems.
- It supports reviewing and lays ground for further learning.

Example 11 Drama　演戏

演戏的活动先从背景介绍和阅读开始。听、说、读、写综合训练。可以选一个小品或集体创作一个剧本。当然需要课堂教学和课后作业的结合。演出可以作为评估的一部分。演出除了角色的分配，还需要准备道具、布景背景，还有导演、摄影等人的工作，是艺术与语言学习的结合，是学生跨学科学习的机会。谈演出的经历还可以作为延伸的语言学习活动。

这个活动要组织好，是以学生为中心的活动的好机会，给学生发挥不同学习特点、能力、风格的余地。

Pre-activity:

Select a scene or act from a drama (or write a script).

Procedure:

Step 1: Study the script

- Pre-reading:

  Discuss the story line.

  Map out the personal relationships between characters.

  Make a vocabulary list.

- Reading:

  Questions and answers on the story.

  Questions and answers on the personal relationships.

  Analyze tones, imageries, and emotions, etc. of the story.

- Writing:

  Outline the personal relationships between characters.

  Describe a character.

  Summarize the story.

Step 2: Rehearse

- Assign roles: Don't forget we need a director and assistants. If the scene has only a few characters, divide the class into small groups.
- Memorize lines individually and in small groups.
- Rehearsals: Practice in class or on stage and practice at home.

Step 3: Perform

- Prepare costumes and prompts.
- Perform (and videotape the performance if possible).

Step 4: Summarize the acting experience

- Talk in class about incidents related to the whole experience.
- Talking about personal feelings.
- Write about the experience.

Analysis of the activity:

- It integrates performing arts into language learning: Students write the script, prompts, background scenes, self-direct and organize, and record the drama.
- It combines reading with writing, combines writing the story, writing about the story and about personal experience.

Comprehensive Language Tasks and Projects 综合项目

Example 12 Task-based Projects 实现具体目的的综合项目

A task-based project is developed around life situations. It usually has a communicative purpose. It requires use of language to gather information and to present information. It can be used at the beginning level of learning the target language.

实现具体目的的综合项目是有的放矢的教学活动。围绕一个生活情景，有目的地交流。需要用目的语去搜寻资料、整理并报告。在语言学习的初级阶段就可以做。

A task-based project for young learners must be clearly structured. The basic instructions include:

- Be clear about the topic and format.
- Lay out detailed content, specifics on sentence patterns, vocabulary, and other required elements.
- Provide examples of writing presentation and rubrics.

年龄小的学生使用此种方法必须步骤明了，包括：

- 明确话题和形式。
- 规定内容、句型、词汇及其他必要成分的使用。
- 提供范文、评估标准等。

The product of a task-based project may include artistic displays, such as picture books, journal entries, display boards, PowerPoint presentations, video productions, performance, etc. in order to accommodate different learning styles.

See below for concrete examples (Examples 13 to 20).

请参照下面的例 13 到例 20。

Example 13 Parody of a Popular TV Show　模仿流行电视节目的滑稽剧

Some classes like to perform. We have asked our students to perform parodies of their favourite television shows, such as a parody of reality shows or sitcoms to take advantage of their story lines, life situations, lively characters and their relationships and communications. This provides realistic but funny examples of language use. It is a way to use what students are familiar with and like in order to motivate, along with students' desire to imitate and perform in order to expand language learning.

有的班级喜欢演戏，但不一定演的都是正剧，演小品也是一个有意思的活动。我们让学生从他们熟悉的电视节目中挑选一个，模仿节目主题、人物编故事和对话演滑稽剧。剧中有故事情节、场景。剧中的人物生动，人物关系活泼，人物之间有交流，有旁白，有评论，是语言运用的具体实例。这个方法利用学生熟悉喜爱的话题、表演的欲望，调动学生的创作积极性，达到设立场景练习日常用语的学习目的。

做法：

- 全班确定小品的内容和所需的语言任务。
- 分组选题，分派角色。
- 集体脑力激荡创作故事情节，分头创作，集体修改。
- 分组排演，合班排练，集体演出。

Procedure：

Step 1：Select stories

- The class brainstorms to select a number of topical stories or scenes.

Step 2：Divide tasks among groups

- The class is divided into groups of two or three.
- Identify group leaders and individual roles (don't forget the director and assistants.)
- Each group is given a number of scenes for which to create dialogue and narration.
- Deadlines and schedules come with each task.

Step 3：Rehearse

- Design props and background scenery (use PowerPoint).
- Prepare props.
- Group rehearsals.
- Class rehearsals.

Step 4：Performs

Notes：

Two of our Chinese III classes wrote scripts and performed a parody of the reality TV show "The Bachelor." The entire group performed the introductory and concluding interview scenes on stage as a whole, and in between performed individual episodes on dating using various locations, such as dining out in a fancy restaurant, seeing a movie in a theatre, visiting parents, dancing, talking at a beach, being interviewed on the red carpet on Oscar night, etc. They portrayed different types of bachelors and women.

The effective language learning topics covered in this example are personal introduction, interpersonal exchanges in various real-life situations and communicative functions such as bargaining, requesting and providing services, commenting on and evaluating behavior, etc.

In the case of our Chinese III class, the students made sure that everything was as authentic to a TV show as classroom conditions allowed. They really had fun creating the show. They even scripted and acted out TV commercials in between scenes.

However, admittedly, the two classes that engaged in this activity were of a smaller size — about 16 students or under. If the class is too large, it becomes difficult for the instructor to supervise everything, like videotaping scenes outdoors as a class. Still, this kind of activity can be scaled down or modified in other ways.

Example 14 A Movie Story Line　电影故事

Using Chinese movies in class often promotes interest in Chinese culture. Using movies to study language is more complicated. We have repeatedly used *A Great Wall* or *Wedding Banquet* for Chinese III classes — Sometimes both.

利用电影可以提高学习语言和文化的兴趣，但不能无的放矢，要用得合理。我们常用 *A Great Wall* 或 *Wedding Banquet* 作为中文三年级的辅助教材。

We use the film *Wedding Banquet* in the thematic unit covering marriage. Afterwards, the class describes personal traits, such as physical appearance, personality, professions, the ideal spouse, traditional and modern values on marriage, and practice of marriage. The movie is shown in three to four segments.

A Great Wall 适合跟讨论教育制度和家庭生活的学习内容联系起来。而 *Wedding Banquet* 跟婚姻、家庭、传统与现代观念的对比有关。以婚宴为例，我们在学完描述人的特征：外表、性格、职业等后，谈理想的爱人、婚姻和婚姻观。开始看电影，分 3 ~4 段看，看一段，讨论一段，描写一段。

The class is asked to make a story book and each student selects a point of view. In other words, they must tell the story from the perspective of the mother, the father, the boyfriend, the wife, or the main character or a friend. Then the whole class compiles the writings into a movie story book.

我们让全班编一本书。每个学生选一个电影人物。从那个人物的角度讲电影的故事。每个故事后都附有一个词汇表。故事包括故事情节和评论。故事完成前有同伴修改的活动，完成后有报告，最后汇集成书。

Procedure:

Step 1: Pre-writing

- The class views the movie an episode at a time and brainstorms on the vocabulary necessary or useful to describe situations in the movie.
- The class creates a must-use vocabulary list. Then they tell story orally and write it down.

Step 2: Peer-editing

- Students exchange drafts of their writing in order to accomplish two things:
  a. Point out strengths in the writing, such as good sentences.
  b. Make suggestions for revision.

Step 3: Presentation

- Students give oral and written presentations individually.

Analysis of the activity:

- A movie is used in conjunction with a thematic unit, and has thus become an extension of the learning experience.
- The movie helps to visualize concepts, views, and practices learned in the thematic unit making the discussed topic more vivid and real.
- The movie touches upon social, cultural, and political issues, which provides a lifelike context for interdisciplinary language learning.
- Students are given the choice to take a position on the issues related to the theme and its topics.

Example 15 Cooperative Learning — Group Project 合作学习——集体项目

A group project is a shared learning experience. It is student-centered learning and gives learners control in learning while demanding that they share responsibilities. Such tasks integrate all learning and language skills, inspire interdisciplinary learning, and are problem-based and task-oriented learning.

合作学习是一个综合性的学习活动，有互动，有交流。而小组集体项目还要求有成员之间的合作互补，为集体成功承担责任。这样的活动激活各种语言知识和交际技能，要求交叉学科的知识，以解决问题为目的。

Here is an example from a Chinese III class. The class is tasked to provide a tourist guide in the form of a book or brochure.

以下是我们中文三年级的一个“合作学习——集体项目”的实例。这个活动的任务是编写一本芝加哥旅游手册。每个小组负责介绍一个旅游点。介绍内容包括旅游点概况、历史与现状、社区及服务、季节气候、旅游时间、旅游须知和交通图。

Group Project: A guide book for Chicago tourists

Language Task: Provide a guide book for visitors to Chicago

Functions: Integrated language use
Connect language learning with cultural learning
Research and cooperative learning

Use: Class activity, homework assignment, assessment

Procedure:

Step 1: Team up

- Divide the class into teams of three to four.

Step 2: Divide tasks

- Each team selects a tourist attraction in the Greater Chicago Area. (Note: Teacher, please prepare a list of suggestions in advance.)

Step 3: Take on roles

Each team member must take on two roles:

- A leadership role: A manager, a resource organizer or a recorder.
- A writing role: Write one section.

Step 4: Gather information

Information must include, but is not limited to:

- A brief introduction to Chicago
- A brief introduction to the selected attraction
- A discussion of the neighbourhood and facilities where the attraction is located
- Visiting times and detailed directions

Step 5: Drafting and editing

- Schedule due dates for: First draft, peer editing and the final revision

Step 6: Putting it together and the team presentation

Elaboration:

- The final presentation may require the wearing of formal attire or historical costume for dramatic effect.
- A competition may be set up to elect the best project (rubric needed).

Caution:

- Don't forget to cite correctly if another's work is used.
- Plagiarism is using another's work without proper citation.
- Plagiarism is also cheating.

Guidelines:

Unit 8 Group Project: A Tourist Guide Book

My Kind of Town Chicago Is⑤

(See Unit 8 Activity 6 above for details)

Example 16 Writing to a Pen Pal 笔友活动

Correspondence is an important form of interpersonal communication. We encourage students to use written formats such as letter writing, e-mail exchanges, or instant messaging.

通信往来是人际交流的一个重要方式。我们可以鼓励学生用三种方式做这个活动：写信、电子邮件或即时信息传递。

A pen pal can be real or imaginary. For the safety of young learners, e-mail and instant messaging should be exchanged in a formally arranged situation and under the instructor's supervision.

笔友可以是真实的或虚构的。出于对年幼学生的安全考虑，电子邮件和即时信息传递的交换应该是在有安排的环境里进行，有老师的监督管理。

---

⑤ The title of the project is borrowed from Cahn and van Heusen's song about Chicago, made famous by Frank Sinatra.

Example 17 Interview　访谈

This is an activity designed for an AP Chinese course. It is a recurring activity used to prepare for a series of interviews that are part of the whole theme-based course entitled "Recording Oral History: Stories of Immigrants" (记录下宝贵的口头历史：移民的故事) The core of the activity is to use real-life situations and tasks to simulate real communicative interactions and scaffold and sustain this learning through cooperative learning. Real-life situations give purpose to language use and connect learners of the target language to their communities, each other, and themselves. Cooperative learning scaffolds the process of learning and using the target language and supports learners with language materials as well as confidence in language use.

这个活动是一个重复使用的活动，是为 AP 中文课程设计的。我们设计的 AP 中文课围绕一个主题"记录宝贵的口头历史：移民的故事"。学生采访一个移民，把他或她的真实生活故事写下来。每一个教学单元学生都集中在一个话题，阅读与话题有关的文章，复习、学习有关词汇和句型，然后采访。先准备采访的问题，再实地进行采访。采访之后，作记录，整理记录、口头报告。

这个活动的中心以真实生活的语言使用为目的引出一系列交际互动。如此的语言实践支持并持续合作形式的语言学习。

真实的语言实践不仅使语言的运用有了真实的意义，而且把目的语与学生的生活、学生的社会环境联系在了一起。

合作学习辅助这样的语言运用，支持学生用目的语，增强学生用目的语的信心。采访是整个教学单元的一部分。先准备采访的问题，再实地进行采访。设计采访问题是这个活动的中心。这个活动是这样展开的：分组脑力激荡→选出最重要的问题→与其他组交换问题→总结。

Language task: Designing Research/Interview Questions

Preparation for the activity:

- Know the task and details of the topic.
- Review general Chinese question formats and vocabulary.

Procedure:

Step 1: Joining a team and taking a role

- The students are divided into pairs or small groups of three.
- They are given the task to design and prepare an interview using appropriate questions.
- Each is assigned a role: A recorder, a reporter, and a note taker.

Step 2: Brainstorming

- The group generates a list of relevant questions through discussion.

Step 3: Sharing ideas

- Each group shares five unique questions with the class.
- The other groups take notes.

Step 4: Wrapping it up

- The instructor gives a brief summary and asks the groups to revise their list as an assignment for the next day.

Follow-up:

The questions will be used for interviews. Also, they are required to be included in later oral and written reports and presentations.

Analysis of the activity:

- Problem Solving:

  a. It is problem-based and goal-specific.

  b. It helps to develop inquiry skills that initiate communicative interactions and is a very important skill for communication.

- Communicative learning:

  This activity involves all three modes of communication. It interactively involves heavy listening and speaking use, along with interpretive reading and writing with presentational components.

- Individual learning through cooperative learning:

  a. It demands active participation and balanced contribution by all participants.

  b. It is also personal since each learner must have a list of his or her own questions for personal projects.

- Connection and learning continuation:

  It is the preparation for further learning, making it an indispensable part of the whole project.

Practicality of the activity:

The subjects to be interviewed may not all be Chinese-speaking. This activity not only prepares for questions needed to conduct real-life interviews, but also provides an opportunity to rehearse questions in Chinese in class.

Example 18 Make a Book　编书

Producing a book is a comprehensive project. A book can be written on any topic, in any format, and may use pictures and drawings. When a book is finished, it can be shared with others. Regardless of the age or language proficiency of learners, they can make a book. Imagine the sense of achievement in language use an author may gain! Moreover, making a book is a good opportunity for self expression and creativity. Nowadays, a book can be electronic: Good for revision as a student's ability progresses.

编一本书是一个综合的项目。因为书的内容可以包罗万象、图文并茂。书写成了还可以跟大家分享。特别是不管学生在什么年龄，有什么语言水平都可以编书。语言运用的成就感可想而知。另外，编书可以根据自己的爱好和想象来做，是一个自由发挥的好机会。在现在这个时代，书也可以是电子形式的，改编加减不在话下。

Example 19 Make a Video Production　制作电视片

If students have access to a video camera and video editing equipment at school or at home, suggest that learners use it for a class project.

学校或学生家若有制作电视片的设备，不妨让他们去用。

The only issue with a video production is that voice can be recorded while taping. In order to guarantee the fairness of oral evaluation, the students will have to give in person oral presentations. Voiceover in a video production should not be a substitute for an oral presentation.

要注意的问题是，电视录影可以同声录制，为了评估学生的口语表达，一定要要求他们作口语展示，不能用录像代替。

Below is a sample rubric of a Chinese II group project: *My School*. This year, three groups made a video production. The best production had the most original design, best picture image, most interesting story, and the most comprehensive language use. Another group, even though the technical aspect of their video was terrific, did not use enough sentence patterns, and therefore received lower group scores.

以下是我们二年级的一个集体项目"介绍我们的学校"。有三个小组做了电视片。有比较才有鉴别。最好的小组的片子构思新颖、画面生动、故事有趣、语言流畅。有一个小组的片子，技术水平虽高可是语言难度不够，影响了全组的得分。

Group Project: Video production
Topic: Promotional marketing material: My school
Content:

- General information about the school:
  Faculty, students, course offerings, extra-curricular activities
- Campus:
  Each floor: Floor plan, departments, activities on location
  Administration offices, facilities outside the building
- Surroundings:
  Immediate surroundings: Front, back, left, right
  Community
- Use positive and negative forms of all sentence patterns
- Complex sentences
- Questions and answers
- Three questions for listening comprehension

Evaluation:

- Group:
  Originality in design
  Artistic design
  Coordination and organization
  Completed on schedule
- Individual:

Content knowledge:
　Linguistic components
　Functional use of the language
　Mechanics (grammatical and technical errors)
Delivery:
　Pronunciation, tones and fluency
　Organization of information
　Presentation/Reference
Contribution to the group

Example 20 My Journal　我的日记/周记

Keeping a weekly journal is a meaningful homework assignment. A journal can be developed gradually as language use grows. We begin using weekly journal assignments after the class begins talking about specific events.

记周记不失为一个有意义的家庭作业。日记/周记的内容跟语言学习一起积累增长。我们在学了表达描述具体事件后让学生记周记。

Each week, we add new required linguistic or functional elements to the journal entry. At the end of a unit, the teacher may ask students to assemble all journal entries into a presentation.

每周，我们要求在日记里加一个语法点或语用的功能。在一段时间后，特别是一个教学单元结束时，老师可以让学生把几周的日记摘选组成一个展示。既复习又提高。

See below sample:

下面是一个实例：

Preparation for the activity:

Designate a small notebook to keep the journal in.

Get started:

Introduce the required journal writing format and elements.

Homework:

- Make it a weekly assignment.

• Make sure to collect it weekly and return it in time for future use.

Progression in writing:

Add new linguistic, functional, stylistic, etc. elements to the requirements as learning progresses.

Elaboration:

• Exchange journal stories in class for speaking and listening practice
• Assemble journal entries into a collection as a project

Analysis of the activity:

• Relate to real-life situations by writing with a purpose.
• Progressive learning with solid and constant review, recycling and spiraling of language materials.

Suggested format and content for journal writing
对日记格式与内容的建议

Date 日期
Weather 天气
General statement: Your mood in general for the day 当天的心情
Record of the activity 记录活动：
    Everyday activities and routine 常规活动
    Specific events 特殊事件

To be added as learning progresses 可增添内容

Plan 计划
Conditions of the activity: Time, place, how 常规活动发生的条件
Recount: Conditions of the event (s): Time, place, how, duration
事件发生的情况
Reasoning, comparison, weather of the day in detail, etc.
评论、比较及其他细节

Part II

下篇 Thematic Unit Design

主题教学单元的设计

Introduction
简介

The content of teaching and learning is divided into thematic units. Theme-based learning is learning with a purpose. Theme-based learning also makes learning real. A theme or topic with lifelike communicative interactions provides a purpose as well as a vehicle to use the language, simply because with a specific theme, all intended and designed classroom learning is connected to real-life situations and tasks. At the same time, it demands employment of all language skills. All grammatical patterns and vocabulary are also merged because the functional usages are relevant to the unit topic. This reflects the purposes and standards of foreign language teaching and learning known as the "5Cs."⑥

本篇把教学内容按交际主题分为十个教学单元。围绕主题的教学使课堂教学目的明确。围绕主题的教学让课堂教学真实。现实生活中的语言交流必需的主体题目能为课堂教学提供真实的目的和途径，不但把课堂教学活动和内容与现实生活情景与语用实际联系起来了，而且要求课堂教学的活动运用和发展各项语言技巧。同时有机地串联了所需的语法要点和词汇，从而体现中小学外语教学大纲的五个目的和标准。

The thematic units introduced in Part II bear several distinctive characteristics in design:

1. They are intended to align with national foreign language teaching and

---

⑥ "5Cs": Communication/Culture/Connection/Comparison/Community. See *ACTFL Foreign Language Learning Standards*. Retrieved from http://www.actfl.org

"5Cs"：语言交流/文化习俗/跨学科联系/比较诠译/社会实践。参照：*ACTFL Foreign Language Learning Standards*. Retrieved from http://www.actfl.org

learning standards.

2. They encourage development of communicative proficiency through problem solving in daily language use.
3. They emphasize student-centered, task-based, problem-solving instructions and activities.
4. They incorporate different learning styles.
5. They aim at accessibility and flexibility in assisting the instructor's lesson planning and can be used with other teaching materials.

本篇介绍的主题教学单元在设计上有以下特点：

1. 以全美外语教学标准为纲。
2. 鼓励通过语言的实际运用发展交际能力。
3. 强调以学生为教学中心，以完成具体任务为目的的实际解决问题的教学策略和课堂活动。
4. 包容不同的学习风格及特点。
5. 体现教案设计的通用性及灵活性。

Mapping of Themes and Topics

教学单元主题题目规划

We provide ten suggested units that are intended for two to four years of instruction for grades 6 ~ 12 middle school and high school Chinese teaching and learning. Each unit may be broken down into smaller building blocks by topic to form more units for elementary school Chinese teaching design.

本篇推出十个教学单元。预计可供初高中学6 ~ 12 年级汉语教学使用。每一单元可按题目分成若干小教学单位成为独立的教学单元，供小学汉语教学课堂教学设计使用。

Each sub-unit can be viewed as one building block, which can be combined with other blocks in other units to form a new unit, or be used with other teaching materials for further expansion.

每个教学单元包括若干从属的小教学单位。每一从属教学单位可作为一个组合块，可与其他教学单元中的组合块重新组合形成新的教学单元，或与其他教材合用扩展教学内容。

The sequence of these suggested units is designed according to their level of grammatical difficulty, progression of vocabulary accumulation, and the logic and need of language use in daily life. Nevertheless, there is room and flexibility for rearrangement.

教学单元的序列取决于语用涉及的语法的难度、词汇的积累和掌握，以及日常语用交流的需要和逻辑。

The Rationale and Practicality of the Design
教学单元设计的原则与实际

Rationale 设计理念

Thematic unit designs constract, map out and plan the content of teaching and learning around themes and topics. The goal is to simulate realistic and practical language and cultural experiences for young students of grades 6 ~ 12.

围绕主题设计教学单元，顾名思义就是根据一个主题编制教学内容与教学指导。目的为6 ~ 12 年级的汉语学生模拟与创造出真实与实用的语言文化学习经历。

The intended learning objectives are to:

1. Align with national and state foreign language standards.
2. Take into consideration the students' cognitive abilities, linguistic and cultural backgrounds and life experiences.
3. Focus on developing understanding and appreciation of the Chinese language and culture through positive learning experiences; developing Chinese language proficiency through functional use and comparative learning; improvement across broad communicative skills through lifelike situations, tasks and interdisciplinary connections.

教学目标的设立：

1. 与全美和本州的世界语言教学标准对齐。
2. 考虑学生的认知能力、语言文化背景及生活经历。
3. 致力于通过正面的、积极的学习经验提高对中国语言文化的理解和肯定，通过实际语用和对比学习提高汉语水平，通过与现实生活近似的情景、语用任务和跨学科的联系全面提高文化素养与交际能力。

Practicality 实际设计

The themes selected in the chapter are selected around the most essential communicative needs and the most familiar and relevant experiences of adolescent students.

本篇所选的教学单元主题都是围绕最基本的交际需求，最贴近青少年生活实际，并为他们所熟悉的。

Central to the themes is "The World and Me." Every topic focuses on communicative interactions beginning with the immediate self and moves on to family, others, school, the outside world, and community, etc. Each topic connects to cultural issues, other subject knowledge and study, and community. Comparative study is encouraged throughout the process and learning content.

具体来说，中心的主题是"我与大千世界"。所有的话题以交际为目的，由"我"展开，从小到大：个人→家庭→他人→外界→社区。每一话题都与文化、其他学科的知识和学习、社区相联系。话题讨论学习始终贯穿语言文化的比较。

Emphasis of the Design　设计强调

1. The progression of the content emphasizes moving from simple language tasks to more comprehensive and sophisticated ones; going from general situations to more specific situations; taking gradual steps to develop in depth.

1. 内容设计强调：从易到难，由浅入深，自普遍至特殊。

2. The teaching and learning process stresses consistent but gradual development of proficiency through constant reviewing, recycling and spiralling of language materials and usage. It emphasizes development of language proficiency through meaningful activities and encourages individual achievement through different learning styles.

2. 教学过程支持实际运用，循序渐进，反复运用，渐次提高。强调语言教学的实践与活动，并鼓励通过各种学习风格达到个体化的学习效果。

3. The design provides users with basic systematic knowledge and comprehensive, conceptualized building blocks for easy and flexible use.

3. 备课使用：把握基本，资料齐备，有据可依，灵活搭配，信手可得。

4. The design provides learners with guidelines for focusing learning, clarifying details, and provides language materials for extended learning.
4. 学习使用：要点明确，难点释义，自控扩展学习。

Steps for Unit Design
教学单元设计步骤

Volume Two Part II suggests the following steps in designing a unit:

1. Decide the theme and sub-topics.
2. Map out teaching and learning:
   - Decide what to teach: Content of teaching and learning;
   - Decide on sequence and depth and design accordingly; and
   - Foresee the learning focus and difficulties: Refer to *Functional and Grammatical Walk Through*.
3. Select relevant and suitable teaching and learning materials.
4. Design and schedule instructional hours and progression of lessons.
5. Design instructional strategies and activities.
6. Design and arrange assignments.
7. Design content, assessment methods and schedule.

本册下篇建议采用以下步骤设计教学单元：

1. 首先提出学习的目的、预期效果，与主题相关的实际交际语用任务。
2. 按题目规划教学内容，做出教学规划蓝图：
   - 决定教学内容；
   - 决定并安排教学步骤、层次和深度；
   - 预测教学重点与难点（参考《什么篇：语用与语法走廊》）。
3. 选择合适的教材。
4. 安排课堂教学时间与进度。
5. 设计教学策略和方法及课堂教学活动。

6. 设计并安排课外作业。
7. 设计并规划教学评估预测方法、内容及时间。

Design Framework
设计构架

- Theme and topic
- Possible sub-units
- Suggested future topical connections
- Grammatical patterns and vocabulary
  (Refer to *Functional and Grammatical Walk Through*)
- Suggested instructional strategies
- Suggested tasks in and out of classroom, activities, and assessment
- 教学单元主体题目
- 从属小单位
- 其他可能的重新组合建议
- 句型与词汇（参考《什么篇：语用与语法走廊》）
- 教学教法建议
- 教学活动建议

Materials
教材

The core of this book advocates designing teaching and learning according to the needs of the students. We suggest that teachers follow the "what" and "how" in this book to customize their currently available materials and possibly add authentic materials to tailor actual classroom practice.

这本书的核心就是倡导根据学生的具体情况设计课堂教与学。我们建议老师们按照这本书“教什么”和“怎么教”的建议，利用现有的教材和可能的真实语言素材组织教学。

Variations of Unit Design
教学单元的变量设置

Volume Two Part II — Thematic Unit Design introduces ten thematic units. Each unit includes three or four variations of a unit design. The intention is that an instructor can customize the unit design according to the needs of the class, the curriculum at large and the course instructional schedule and available instructional hours.

本册下篇介绍十个主题贯连教学单元。每一单元建议了3～4个可能的加减变量。宗旨是教学单元应根据课堂教学的需求、课程设置的全局情况及课时的限制酌情加减，或拆散重新组合。

Variables that can be taken into consideration are：

- Number of grammatical patterns involved,
- Extensiveness of vocabulary,
- Depth of communication tasks, and
- Proficiency of language skills.

应考虑的变量如下：

- 语法点的数量，
- 词汇的覆盖面，
- 语用实践活动的深度，
- 语言技巧的水平。

Suggested variations of the intensity levels：

Variation A：Accelerated

9～12 classes with more instructional hours or learning intensity

Variation B: Medium

6 ~ 8 classes with more instructional hours or learning intensity

9 ~ 12 classes with fewer instructional hours or learning intensity

Variation C: Moderate

6 ~ 8 classes with fewer instructional hours or learning intensity

9 ~ 12 classes with fewer instructional hours or learning intensity

三个不同进度和程度的单元设置方案的难度：

方案 A：强化

适用于 9 ~ 12 年级课时充裕、进度快的教学

方案 B：中等

适用于 6 ~ 8 年级课时充裕、进度快的教学

适用于 9 ~ 12 年级课时相对少、进度略缓的教学

方案 C：普通

适用于 6 ~ 8 年级课时较少、进度缓的教学

适用于 9 ~ 12 年级课时相对少、进度慢的教学

Suggested Activities
教学活动

The suggested activities focus on two aspects of teaching and learning: Functional and meaningful language use and development of basic language skills. They implement the principles of making learning easy, fun and understandable. They emphasize student-centered, task-based, and structured learning.

建议的教学活动着重于两个方面的学习：语言的有意义的实际运用和基本技能的培训培养。力图贯彻化难为易、寓教于乐、举一反三的教学原则；强调以学生为中心、以语用实践为基础、指导明确的教学。

Suggested Assessment
建议测试评估形式

We recommend performance-based assessments. Using fixed, structured, and open-ended formats, we may assess a wide range of modality with regard to students' skills, knowledge and proficiency of language use[⑦].

建议根据语言运用的表现来评估测试教与学的成效。使用各种形式来评估学生的语言技能、语言文化知识和语用水平。

Assessment 1: Daily dictation

Use: Listening or listening and writing

- For *pinyin*: spelling, tones and correctly placing tone marks
- For characters: form/writing of character itself; meaning/English translation; phonetic spelling/*pinyin* with tone mark
- For listening comprehension: translation of accurate or main ideas

Assessment 2: Multiple choice

Use: Listening or reading

Assessment 3: Reading texts

Use: Reading comprehension, vocabulary, or interpretational

Assessment 4: Report/Presentation

Use: Speaking/Writing
Presentational

Assessment 5: Asking and answering questions

Use: Listening/Speaking/Reading/Writing
Interpersonal

Assessment 6: Open-ended tasks

Use: Listening/Speaking/Reading/Writing

---

⑦ Bachman, L. F. & A. S. Palmer. *Language Testing in Practice*. Oxford: Oxford University Press, 1996.

Interpersonal

Presentational

Assessment 7: Other traditional paper-pencil tests

Use: Listening/Speaking/Reading/Writing

测试形式一：听写

使用：听力理解或听写

- 拼音要求拼写，声调标号正确
- 汉字听写要求形、音、义均正确
- 听力理解：翻译或理解大意正确

测试形式二：多项选择

使用：听力理解，阅读理解

测试形式三：阅读

使用：阅读理解，词汇，诠释

测试形式四：报告/展示

使用：说写，报告

测试形式五：问答

使用：听、说、读、写，人际交流

测试形式六：有发挥扩展余地的语言实践活动任务

使用：听、说、读、写，人际交流，展示报告

测试形式七：其他传统的笔纸测试方法

使用：听、说、读、写

Rubrics for Assessment
测试标准

According to the content coverage of the day or lesson, make a clear rubric to specify expectations and required elements for homework assignments and assessments.

根据每日课堂的学习进度，制定明确、清晰的测试评分标准，应申明期待和要求。

For grades 6 ~ 12 classroom teaching and learning assessment, requirements should be clearly communicated, language of the rubric should be general and simple, benchmark performance should be provided and comments for further improvement should be specified. Here are some examples from www. teach-nology. com — The Web Portal For Educators!

评分测试是为了检验教与学的效果。中小学课堂使用的评分细则标准应该要求明确，语言简单易懂，提供范例让学生效仿，并附有建设性意见让学生改进提高。

请参照以下两个范例。均由 www. teach-nology. com（The Web Portal For Educators!）制作。一个是阅读理解的评分标准，一个是报告展示的评分标准。

A Generic Rubric for Reading Comprehension: 阅读理解评估

Name: ____________________ Teacher: ____________________

Date Submitted: ____________________ Title of Work: ____________________

	Criteria				Points
	1	2	3	4	
Organization	Sequence of information is difficult to follow.	Reader has difficulty following work because student jumps around.	Student presents information in logical sequence which reader can follow.	Information in logical, interesting sequence which reader can follow.	——
Content Knowledge	Student does not have grasp of information; student cannot answer questions about subject.	Student is uncomfortable with content and is able to demonstrate basic concepts.	Student is at ease with content, but fails to elaborate.	Student demonstrates full knowledge (more than required).	——

Grammar and Spelling	Work has four or more spelling errors and/or grammatical errors.	Presentation has three misspellings and/or grammatical errors.	Presentation has no more than two misspellings and/or grammatical errors.	Presentation has no misspellings or grammatical errors.	____
Neatness	Work is illegible.	Work has three or four areas that are sloppy.	Work has one or two areas that are sloppy.	Work is neatly done.	____
References	Work displays no references.	Work does not have the appropriate number of required references.	Reference section was completed incorrectly	Work displays the correct number of references, written correctly.	____
				Total →	____

Teacher Comments:

Powered by www. teach-nology. com — The Web Portal For Educators!

A Generic Rubric for Presentations　报告展示评估

Name: ______________________　　Teacher: ________________

Date of Presentation: ______________　　Title of Work: ______________

	Criteria				Points
	1	2	3	4	
Organization	Audience cannot understand presentation because there is no sequence of information.	Audience has difficulty following presentation because student jumps around.	Student presents information in logical sequence which audience can follow.	Student presents information in logical, interesting sequence which audience can follow.	____

Content Knowledge	Student does not have grasp of information; student cannot answer questions about subject.	Student is uncomfortable with information and is able to answer only rudimentary questions.	Student is at ease with content, but fails to elaborate.	Student demonstrates full knowledge (more than required) with explanations and elaboration.	——
Visuals	Student used no visuals.	Student occasionally used visuals that rarely support text and presentation.	Visuals related to text and presentation.	Student used visuals to reinforce screen text and presentation.	——
Mechanics	Student's presentation had four or more spelling errors and/or grammatical errors.	Presentation had three misspellings and/or grammatical errors.	Presentation has no more than two misspellings and/or grammatical errors.	Presentation has no misspellings or grammatical errors.	——
Delivery	Student mumbles, incorrectly pronounces terms, and speaks too quietly for students in the back of class to hear.	Student incorrectly pronounces terms. Audience members have difficulty hearing presentation.	Student's voice is clear. Student pronounces most words correctly.	Student used a clear voice and correct, precise pronunciation of terms.	——
				Total →	——

Teacher Comments:

Powered by www. teach-nology. com — The Web Portal For Educators!

For further information, please visit The Rubric Bank at www. cps. k12. il. us.

若需更多的可借鉴的样本，请参阅芝加哥公立学校网站所提供的评分细则库 www. cps. k12. il. us。

List of Suggested Units
教学单元表

The units are designed by theme or topic. The theme is centered on "The World and Me." Every topic focuses on communicative interactions, beginning with the immediate self and moving on to family, others, school, the outside world, and community, etc. Each topic connects to cultural issues, other subject knowledge and study, and community. Comparative study is encouraged throughout the process and learning content.

教学单元均围绕主题设计。所有的话题以交际为目的，由“我”展开，从小到大：个人→家庭→他人→外界→社区。每个话题都与文化、社区及其他学科的知识相联系。话题的讨论、学习始终贯穿语言文化的比较。

All content of teaching and learning is adjustable. It is essential to use *Functional and Grammatical Walk Through* because the book provides grammatical patterns and categorizes vocabulary by similar themes and topics. It also contains critical grammatical explanations and clarifies difficulties from the perspective of English speaking learners.

教学内容可灵活加减、重新组合。关键是要参照《什么篇：语用与语法走廊》一书的教学内容。《什么篇：语用与语法走廊》有关的语法点、词汇都按小题目汇集、分类。同时还有英语学生学习汉语的重点和难点的提示与注释。

Unit One: My Friends and Me　第一教学单元：我跟我的朋友

Phonetics	语音
Characters	汉字介绍
Greetings	问候
Personal Physical Condition	个人状况
Names	姓名
Basic Numbers	基本数字
Age	年龄
Address and Telephone Number	家庭住址与电话
Family Members	家庭成员
Nationality/Language	国籍/语言

Unit Two: My Family　第二教学单元：我家

Family Members	家庭成员
Family Relationships/Relatives	家庭关系/亲友
Work/Job/Workplaces	职业/工作/工作地点

Unit Three: My Hobbies and My Day　第三教学单元：我的喜好和我的一天

Daily Activities	日常活动
Time/Place/Manner and Means	时间/地点/方式
Hobbies/Preferences/Obligation and Duty	喜好/选择/责任
Evaluating Ability and Performance	评估能力及其表现
Plans	活动计划

Unit Four: Going Shopping　第四教学单元：买东西

Large Numbers	大数字
Money/Colors/Clothing/Tools	钱/颜色/服装/用具
Describing things/Identifying objects	描述/识别
Bargaining	讨价还价

Comparing and judging 比一比

Complex Noun Phrases 复杂名词词组

Unit Five：My Stories 第五教学单元：我的故事

Telling Stories 讲故事

Conditions of Events 复杂状语

Duration 时间段

Reasons 原因和理由

Requisites，Ability and Permission 条件、能力和许可

Unit Six：I Love Spring in Chicago 第六教学单元：我爱芝加哥的春天

Change in The Weather 天气变化

Duration 时间段

Seasons/Weather/Temperature 季节/天气/温度

Geographic Location 地理方位

Comparisons 比较

Daily Activities 日常活动

Unit Seven：My Life at School 第七教学单元：我的校园生活

Directions and Positions 方位

School Life 学校的生活

Campus 校园

Curriculum and Subjects 课程科目

Extra-curricular Activities 课外活动

Unit Eight：I Live in Chicago 第八教学单元：我家住在芝加哥

Buildings 建筑

Neighborhood 邻里

My House 我家

Visit My House	请你来我家

Unit Nine: My Favorite Dish: Eating in Chicago

第九教学单元：我最爱吃的菜：吃在芝加哥

Food	食物
Drinks	饮料
Vegetables	蔬菜
Animals	动物
Cooking	做饭

Unit Ten: My Past and Present: The Body and Health

第十教学单元：我的过去与现状：身体与健康

Body	身体部位
Physical Health	身体状况
Illness	疾病
Visiting a Doctor	看病
History and Past Experience	过去的经历

Unit Design
教学单元设计

Unit One：My Friends and Me
第一教学单元：我跟我的朋友

Theme 主题

My Friends and Me 我跟我的朋友

Topics 交谈要点与话题

- Greetings 问候
- Introducing Personal Physical Condition 介绍个人状况
- Introducing Names 介绍姓名
- Basic Numbers 基本数字
- Talking about Age 谈年龄
- Talking about Home Address and Telephone Number 谈家庭住址与电话
- Talking about Family Members 谈家庭成员
- Talking about Nationality 谈国籍
- Talking about Language 谈语言

Content of Teaching and Learning　教学内容

Linguistic Functions　语用

- Self introduction　自我介绍
- Exchanging personal information　互换个人简介
- Phonetics: Pronunciation/Tones/Phonetic reading and spelling
  语音：发音、声调、拼读与拼写
- Writing Chinese characters　汉字书写
- Simple narration　简单表述
- Simple interaction　简短问答
- Use of a Chinese word processor　使用中文处理软件

Grammatical Patterns and Vocabulary　语法点与词汇

(Refer to *Functional and Grammatical Walk Through*)

（参阅《什么篇：语用与语法走廊》：（索引：A/B/1/2/3/4/9/13））

Vocabulary　词汇	Grammatical Points　语法点
Pronouns　代词（2） Adjectives　形容词（9） Numbers　数字（1） Family Members　家庭成员(3) Countries　国家（4） Languages　语言（4）	Phonetics　语音（A） Chinese characters　汉字（B） Adjective as predicate　形容词谓语句(2) "不" as negative　"不"表示否定(13) Yes/No questions　是非疑问句（13） Wh-questions　特殊疑问句： 谁/什么/哪（13） "是/说/在"（4）

Cultural Studies and Connections　文化及跨学科联系

- Geography　地理
- Ethnicity　民族
- Social Studies　政治与历史

Who are Americans? 美国人

Chinese American 美籍华人

- Evolution of language: Chinese characters 语言的变迁：汉字

  Social and cultural variation and diversity in language use: Titles

  语言运用中的社会文化多样化：称谓

Variations of Unit One 第一单元的变量设置

The instructor can customize this unit design according to the needs of the class, curriculum at large, the course instructional schedule and number of contact hours.

教学单元应根据课堂教学的需求、课程设置的全局情况及课时的限制酌情加减。

Variables that can be taken into consideration are:

- Number of grammatical patterns involved,
- Extensiveness of vocabulary,
- Depth of communication tasks, and
- Proficiency of language skills.

应考虑的变量如下：

- 语法点的数量，
- 词汇的覆盖面，
- 语用实践活动的深度，
- 语言技巧的水平。

Suggested Variations of the Unit by Topic 建议参考如下

Variation A: The unit can be easily divided into three sub-units.

方案 A： 分三个从属教学单位。

Sub-Unit One: Self Introduction　教学单位一：自我介绍		
Vocabulary **词汇**	**Grammatical Points** **语法点**	**Linguistic Functions** **语用**
Pronouns 代词（2） Adjectives 形容词(9) Numbers 数字（1）	Phonetics　语音（A） Characters　汉字（B） Adjective as predicate 形容词谓语句（2） "不" as negative "不"表示否定(13) Yes/No questions 是非疑问句（13）	Greetings　问候 Personal physical condition 介绍个人家庭成员状况 Basic numbers 基本数字 1 ~ 99

Sub-Unit Two: Family　教学单位二：家庭		
Vocabulary **词汇**	**Grammatical Points** **语法点**	**Linguistic Functions** **语用**
Family members 家庭成员(3)	Phonetics　语音（A） Characters　汉字（B） Wh-questions 特殊疑问句： 谁/什么（13）	Introducing names 介绍姓名 Talking about age　谈年龄 Talking about home address and telephone number 谈家庭住址与电话 Talking about family members 谈家庭成员

Sub-Unit Three: Country and Language　教学单位三：国家与语言		
Vocabulary　词汇	**Grammatical Points　语法点**	**Linguistic Functions　语用**
Countries 国家（4） Languages 语言（4）	"是/说/在"（4） Wh-questions 特殊疑问句：哪（13）	Talking about nationality 谈国籍 Talking about language 谈语言

Variation B: **The unit can be divided into two sub-units.**

方案B： 分两个从属教学单位。

Sub-Unit One: Self-Introduction 教学单位一：自我介绍		
Vocabulary 词汇	**Grammatical Points 语法点**	**Linguistic Functions 语用**
Pronouns 代词（2） Adjectives 形容词（9） Family members 家庭成员(3)	Phonetics 语音（A） Characters 汉字（B） Adjectives as predicate 形容词谓语句（2） “不” as negative “不”表示否定（13） Yes/No questions 是非疑问句（13）	Greetings 问候 Personal physical condition 介绍个人家庭成员状况 Introducing names 介绍姓名

Sub-Unit Two: Country and Language 教学单位二：国家与语言		
Vocabulary 词汇	**Grammatical Points 语法点**	**Linguistic Functions 语用**
Countries 国家（4） Languages 语言（4）	“是/说/在”（4） Wh-questions 特殊疑问句： 谁/什么/哪（13）	Talking about nationality 谈国籍 Talking about language 谈语言 Talking about geography 谈地理

Variation C: **This unit can be divided into several smaller and simpler units.**

方案C： 分四个从属教学单位。

Sub-Unit One 教学单位一	**Sub-Unit Two 教学单位二**	**Sub-Unit Three 教学单位三**	**Sub-Unit Four 教学单位四**
Greetings 问候(2) Names 姓名(2)	Numbers 数字(1) Simple math 简单算术(1) Date and age 日历和年龄(1/6)	Family 家庭成员(3) Relatives 亲属关系(3)	Nationality 国籍(4) Language 语言(4) Geography 地理(4)

Instructional Tips　教学指导策略提示

Tip 1:

Phonetics learning will be a main focus throughout the unit.
Phonetics includes sound, tones, and spelling.

语音的学习要贯穿始终。强调语言、声调和拼读。

Tip 2:

Teach tones and sounds with real words, meaningful utterances, and tone changes in short sentences.

语音和声调最好与实际用语结合。在短句中教声调变化。

Tip 3:

Emphasize the importance of tones in Chinese language by dramatizing the effects of different tones.

教声调可以夸张不同，用以强调。

Tip 4:

Find ways to help students to pronounce Chinese sounds and tones correctly by identifying sounds and tones that students use in their mother tongue.

尽量找与学生母语或其他学生熟悉的音与调来帮助学生正确发音发声。

Tip 5:

Sentence patterns and vocabularies should be repeated and recycled in language tasks of every sub-unit and sub-topic.

学会的词句要不断反复运用。

Tip 6:

The number of characters taught can be customized. Selection of the characters to be taught each day should be well thought out. However, they should come from the context of the language used in class. Once characters are taught, encourage writing whenever possible. Also, testing of characters should be cumulative. That is to say, old characters should be tested repeatedly.

汉字的数量可根据情况加减。每天教的汉字应仔细挑选，与所学内容有关。汉字一旦教过，要反复使用，不断复习测试。

Tip 7：

Reading Chinese characters in texts and writing do not have to be developed at the same time. Reading skills such as understanding meaning with common sense and understanding meaning with contextual cues should be developed first. Pre-reading activities are essential for reading comprehension.

阅读与书写不一定非要同步，阅读能力的发展应领先。

Tip 8：

Integrate creation of *pinyin* texts with the development of listening and speaking skills. However, do not worry that speaking and listening may progress quicker than reading and writing. Take advantage of the fact that Chinese speaking can be developed quickly at an early stage of learning.

听说能力不应受读写能力的牵制，相反听说可带动促进读写。在学习的初期不要错失可大力快速发展说的良机。

Tip 9：

When introducing a new concept or a new pattern, make sure that the content and method of introduction is age appropriate. That is to say, teaching and learning in class must make sense to students.

介绍一个新概念或一个新句型时，一定要考虑教与学的内容和引入的方式、方法要与学生的年龄、认知水平、理解接受能力等相适合。

Suggested Activities 建议教学活动

Phonetics 语音教学

Activity 1 Teaching with Rhymes — A Class Song 韵律——班歌

Language task：Create a simple rhyme and sing it

Functions：Practice sounds, tones, tone changes and adjective as predicate

Use:　Class activity, homework assignment, assessment

Create a simple rhyme and sing it. This fosters practice of sounds, tones, tone changes and adjective as predicate. It requires the use of all language skills, and can be used as a class activity, a homework assignment, or even an assessment. Students may create their own versions in writing and speaking.

这个活动是全班编个歌谣，念熟背会。用于语音阶段的发音与声调及形容词谓语句的练习，可以扩充成听、说、读、写的全面学习。可以让学生继续创造自己的歌词。课上、课下都能用，也可作测试。

Preparation for the activity:

- Know *pinyin*.
- Know positive and negative patterns used to describe things.
- Know tone changes.

Procedure:

Step 1: Create a class song

- As the class progresses, a rhyme comes into being sentence by sentence:

  傅老师不饿。
  傅老师不渴。
  傅老师很忙。
  傅老师很好。

Step 2: Rehearse

- The whole class says or sings it aloud (with attitude!).
- Small groups repeat until memorized.

Step 3: Write from memory

- A volunteer goes to the board to write it down.
- Others write it out in *pinyin*, too.

Step 4: Peer editing

- Check each other's work.

Step 5: Create another verse

- Go home and write another verse using other subjects and adjectives.

Follow-up:

Come back to class with a new verse memorized, and perform it.

Listening and Speaking　听说练习

Activity 2　Real Communication — "How Are You?"　你好
Language task:　Greetings
Functions:　Interpersonal: Practice simple interactive exchanges
Elaboration:　Presentational: Report
Use:　Class activity or homework assignment

这个活动有两步。在学习问候后，让学生互相问候。然后，让他们汇报交谈的内容。既有交流又有成句表达叙述，既学习问与答又使用直接和间接引语。课堂口头使用后，可要求作为课后作业写下来，加固学习。

Preparation for the activity:

- Know adjectives for greetings/Pronouns/How to ask questions.
- Teacher models the interactive exchange.
- Teacher provides clear instruction about procedures and expectations.

Procedure:

Step 1: Greet your neighbor

- Ask students to greet each other in pairs.
- Each must ask questions and answer as well.

Step 2: Present the dialogue to the class

Elaboration:

Report to class use these patterns:

我问他/她……

他/她说……

to transform the question and answer session into a report.

Follow-up:

Repeat the activity in writing as a homework assignment.

Character Writing　写汉字

Activity 3　Do You Know the Right Way?　你会正确的笔顺吗?
Language task: Write characters
Functions: Learning stroke orders when writing characters
Use: Class activity

这个活动教汉字书写的笔顺。老师示范，学生模仿。之后，请学生上黑板，按所教的规律自己书写汉字，其他学生看笔顺是否合要求。经过反复几次后，当场测试。这样的活动在教学初期，每天都可用。教笔顺的同时也要强调字形的外表，其他记忆汉字的方法。

Preparation for the activity:

Recognition of the characters to be written/Teacher modeling

Procedure:

Step 1: Teacher demonstration
- Teacher introduces the writing, the stroke orders, etc.

Step 2: Students write following the demonstration

Step 3: Have a student come to the board to demonstrate
- Have the whole class observe and critique it.

Step 4: Repeat Step 3 using other examples

Optional:

The whole class comes to the board in groups of five or six to have a quick on the spot dictation.

Follow-up:

This activity can be a daily routine at the early stages of learning characters.

Practicality of the activity:

- Besides teaching stroke order, the teacher may also emphasize appearance of the writing.
- The teacher may also use other strategies to help learners to remember characters.

Activity 4 Creating Art 艺术创作

Language task: Create posters as classroom wall decorations
Write characters on 8.5 × 11cm sheets and post them on the wall

Functions: Write characters

Use: Class activity or homework assignment

活动的目的是让学生把汉字写在大纸上，然后张贴在教室里。做法是先把所学的汉字让学生写在黑板上，让每人挑选数个（根据情况规定数额）。分发纸张与彩笔。提出要求并示范样本，让学生发挥艺术才能写出漂亮的汉字。随汉字量的增加，可再次使用这个活动。

Preparation for the activity:

- Know some characters.
- Paper, colored markers.

Procedure:

Step 1: Give instructions and show examples
Step 2: Students write all previously learned characters on the board to review
Step 3: Students go to the board individually to indicate the ones that they plan to write
Step 4: Student chooses the colors of markers to be used
Step 5: Students create posters
Step 6: Class goes over all posters to select the best ones
Step 7: Post the characters on the wall

Follow-up:

This activity can be repeated a couple of times during the school year.

Activity 5 Team Competition — "Smashing the Board" 比赛写汉字

Language task: Write characters

Functions: Review characters, making connections between characters

Use: Class activity

把学生分成两组。每组做一个汉字的清单：按一个规律排列所有的汉字。（自选一个方法。老师可给不同的建议，例：按偏旁或字义等）然后按两队，逐个上前按顺序写在黑板上。看哪队先写完、写的汉字最多、错误最少。一次只可有一人写，每人机会均等。预备活动也可包括让每个学生事先把所有学的汉字列一个自己的表以备小组用。

Preparation for the activity:

Know enough characters to play for at least 5 minutes.

Procedure:

Step 1: Divide the class into two teams

Step 2: Each team creates a list of all their previously learned characters

Step 3: Timed competition (5 ~ 10 minutes)

The winning team finishes with the most characters with fewest mistakes.

Rules:

- The characters must be connected with a characteristic: either they are connected by a shared part, or meaning, etc.
- Each team can only have one player writing at the board.
- Each player can only write one character at a time.
- Correcting a mistake counts as one turn of playing.
- Each player can go another round only when all players on the team take a turn.

Tips:

- Players must have time-saving strategies! Organization is important:
  - the writing order of players, and
  - the presentation of the writing on the board.
- Players may create a list individually beforehand, but they still need to create a list as a group.

Critical Thinking and Comparative Study 评判和比较

Activity 6 Guessing Game — Winning Bonus 猜猜看：有奖活动

Language task: Learn the differences in language use

Ask the students to compare English and Chinese

Identify the differences

Functions: Critical thinking

Use: Class activity

老师提问，学生对比与英文的不同，用自己的话归纳句型和使用。促使学生在学习的同时有一定的思考。给分奖励，鼓励踊跃思考、发言。

Procedure:

Step 1: Pose questions

Step 2: Solicit answers

Step 3: Summarize the correct answers

Step 4: Award bonus points to winners

An Example:

Introduction: 我是“傅老师”。

Question: What do you call me in English?

Answer: “Ms. Fu” or “Dr. Fu”.

Question: Can anyone tell me what is the difference between English and Chinese?

Answer: 1. In Chinese, a title goes after the family name; in English, a title comes before the family name.

2. There are accents (tones).

Analysis of the activity:

- It engages student learning by drawing attention to instruction and language use.
- It provokes critical thinking through comparative learning.
- It generates curiosity and interest.
- It is age appropriate.

Activity 7　Discovering Rules　找出规律

Language task: Summarizing rules

Functions: Critical thinking, generalizing grammatical patterns, tone changes, spellings, grammatical patterns, functional use

Use: Class activity or homework assignment

老师提问，学生想一想，用自己的话归纳句型和使用。促使学生在学习的同时有一定的思考。给分奖励，鼓励踊跃思考、发言。老师总结后可以让学生课后把总结写下来。

Preparation for the activity:

- Presentation of enough language materials.
- Emphasis on rules in practice.
- Ask leading questions.

Procedure:

Step 1: Pose questions

Step 2: Solicit answers

Step 3: Summarize the correct answers

Follow-up:

If the rules are to be stressed, after rules are summarized in class, make sure to include the summary in a homework assignment and assessment.

An Example:

Use the example in Activity 6. Ask the students to describe what they have learned in class in their own words as homework.

Cultural Study　文化学习

Activity 8　Do You Want a Chinese Name?　起中文名字

Language Task: Get a name in Chinese

Functions: Self-introduction: Cultural information

Learning *pinyin* and characters

Elaboration: Introduce use of Chinese word processors and dictionary

Use: Class activity

起中文名可以作为一个活动。老师介绍一般中文名字的几种起法，用字典、网上的中文名网站或中文名书籍等。让学生根据介绍的办法，选一个理想的名字。老师帮助定一个合适的名字，用汉字写下来，经常用中文名字。起中文名应由学生自己决定。

Preparation for the activity:

- Dictionary.
- Reference books or handouts on Chinese names.
- Computer with Chinese word processor.
- Internet connection/websites for Chinese names.

Procedure:

Step 1: Cultural information

- Teacher introduces the Chinese ways of naming a child.

Step 2: Provide tools

- Introduce the use of a Chinese word processor or dictionary to find a word.

Step 3: Find a name for you

- Student decides what method he/she prefers to obtain a name in Chinese and uses the tools provided to search for a name.

Step 4: Finalize it

- Student consults teacher with final decision on the name.

Step 5: Write it in characters

Follow-up:

Encourage students to use their Chinese names daily in writing.

Practicality of the activity:

If a student refuses to have a Chinese name for a reason other than that he or she does not want to do the work, then the wish should be respected.

Activity 9 Where in the World Is Carmen San Diego?　卡门在哪儿?
Language Task: Locate a country on map
Functions: Cultural information (geography)
Specify location by using 在 and related vocabulary
Use: Class activity

在地图上指出并说出一个国家的地理位置，还可加语言。这是一个游戏（游戏名来自学生熟悉的电视儿童游戏节目），先学国名和语言及表述，然后分组。小组分头做卡片，每张卡上写国名或语言。比赛开始：参赛小组派人抽卡。抽卡人必须立即说出："她是哪国人?""那个国家在哪儿?""她说什么语?"说对得分。一（两）分钟一换队。在指定时间内得分多的队获胜。复杂一点，还可以问答形式进行。

Preparation for the activity:

- Glossary, paper, index cards.
- Enough practice using the sentence patterns and vocabulary.
- Clarify rules of the game.
- Cards may also be prepared the day before as a homework assignment.

Procedure:

Step 1: Pre-game prep
- Equip students with vocabulary on countries and languages.

Step 2: Form a team
- Divide the class into two or more teams.

Step 3: Prepare your clues
- Each team prepares a stack of cards.
- Each card has a country or a language written on it (either in Chinese characters or in *pinyin*).

Step 4: Who is Carmen? Where is she?
- Team members take turns to draw cards randomly.
- Then make statement according to the information provided.
- Must provide the answers to the following questions:
  (not necessarily in this order)

她是哪国人？
那个国家在哪儿？
她说什么语？

Step 5: Score! Within 1 minute (or 30 seconds)

- 3 points for the team: All three sentences are correct.
- 2 points for the team: Two sentences are correct.
- 1 point for the team: One sentence is correct.

Elaboration:

Bonus points: Instead of giving an statement, you may provide both a question and an answer.

Note:

The name of game comes from an old but popular children's TV show on PBS.

Suggested Assignment Focus 建议作业的重点

• Using phonetic spelling	练习拼音书写
• Writing and using characters	用汉字
• Developing all four language skills	发展听、说、读、写技能
• Completing basic language tasks in Chinese	用目的语完成语言任务
• Asking questions	会提问

Suggested Assignments 建议作业

- Assign listening materials: Listening.
- Copy words or characters: Reading and writing.
- Memorize language materials, and prepare to perform during the next class: Reading and speaking.
- Produce language materials as instructed, and prepare to perform during the next class: Writing and speaking; open-ended tasks.
- Interview a family member and make a report or a dialogue: Speaking and writing; task-based presentation.
- Bring a picture of a person or people and prepare to introduce to the class:

Speaking and task-based presentation.

- 听力练习。
- 读写练习。
- 记忆语言材料，准备测试：读写。
- 创造性地运用语言材料，预备课上展示：说写，语言实践任务。
- 访问家庭成员并报告情况或对话：说写，语言实践任务。
- 带照片当堂介绍：准备即席会话交流。

Suggested Assessment Focus　建议评估重点

Listening comprehension　听力理解

- Differentiation of sounds and tones　辨音辨调
- Comprehension of learned words　听懂所学的词
- Comprehension of short sentences　听懂短句
- Comprehension of short dialogues　听懂小对话

Speaking　说

- Emphasis on correct pronunciation　发音正确
- Emphasis on correct tones　声调正确
- Emphasis on fluency　流利
- Emphasis on producing correct sentences　能说句子
- Emphasis on the ability to initiate and respond properly to interactions　发问并回答

Reading　阅读

- Words, sentences and short texts in *pinyin*　阅读拼音形式的词、句子、短文
- Words, sentences, and short texts using Chinese characters　阅读汉字形式的词、句子、短文
- Guess meanings with common sense and contextual clues　根据背景知识和上下文猜断语义

Writing 写

- Use correct spelling of *pinyin* 正确用拼音书写
- Write characters correctly 正确用汉字书写
- Create texts in *pinyin* 用拼音写作表达
- Create texts using known Chinese characters 用已知汉字写作表达

Suggested Assessment 建议测试评估形式

See page 90.

见 90 页。

Rubrics for Assessment 测试标准

Make a clear rubric specifying expectations and the required elements according to the content coverage of the day or lesson.

根据每日课堂的学习进度，制定明确、清晰的测试评分标准，以申明期待和要求。

Sample Unit Project 教学单元综合项目测试例案

Unit One Project: Self-Introduction

第一教学单元综合项目：自我介绍

Format:

Oral and written presentation

Topic:

Self-introduction

Content:

- Name (English and Chinese names) (family, first and full names)
- Physical condition

  Adjectives: (好，饿，渴，累，忙，etc. with 也，都，很，不)
- Family

  Verb: to have

  Measure word: quantity +个

- Address and telephone number
- Nationality and language

  Verb: to be and to speak
- A dialogue
- Three questions for listening comprehension

Requirements:

- Each presentation must contain positive as well as negative sentences.
- Each presentation must contain questions (Yes/No, Wh) and answers.

Evaluation:

- Content knowledge:

  Linguistic components

  Functional use of the language

  Mechanics (grammatical and technical errors)
- Creativity in presentation:

  Overall design

  Visual aids or artistic expressions
- Delivery:

  Pronunciation, tones and fluency

  Organization of information

  Presentation

  Reference
- Effort

Writing Sample　范文

我姓 W。我叫欧娜。

我很好。我很忙。我不懒。我不笨。

我十四岁。

我是美国人/中国人/爱尔兰人/法国人/德国人。

我说英语、西班牙语和一点儿汉语。

我有妈妈和一个弟弟，也有爷爷和奶奶。我还有姥姥，三个叔叔和三个舅舅，一个婶和两个舅妈，三个表弟和两个表妹。我没有哥哥、姐姐和妹妹。

我是中学生。我家住在芝加哥。

我在芝加哥北部大学预科高中上学。

我的电话是7734567890。

我家的电话是7733219786。

Sample Questions　问题

1. 你姓什么？
2. 你叫什么？
3. 你是哪儿人？
4. 你说不说汉语？
5. 你家有几个人？
6. 你家都有谁？（你家有什么人？）
7. 你父母有几个孩子？
8. 他们怎么样？
9. 你弟弟呢？

（By Ona W.，Northside College Preparatory High School，Chinese 1）

Unit Two: My Family
第二教学单元：我家

Theme　主题

My Family 我家

Topics　交谈要点与话题

- Family Members　家庭成员
- Family Relationships　家庭关系
- Relatives　亲友
- Work/Job　职业/工作
- Workplaces　工作地点

Content of Teaching and Learning　教学内容

Linguistic Functions　语用

- Using phonetics correctly: Pronunciation, tones, phonetic reading and spelling　正确使用发音、声调、拼读与拼写
- Writing Chinese characters　汉字书写
- Describing with simple narration　简单表述
- Initiating and responding in simple interactions　简短问答
- Listening with comprehension to short sentences 简短句子的听力理解
- Reading short passages with comprehension　简短段落的阅读理解
- Using a Chinese word processor　使用中文处理软件
- Seeking and exchanging personal information　交换个人简介

Grammatical Patterns and Vocabulary　语法点与词汇

(Refer to *Functional and Grammatical Walk Through*)

（参阅《什么篇：语用与语法走廊》（索引：B/3/4/5/13/16））

Vocabulary 词汇	Grammatical Points 语法点
Immediate family 直系亲属（3） Extended family 亲戚（3） Family relations 家庭关系（3） Work/Job 职业/工作（5） Workplaces 工作地点（5/16）	To have 有没有（3） Measure word “个”（3） Use of “也”“和”（4） “不”“没”as negative（13） Yes/No questions 是非疑问句（13） Wh-questions 特殊疑问句（13） Identification “是”（5） Asking about occupation 工作（5） Specify location using “在”（5） Chinese Characters 汉字（B）

Cultural Studies and Connections 文化及跨学科联系

- Family and culture 家庭及文化
- Various kinds of families 多样化的家庭组成
- Work and occupation 工作与职业
- Chinese cultural origins and history 中国的文化起源和历史

Variations of Unit Two 第二单元的变量设置

The instructor can customize this unit design according to the needs of the class, curriculum at large, the course instructional schedule and number of contact hours.

教学单元应根据课堂教学的需求、课程设置的全局情况及课时的限制酌情加减。

Variables that can be taken into consideration are:

- Number of grammatical patterns involved,
- Extensiveness of vocabulary,
- Depth of communication tasks, and
- Poficiency of language skills.

应考虑的变量如下：

- 语法点的数量，
- 词汇的覆盖面，
- 语用实践活动的深度，
- 语言技巧的水平。

Suggested Variations of the Unit by Topic　建议参考如下

Variation A： **The unit can be easily divided into two sub-units. Each unit can include an expandable, related vocabulary list.**

方案 A： **这个单元可以分成两个教学单位。每个教学单位的词汇表可增减。**

Sub-Unit One：Who are your family members?　教学单位一：家庭与亲属		
Vocabulary **词汇**	**Grammatical Points** **语法点**	**Linguistic Functions** **语用**
Immediate family 直系亲属(3) Extended family 亲戚（3） Family relations 家庭关系(3)	To have　有没有（3） Measure word“个”（3） Use of“也”“和”（4） “不”“没”as negative(13) Wh-questions 特殊疑问句：谁/什么(13)	Physical condition 谈家庭成员状况 Introducing names　谈姓名 Talking about age　谈年龄 Talking about home address and telephone number 谈家庭住址与电话 Talking about nationality and language 谈国籍与语言

Sub-Unit Two：What do your family members do？ 教学单位二：职业、工作和地点		
Vocabulary **词汇**	**Grammatical Points** **语法点**	**Linguistic Functions** **语用**
Work/Job 职业/工作(5) Workplaces 工作地点(5/16)	Identification“是”（5） Asking about occupation 工作（5） Specifying location using“在”（5）	Talking about work/job 谈职业/工作 Specify workplaces 谈工作地点、工作单位

Variation B： **The unit can be simply about the family.**

The unit can be easily divided into two sub-units.

方案 B： **这个教学单元可以把“谈家庭”作为教学重点。**

这个单元可以分成两个教学单位。

Sub-Unit One：Family 教学单位一：家庭与亲属	
Vocabulary 词汇	**Grammatical Points 语法点**
Immediate family 直系亲属(3) Extended family 亲戚（3） Family relations 家庭关系(3)	To have 有没有（3） Measure word“个”（3） Use of“也”“和”（4） “不”“没”as negative（13） Wh-questions 特殊疑问句：谁/什么(13)

Sub-Unit Two：Family 教学单位二：家庭与亲属
Linguistic Functions 语用
Physical condition 谈家庭成员状况 Introducing names 谈姓名 Talking about age 谈年龄 Talking about home address and telephone number 谈家庭住址与电话 Talking about nationality and language 谈国籍与语言

Variation C:　Reduce the vocabulary coverage in each sub-unit.

方案 C:　减少方案 A 或方案 B 每个教学单位的词汇量。

Instructional Tips　教学指导策略提示

Tip 1:

Phonetic learning will still be a main focus throughout the unit.

语音的学习还要贯穿始终。

Tip 2:

Sentence patterns and vocabularies from the previous unit should be repeated and recycled in the new unit to maintain continuity in language use and to sustain learning. Include old topics as required elements for new language tasks.

学会的词句要不断反复运用，话题不断反复增新，词汇的学习以老带新。

Tip 3:

Encourage use of characters in writing and reading. Don't be afraid of using characters in combination with *pinyin*. Use *pinyin* as an assistant until the *pinyin* is internalized. Don't forget to give bonus points to learners who put effort into using more characters in writing.

鼓励学生用汉字阅读和写作，混用拼音和汉字也没关系，强调拼音拼写正确了对将来用计算机输入有好处。奖励在作业中自觉多用汉字的学生。

Tip 4:

Reading texts in characters and writing do not have to be developed at the same time. Reading skills such as reading meaning with common sense and reading meaning with contextual clues should be developed first. Pre-reading activities, such as stimulating prior knowledge about the topic and reviewing related vocabulary are essential for reading comprehension.

阅读与书写不一定非要同步，阅读能力的发展应领先。读前的预热活动对阅读理解至关紧要。

Tip 5：

Encourage interactive information exchange. Inquiry is essential to communication. Provide opportunities for learners to be familiar with and be fluent in asking questions.

提问是交流的重要手段，从一开始就应注重让学生练习提问。

Tip 6：

In order to develop task-based projects as major assignments and assessments, make sure the language materials used are developed gradually and cumulatively with clear guidance and structured instruction.

逐步扎实地发展语用的能力，利用语言实践任务鼓励运用所学语言。但要注意教学指导明确清晰，有铺垫。

Tip 7：

Accept and appreciate social and cultural diversity and various kinds of family arrangements.

接受和肯定不同社会和文化的家庭结构。

Tip 8：

Cultural and language studies can be intertwined. Language use may reflect cultural views and practices, while cultural issues may introduce and emphasize new language use.

文化的学习和讨论可以与语言学习紧密相连。既可由语言使用本身反映文化内涵并加以强调，又可由文化问题引出语言的使用，交融学习。

Suggested Activities 建议教学活动

Activity 1 Describe a Picture 描述照片图画

Language task： Introduce a person and the family

Functions： Reporting and presenting information in narration

Writing and speaking

Use： Class activity, homework assignment, assessment

让学生带照片或图画，介绍一个人或一个家庭。可以事前准备或即席报告。把学生熟悉的生活和本人的经历带进课堂。

Procedure:

Step 1: Bring or draw a picture of a person

Step 2: Report and present information about the person

- Use the student's experience as target language material to make learning personal.

Activity 2　　Interview and Report　访谈和报告
(Elaboration on Activity 1.)

Language task: Introduce a person and the family

Functions: Gather information through inquiry
Report and present information as a narration
Interactive communication
Listening, speaking and writing

Use: Class activity, homework assignment, assessment

这是上一活动的扩展。学生带来照片后，互相练习对话。

这个活动完成后还可根据听说的结果进行写作练习。

Preparation for the activity:

- All vocabulary and grammatical patterns needed for the task.
- A picture

Procedure:

Step 1: Bring or draw a picture of a person

Step 2: Pair up

Step 3: Interview your partner and gather as much information as possible about the person in your partner's picture

Step 4: Report to class briefly

Follow-up:

Write up the information gathered in class (including the questions you have asked to gather information).

Activity 3 Real Communication — Family 谈家庭

"Who are your family?" 你家有谁/什么人？

"What do they do?" 他们做什么？

"Where do they work?" 他们在哪儿工作？

Language task: Seek information about family

Functions: Interpersonal: Practice simple interactive exchange

Elaboration: Presentational: Report

Use: Class activity or homework assignment (with current topic of the day)

学生针对当天的话题，互相交流有关各自家庭的情况。然后或表演对话，或报告对话的结果。要求根据话题正确使用各种问句。活动前老师应示范，也要把要求交代清楚。这个活动也可扩展成家庭作业的一部分。

Preparation for the activity:

- Know adjectives for greetings.
- Know pronouns.
- Know how to ask questions.
- Teacher models the interactive exchange.
- Teacher provides clear instructions for procedures and expectations.

Procedure:

Step 1: Pair up students

- Pair them up randomly.

Step 2: Greet your partner

- Ask students to exchange information in pairs.
- Each must ask questions and give answers.

Step 3: Perform the dialogue to the class

Elaboration:

Report to class, using these patterns:

我问他/她……

他/她说……

to change the question/answer session into a report by using either direct or indirect quotes.

Follow-up:

Repeat the activity in writing as a homework assignment.

Activity 4　　Team Competition — "Smashing the Board"　比赛写汉字

(See Unit One, Activity 5)

(请参照第一教学单元活动5)

Critical Thinking and Comparative Study　评判和比较:

Activity 5　　Guessing Game — Winning Bonus　猜猜看：有奖游戏

Activity 6　　Discovering Rules　找出规律

(See Unit One, Activity 6 and Activity 7)

(请参照第一教学单元活动6和活动7)

Cultural Study　文化学习

Activity 7　　Chinese Family Relations　中国家庭关系

Language task: Draw a family tree

Functions: Cultural learning

Comparative learning

Reinforce vocabulary and sentence patterns

Writing, speaking and listening

Use: Class activity, homework assignment, assessment

这个活动把中国文化的学习与学生自己的生活经验和文化背景结合起来，并介绍文化与地区差异。

先由老师介绍中国家庭关系，指出有关词汇的用法、与英文的不同和地方差异。然后让学生用汉语词汇画出自己的家族图。学生向全班介绍、讲述自己画的图，用“这是……那是……”等句型。

Procedure:

Step 1: Lecture

- Teacher introduces family relation terms in Chinese and compares with English.
- Teacher introduces regional variations, formal and informal usages.

Step 2: Students draw a family tree using Chinese terminologies

Step 3: Elaboration

- Use drawings to add artistic flavor to the tree.
- Use a computer to brush up on Chinese typing.

Step 4: Present to class by using

这是……

那是……

Analysis of the activity:

1. Personalize it
   - Help students to make connections with Chinese using their own lives.
2. Integration
   - Provide an opportunity for students to use a Chinese word processor or their artistic talent to reinforce learning.
   - Require use of multiple language skills.
3. Cultural Connection
   - Students learn about Chinese family relationships in a comparative way.

Activity 8	Task-based Projects　语言实践任务项目
Language task:	Introduce a family
Format:	Oral presentation and written presentation
Function:	Demonstrate language proficiency through use
Use:	Class activity, homework assignment, assessment

这个活动要求学生介绍一个家庭。这个家庭可以是学生自己的，也可以是学生挑选的（如很多学生喜欢谈 the Simpsons）。

见下范例：教学单元综合项目测试标准例案。

A task-based project must be clearly structured. The basic instructions include:

- Be clear about the topic and format.
- Lay out detailed content, specifics on sentence patterns, vocabulary, and other required elements.
- Provide examples of writing presentation and rubrics.

指导学生完成语言实践任务项目应有明确的指示。基本教学指导应包括：

- 明确话题和形式。
- 规定内容、句型、词汇及其他必要成分的使用。
- 提供范文、评估标准等。

See Part I: Teaching Tips — Best Practices, Question 13: How do I design a good project?

请参照上篇：教学小诀窍——好经验，问题13：怎么设计一个好的综合性的学习项目？

Suggested Assignment Focus　建议作业的重点

- Reading with increasing number of characters　阅读加大汉字数量
- Writing in sentences and using *pinyin* and characters　用汉字和拼音写句子
- Developing all four language skills　发展听、说、读、写技能
- Completing basic language tasks in Chinese　用目的语完成语言任务
- Asking questions　会提问

Suggested Assignments　建议作业

- Assign listening materials: Listening.
- Copy words or characters: Reading and writing.
- Memorize language materials, and prepare to perform during the next

class: Reading and speaking.

- Produce language materials as instructed, and prepare to perform during the next class: Writing and speaking; open-ended tasks.
- Interview a family member and make a report or a dialogue: Speaking and writing; task-based presentation.
- Bring a picture of a person or people and prepare to introduce them to the class: Speaking and task-based presentation.
- Create oral and written presentations as a project: All language skills.
- 听力练习。
- 读写练习。
- 记忆语言材料，准备测试：读写。
- 创造性地运用语言材料，预备课上展示：说写，语言实践任务。
- 访问家庭成员并报告情况或对话：说写，语言实践任务。
- 带照片当堂介绍：准备即席会话交流。
- 创作口语和书面报告：综合训练。

Suggested Assessment Focus　建议评估重点

Listening comprehension　听力理解

- Differentiation of sounds and tones　辨音辨调
- Comprehension of learned words　听懂所学的词
- Comprehension of short sentences　听懂短句
- Comprehension of short dialogues　听懂小对话

Speaking　说

- Emphasis on correct pronunciation　发音正确
- Emphasis on correct tones　声调正确
- Emphasis on fluency　流利
- Emphasis on producing correct sentences　能说句子
- Emphasis on the ability to initiate and respond properly to interactions　发问并回答

Reading　阅读

• Words, sentences and short texts in *pinyin*	阅读拼音形式的词、句子、短文
• Words, sentences, and short texts using Chinese characters	阅读汉字形式的词、句子、短文
• Guess meaning with common sense and contextual clues	根据背景知识和上下文猜断语义

Writing　写

• Use correct spelling of *pinyin*	正确用拼音书写
• Write characters correctly	正确用汉字书写
• Create texts in *pinyin*	用拼音写作表达
• Create texts with known Chinese characters	用已知汉字写作表达
• Write with a Chinese word processor	会用中文处理软件

Suggested Assessment　建议测试评估形式

See page 90.

见 90 页。

Rubrics for Assessment　测试标准

Make a clear rubric specifying expectations and the required elements according to the content coverage of the day or lesson.

根据每日课堂的学习进度，制定明确、清晰的测试评分标准，以申明期待和要求。

Sample Unit Project　教学单元综合项目测试例案

Unit Two Project: Family and Occupations

第二教学单元综合项目：家庭和职业

Format:

Oral and written presentation

- Narration and dialogue
- With artistic display or a PowerPoint presentation

Topic:

Family and profession

Content:

- Self-introduction
  - Name (family, first and full names)
  - Physical condition
    - Adverbs + adjectives
  - Address and telephone number
  - Nationality and language
    - Verb: to be and to speak
- Family
  - Immediate family members and relatives
    - Verb: to have
  - Measure word: Quantity + 个
- Professions:
  - Job titles
  - Locations
- Three questions for listening comprehension

Requirements:

- Each presentation must contain positive and negative sentences.
- Each presentation must contain questions (Yes/No, Wh) and answers.

Evaluation:

- Content knowledge:
  - Linguistic components
  - Functional use of the language
  - Mechanics (grammatical and technical errors)

- Creativity in presentation:
  - Overall design
  - Visual aids and artistic expression
- Delivery:
  - Pronunciation, tones and fluency
  - Organization of information
  - Presentation
- Effort

Writing Sample　范文

我　　家

你家住在哪儿？	我家住在芝加哥。
你的电话是什么？	我的电话是7736316707。
你家有没有四个人？	我家有四个人。
你家有什么人？	我家有妈妈、爸爸、弟弟和我。
	我父母有两个男孩子，没有女孩子。
	我家有爷爷、姥姥、姥爷和奶奶。
	我家还有两个伯伯和一个伯母。
你家没有什么人？	我家没有表哥、表妹和表弟，我家没有妹妹、姐姐和哥哥。
她是谁？	这是我的表姐。
谁是五十岁？	我爸爸是五十岁。
你的亲戚好吗？	我姥爷不忙，我姥姥很好。
你家是哪国人？	我家是日本人/乌克兰人/波兰人/中国人。
	我爸爸是中国人，我妈妈是乌克兰人。
你说不说法语？	我说。我也说汉语和英语。
谁是学生？	我弟弟、表姐和我都是学生。

(By Joseph. W., Northside College Preparatory High School, Chinese 1)

Unit Three：My Hobbies and My Day
第三教学单元：我的喜好和我的一天

Theme 主题

My Hobbies and My Day 我的喜好和我的一天

Topics 交谈要点与话题

- Daily Activities 日常活动
  (Time 时间/Place 地点/Manner and Means 方式)
- Hobbies/Preferences/Obligations and Duty 喜好/选择/责任
- Evaluating Ability and Performance 评估能力及其表现
- Plans 活动计划

Content of Teaching and Learning 教学内容

Linguistic Functions 语用

- Describing daily activities 描述日常活动
- Planning daily activities 计划日常活动
- Negotiating time, place, means 交涉时间、地点、方式和工具
- Evaluating ability and performance 评估能力及其表现

Grammatical Patterns and Vocabulary 语法点与词汇

(Refer to *Functional and Grammatical Walk Through*)

(参阅《什么篇：语用与语法走廊》（索引：B/6/7/8/9/12/13/16/17))

Vocabulary 词汇	Grammatical Points 语法点
Calendar 日历（6） Time of day 钟点（6） Verbal phrases detailing daily actions 日常行为动词（7） Locations 地点（16） Methods 方式（17） Modal verbs 情态动词（8） Adverbs 副词（9） Conjunctions used for complex sentences 复句连词(12)	Formation of time expressions 时间表达(6) Adverbial phrases in sentences 状语在句中的位置（16/17） Time 时间（6） Location 地点（16） Methods 方式（17） Action as time 行为表示时间（6） Yes/No questions 是非疑问句（13） Wh-questions 特殊疑问句（13） Complements of degree 程度补语（9） Use of modal verbs 情态动词的使用（8） Use of complex sentences 复句（12） Chinese characters 汉字（B）

Cultural Studies and Connections 文化及跨学科联系

- Cultural Variations：Celebrating birthdays
  文化：过生日的习俗
- Anthropology：Evolution of transportation
  人类学：交通工具的变迁

Variations on Unit Three 第三单元的变量设置

The instructor can customize this unit design according to the needs of the class, curriculum at large, the course schedule and available instructional hours.

教学单元应根据课堂教学的需求、课程设置的全局情况及课时的限制酌情加减。

Variables that can be taken into consideration are：

- Number of grammatical patterns involved,
- Extensiveness of vocabulary,
- Depth of communication tasks, and

- Proficiency of language skills.

应考虑的变量如下：

- 语法点的数量，
- 词汇的覆盖面，
- 语用实践活动的深度，
- 语言技巧的水平。

Suggested variations of the Unit by Topic 建议参考如下

Variation A: **The unit can be easily divided into four sub-units. Each unit can include an expandable vocabulary list.**

方案 A: **分四个从属教学单位。每个教学单位的词汇可以增减。**

Sub-Unit One: Discussing a schedule or a routine 教学单位一：时间表/日程		
Vocabulary **词汇**	**Grammatical Points** **语法点**	**Linguistic Functions** **语用**
Calendar 日历（6） Time of day 钟点(6) Parts of a day 一天的组成部分(6) Verbs related to daily actions 日常生活动词(7)	Action verb as predicate 动词谓语句（7） Time as adverbial 时间词做状语（7） Wh-questions 特殊疑问句:哪(13)	Time 时间 Place 地点 Daily activities 日常活动 Manner and means 方式

Sub-Unit Two: What do you like to do? 教学单位二：喜欢做什么		
Vocabulary **词汇**	**Grammatical Points** **语法点**	**Linguistic Functions** **语用**
Modal verbs 情态动词（8） Verbs related to daily actions 日常生活动词(7)	Use of modal verbs 情态动词的使用(8)	Hobbies 喜好 Preferences 选择 Obligations and duty 责任

Sub-Unit Three: How well can you do it?　教学单位三：做得怎么样		
Vocabulary 词汇	Grammatical Points 语法点	Linguistic Functions 语用
Adjectives　形容词（9） Adverbs　副词（9） Verbs related to daily actions 日常生活动词(7)	Modal verb: Know how 情态动词:会（8） Complements of degree 程度补语（9）	Evaluating ability and performance 评估能力及其表现

Sub-Unit Four: Preferences and Reasoning　教学单位四：选择与原因		
Vocabulary　词汇	Grammatical Points　语法点	Linguistic Functions　语用
Modal verb 情态动词(8)	Use of modal verb 情态动词的使用（8）	Plans　活动计划

Variation B:　**This unit can be simply divided into three sub-units.**
Map vocabulary and grammatical patterns according to language use; and
Keep vocabulary and grammatical patterns to a minimum and focus on the functions.

方案 B:　分三个从属教学单位。把握每个教学单位的词汇量和语法点。

Sub-Unit One: Discussing a schedule or a routine 教学单位一：谈时间表/日程		
Vocabulary 词汇	Grammatical Points 语法点	Linguistic Functions 语用
Calendar　日历（6） Parts of a day 一天的组成部分（6） Time of day　钟点（6） Verbs related to daily actions 日常生活动词(7)	Action verb as predicate 动词谓语句（7） Time as adverbial 时间词做状语(7) Wh-questions 特殊疑问句:哪(13)	Time　时间 Place　地点 Hobbies　喜好 Preferences　选择 Daily activities 日常活动 Manner and means 方式

Sub-Unit Two：How to and Evaluation of Actions 教学单元二：怎么做，做得怎么样		
Vocabulary **词汇**	**Grammatical Points** **语法点**	**Linguistic Functions** **语用**
Adjectives 形容词（9） Adverbs 副词（9） Verbs related to daily actions 日常生活动词(7) Modal verbs 情态动词(8)	Modal verb：Know how 情态动词：会(8) Complement of degree 程度补语（9）	Hobbies 喜好 Preferences 选择 Evaluating ability and performance 评估能力及其表现

Sub-Unit Three：Preferences and Reasoning 教学单位三：选择与原因		
Vocabulary 词汇	**Grammatical Points 语法点**	**Linguistic Functions 语用**
Modal verbs 情态动词(8)	Use of modal verbs 情态动词的使用（8）	Preferences 选择 Plans 活动计划

Variation C： **This unit has four simpler sub-units.**

Map vocabulary and grammar according to functional language use；and

Keep vocabulary and sentence patterns to a functional minimum.

方案 C： **分四个简单教学单位。把握每个教学单位的词汇量和语法点，限制在最少。**

Sub-Unit One：Time 教学单位一：时间
Vocabulary 词汇
Calendar 日历（6） Parts of a day 一天的组成部分（6） Time of day 钟点（6） Verbs related to daily actions 日常生活动词（7）

Sub-Unit Two: Actions　教学单位二：活动		
Vocabulary 词汇	Grammatical Points 语法点	Linguistic Functions 语用
Action verbs　动词(7) Places　地点（16） Methods　方式（17）	Action verb as predicate 动词谓语句（7）	Time　时间 Place　地点 Manner and means　方式 Daily activities　日常活动

Sub-Unit Three: Plan Hobbies and Preferences　教学单位三：喜好与选择		
Vocabulary 词汇	Grammatical Points 语法点	Linguistic Functions 语用
Verbs related to daily actions 日常生活动词(7) Modal verbs　情态动词（8）	Modal verb: Want 情态动词:想要(8)	Hobbies　喜好 Preferences　选择

Sub-Unit Four: Evaluation of Actions　教学单位四：做得怎么样		
Vocabulary 词汇	Grammatical Points 语法点	Linguistic Functions 语用
Verbs related to daily actions 日常生活动词(7) Modal verbs　情态动词(8)	Modal verb: Know how 情态动词：会（8） Complements of degree 程度补语（9）	Evaluating　评估 Commenting　评论

Instructional Tips　教学指导策略提示

Tip 1:

Use life-like tasks to stimulate new language use. Use authentic materials when possible.

与现实生活相似的语言实践活动能激励新语言的学习，尽可能地用真实的语言材料。

Tip 2：

Sentence patterns and vocabularies from the previous units should be repeated and recycled in new units to maintain continuity in language use and to sustain learning. Include old topics as required in addition to new language tasks.

学会的词句要不断反复运用，话题不断反复增新，词汇的学习以老带新。

Tip 3：

Develop reading through use of visual aids, hands-on materials and activities, and authentic materials. Visual exposure is good for visual learners and hands-on activities are most helpful to active learners.

通过尽可能多的视觉辅助、直观和身体力行的材料和活动，以及真实生活语言教材来加强阅读能力，使学习风格特点不同的学生各得其所。

Tip 4：

Encourage interactive information exchange. Inquiry is essential to communication. Provide opportunities for learners to be familiar with and become more fluent in asking questions. Communicative exchanges can happen through games and task-based activities. Teacher modeling is important.

提问是交流的重要手段，从开始就要注重让学生练习提问，给学生创造机会熟悉和熟练提问。交际活动可以通过游戏和生活活动展开，老师的示范至关紧要。

Tip 5：

In order to develop task-based projects as major assignments, make sure language materials are developed gradually and cumulatively with structured instruction and clear guidance. This also applies to assessments.

逐步扎实地发展语用的能力，利用语言实践任务鼓励运用所学语言。但要注意教学指导明确清晰，有铺垫。作业和测试都如此 。

Tip 6:

Maintaining knowledge is one way to motivate learning. However, in order to achieve this, a teacher must repeatedly emphasize critical instructions and assignments. Not all students pay close attention to everything at all times. The teacher must create the right circumstances and use a variety of methods to gain the attention of students. It is also important to emphasize and reinforce instruction through note taking training. Students who take good notes are more likely to accomplish tasks efficiently and in a timely fashion.

要保证教学质量，让学生保持学习劲头，让他们成功，就得让学生学懂会用。任何教学的重点或教学的要求都要反复强调。一班学生不是每个学生在课堂的每一分钟都集中精力听讲的，总有人没听见或没用心或忘记了。老师一方面要设法抓住学生的注意力，另一方面要适时多方式地重复和强调，特别是教学的要求和作业，一定帮助学生记在脑子里同时也得记在本子上。

Suggested Activities　建议教学活动

Learning Time Expressions　学习时间词

Activity 1　Use Authentic Materials — What Time Is It?　几点了？

Language task: Tell time

Functions: Ask and tell the time
Listening, speaking, reading and writing

Use: Class activity, homework assignment, assessment

Present authentic materials and ask students to tell the time; May use English materials first, then use Chinese materials.

这个活动用来学习时间，主要是钟点。先可以看实物说，然后可以练习问答。还可以结合学习当地的历史、文化事件等。也可以跟学生、家庭成员的生日等话题结合。

Suggested materials for teaching time expressions (most of the materials can be found online)：

Calendars：

- City cultural events calendar
- School events calendar
- Historical events calendar

Time schedules：

- Bus, train, flight schedules
- Movie theater schedules

建议使用的教材——英文的、中文的各种时间表：（可从网上下载）

日历：

- 城市文化活动日历时间表
- 学校课程、课外活动时间表
- 历史事件时间表

时刻表：

- 汽车、火车、航班时刻表
- 电影、戏剧演出时刻表

Preparation for the activity：

Print out authentic materials for class use.

Elaboration：

- Students may also list the birthdays of family members.
  (Use with Activity 2 in Unit One)
- Have students make a calendar on a specific topic, such a "Major Events Calendar."

Analysis of the activity：

- Gathering events and presenting time with a purpose makes learning meaningful.
- Use of authentic materials in Chinese nurtures development of language proficiency in real-life situations.
- Use the opportunity to make connections with Social Studies or current affairs.

Learning Action Verbs　学动词

Activity 2　Charades　打哑谜

This game derives from a traditional game of guessing movie titles. In the Chinese classroom, it can be played with different levels of sophistication.

这个游戏常用来猜电影名。在汉语课堂上可以用来做各种语言学习的活动。

Simple version: Verbs are actions

A person or two people go to the front of the class and use body language to demonstrate a concept. The class guesses the meaning in Chinese.

Note:

As the topic suggests, we usually use this for learning verbal phrases.

Materials:

A list of verbal phrases to be learned will be helpful.

简单玩法:

顾名思义，学生到教室前边，做一个动作，请全班猜意思。

若学习动词，最好事先给一张词汇表。

Complex version: Guess what they are trying to tell us?

You may have teams plot a sentence or a scenario and act it out for others to guess.

Note:

It is not recommended to make the game too complex.

复杂玩法:

分队用肢体语言表演一句话或一个故事情景，请对方猜。

情节不宜太复杂。

Activity 3　Artistic Interpretations of Actions: Drawing Verbs　画动词

Language task: Drawing verbs

Functions: Writing characters

Use: Homework assignment or class activity

这个活动用以学习动词。让学生动脑筋，将动词的意思用图画表现出来。以形象思维带动汉字的学习。做法：学生每人挑六个动词组（可用《什么篇：语用与语法走廊》（7）），写汉字并配以图画。课上展示。

Preparation for the activity:

A list of verbs from which to choose.

(Reference: *Functional and Grammatical Walk Through* (7))

Procedure:

Step 1: Assignment

- Each student writes six self-chosen verbal phrases and draws pictures expressing them.

Step 2: Present in class

Follow-up:

- Post the artwork on the classroom walls.
- Compile the artwork into a book.

Learning Time and Action　学习时间和行为

Activity 4	Think about Your Day's Schedule in Chinese 每日活动时间表
Language task:	Create a schedule in Chinese
Functions:	Relate time expressions with actions Writing, speaking, listening, reading
Elaboration:	Presentational mode: Report
Use:	Class activity, homework assignment, assessment

做法：

- 先全班谈论每日活动时间表。
- 然后与人对话。
- 找出一两个活动的时间向全班汇报。
- 接下来还可以扩展成家庭作业的写作部分。

Preparation for the activity:

- Know weekdays and clock time.
- Know verbal phrases used in school life.
- Know how to ask questions.

Procedure:

Step 1: Talking about a daily schedule in class

- In combination with Activity 2 in Unit One: Students share one or two schedule activities with a partner and report to class.

Step 2: Take it home

- Ask students to write down the typical schedule of a school day

Elaboration:

Use question and answer format.

Follow-up:

The resulting schedule may serve as a partial draft for a later project.

Comprehensive Review　综合复习

Activity 5　Game: Win-Lose-or Draw　输赢在此一画

Language task: Use drawings to prompt meaning

Functions: Review vocabulary and sentence patterns

Use all four language skills

Use: Class activity

The name of this game comes from an old TV game show from the late 1980s because the game models the show's format.

One player draws pictures on the board, while the others guess the meaning out loud. This game prompts writing, reading, speaking and listening of Chinese. It involves competing teams of three to five players. The goal of game is to earn the most points and win the game. Points are earned by guessing the meaning of pictures drawn from words or sentences written on a card. The cards are created by students.

这个游戏模仿 20 世纪 80 年代一个有名的电视游戏节目的形式，因此借用了游戏的名字。这个游戏就是画画儿猜字。要求学生听、说、读、写汉语。玩这个游戏可以有数个队参加。每队 3 ~ 5 个队员。得分高的队是赢家。

游戏的玩法：

- 分队。每个队员做五张卡片。卡片上写一个中文词或中文句子。
- 检查卡片是否正确。收齐卡片，按组分放。
- 轮流以队为单位玩。一队一次派一个队员上前抽他队一张卡片。（给老师看卡片上的句子和字数。由老师在黑板上画出表示字数的横线）见卡后，按卡片上的汉语在黑板上画画儿，其他队员猜意思，直到每个字都被猜出为止。时间限制：一分钟。

游戏规则：

- 轮流玩。直到每队每人都玩过才可进第二轮。
- 画的人不能说话，不可用数字，不能用手势。
- 如卡片上有错字，被抽卡人发现，抽卡人自动得分。

窍门：

- 一队只有一分钟可以得胜。如该该队队员画画儿，大声和快速说出所有跟图画有关的可能的词，老师听见就会写在黑板上了。

游戏的使用：

- 复习词汇和句型。
- 听、说、读、写全面练习。
- 需要老师的辅助，课上使用。

Requirements：

- Teams of three to five players
- Instructor
- A time keeper

Materials：

- Index cards or small pieces of paper

Procedure:

Step 1: Form teams

- Three to five players form a team. There must be at least two teams to play.

Step 2: Preparation

- Each player creates five cards, each card bears a sentence or several words using previously learned sentences and characters.
- Each team must brainstorm sentences as a team to avoid duplication. Then each individual writes words or sentences.
- Each team reviews to ensure that each card is written correctly.

Step 3: Play

- The cards are gathered and piled face down according to team.
- Teams take turns to send one player at a time to draw the meaning of cards made by a different team. (Team 1 draws from Team 2's pile, Team 2 from Team 3's, and so on.)
- The drawing player **silently** reads the sentence on the card and shows the contents only to the teacher. (The teacher confirms that the player understands the sentence.)
- The instructor draws blank lines on board indicating the number of characters in the sentence.
- The player goes to the board to draw pictures while the rest of the team guesses, shouting out possible answers.
- The time keeper starts the clock as soon as the player begins drawing.
- The instructor, upon hearing any word in the sentence, writes over the appropriate line.
- The team wins a point if all the blanks are filled within one minute.
- The instructor cleans the board quickly and keeps score on board.

Rules:

- Teams take turns to play.
- Each player plays in turn until everyone on the team gets a chance to play.

- The player who draws is not to utter a sound at any time (except when confirming the meaning with the instructor before drawing).
- Each round must be completed in one minute. A team that is unsuccessful loses the point to the team that produces the card.
- The team that discovers a card bearing a sentence with incorrect characters or grammatical errors automatically wins a point.
- Only drawings are accepted. No numbers. No gestures.

Tip:

The team should try to shout all possible answers in order to score in time. For example, if the player draws a person, the rest of the team should quickly say all possible vocabulary related to a person.

Use:

- This game is good for reviewing sentence patterns and vocabulary.
- It can be used periodically.
- It is an in-class activity because it requires an instructor's facilitation.

Hobbies and Preferences 喜好与选择

Activity 6 What Do You Llike to Do? 你喜欢做什么？

We may use the format and routine of Activity 4, above, but change the topic. Expand the discourse by adding:

With whom do you like to play? 你跟谁玩？
Where do you usually play? 你常在哪儿玩？

这是上面活动4的演变。用活动4的形式和程序。把话题变成“你喜欢做什么”“怎么玩”，还可加“你常跟谁玩”“在哪儿玩”等。

Activity 7 Tongue Twister 绕口令

Pronunciation and fluency are also related to the physical part of speaking. This activity is introduced to exercise the “speaking muscles.”

这是一个练嘴的活动。强调的是发音与声调的准确和说话的流利程度。

做法：

- 发一个词 、词组或短句的单子。
- 练习：默念，听老师读，跟老师读，加快语速。
- 背诵：集体，个人。
- 挑一条或两条计时背诵。有错重来。

Preparation for the activity：

Handouts：Practice rhyme sheet.

Procedure：

Step 1：Create a vocabulary list of rhyming words，phrases or sentences.

Step 2：Pre-speaking practice

- Read the list of rhymes to review the vocabulary.

Step 3：Read aloud

- The teacher leads reading rhymes aloud in class with increasing speed.

Step 4：Class memorization

- The class tries to say one rhyme from memory.

Step 5：Individual experiment

- Select individuals to perform from memory.

Step 6：Time the speech

- Ask the students to time the teacher reciting one rhyme to see how fast it can go.
- Have students try to set personal records.

Follow-up 1：Homework

Select two or three rhymes to practice：Memorize and time.

Follow-up 2：In-class competition

- Students select one best-practiced rhyme to perform.
- The performance is timed.

Sample：

Here is a sample practice sheet for modal verbs and verbal phrases.

顺口溜：

想看电影，想看电视，想打球，想游泳，想睡觉，想吃中国饭，不想看书。

要玩电脑，要去中国，要做功课，要回家，要骑马，要坐车，不想喝可口可乐。

喜欢看书，喜欢喝咖啡，喜欢吃水果，喜欢打电话，喜欢跳舞，喜欢唱歌，不喜欢说法语。

会说英语，会说日语，会打篮球，会打排球，会做饭，会开车，不会用电脑。

跑步跑得快，写字写得慢，吃饭吃得多，喝水喝得少。

起床起得早，睡觉睡得晚，走路走得快，骑车骑得慢。

Making Comments 评论

Activity 8 Convert A Reading 读后说
Language task: Adapt the reading according to your own life experience
Functions: Reading, speaking and writing with a sample
Elaboration: Presentational mode: Report
Use: Class activity, homework sssignment, assessment

这个活动以阅读为主，阅读带动说话，阅读与说话为写作铺垫。可课上完成，也可部分做课外活动。累计为综合项目打基础。

做法：

- 在讨论日常活动和喜好的基础上阅读一篇短文。
- 阅读后问答检查阅读理解。
- 以问答为起点一句一句地把答案变成叙述。
- 背诵。
- 写下来。

Procedure:

Step 1: Based on a class discussion, read a passage about a person's hobby

Step 2: Talking about it

- Check comprehension by asking questions.

Step 3: Talking about it more

- Repeat answers one after another and develop into a narration.

Step 4: Deliver the narration from memory

Step 5: Take it home

- As a homework assignment, students rewrite the passage changing key information according to their own experiences.

Elaboration:

Include questions and answers

Follow-up:

The resulting narration can serve as a partial draft for a later project.

Making Plans　计划

Activity 9　Creative Writing: "A Day in My Life"　写作：我的一天

Language task: Write about your life

Functions: Relate time expressions with actions

Writing

Elaboration: Presentational: Report

Use: Class activity, homework assignment, assessment

根据以上几个活动，发展成写作“我的一天”，或其他话题的习作，例如：谈计划等。先说再写。还可以加问答，加写成对话。可以发展成综合项目的一部分。

Procedure:

Step 1: Talk about schedules, hobbies, preferences in class

- In combination with Activity 2 in Unit One: Students share 1or 2 schedule items with a partner and report to class.

Step 2: Take it home

- Ask students to write about the topics discussed.

Elaboration:

Include questions and answers.

Follow-up:

- It lays ground for presentation.
- It also lays ground for a peer editing and re-writing activity.
- It can also serve as a partial draft for a later project.

Activity 10	Peer Editing and Re-writing: "A Day in My Life" 同伴相互修改文章
Language task:	Combine individual writings to make dialogues
Functions:	Make plans Interpersonal communication: Writing, speaking, listening, reading
Elaboration:	Presentational: Report or presentation
Use:	Class activity, homework assignment, assessment

这个活动是以上几个写作活动的继续。也可用于综合项目的一部分。

做法：

- 同伴相互审阅初稿，各自选出对方好的句子，并提出一到两条修改建议。
- 综合两人的作文，共同创作一个对话。

Preparation for the activity:

Must have completed Activity 9.

Procedure:

Step 1: Instructions

- Clarify task.
- Lay out specific required elements.

Step 2: Form a team

- Pair up learners randomly.

Step 3: Create a dialogue

- Ask students to read each other's writing and select the best sentences to form a base for a dialogue or two.

Follow-up:

It can serve as a draft for a later project (see below Unit Three Project B).

Critical Thinking and Comparative Study　评判和比较

Activity 11　Guessing Game — Winning Bonus　猜猜看：有奖游戏

Activity 12　Discovering Rules　找出规律

(请参照第一教学单元活动 6 和活动 7)

Don't forget to use these activities in class repeatedly.

Project　综合项目

Activity 13　Task-based Projects　语言实践任务项目

Language task: Talk about a hobby/Make a plan

Format: Oral presentation and written presentation

Functions: Demonstrate language proficiency

Use: Class activity, homework assignment, assessment

A task-based project must be clearly structured. The basic instructions include:

- Be clear about the topic and format.
- Lay out detailed content, specifics on sentence patterns, vocabulary, and other required elements.
- Provide examples of writing presentation and rubrics.

指导学生完成语言实践任务项目应有明确的指示。基本教学指导应包括：

- 明确话题和形式。
- 规定内容、句型、词汇及其他必要成分的使用。
- 提供范文、评估标准等。

See Part Ⅰ: Teaching Tips — Best Practices, Question 13: How do I design a good project?

请参照上篇：教学小诀窍——好经验，问题13：怎么设计一个好的综合性的学习项目？

Suggested Assignment Focus 建议作业的重点

- Reading with increasing number of characters 阅读加大汉字数量
- Writing in sentences using characters 用汉字写句子
- Developing all four language skills 发展听、说、读、写技能
- Completing basic language tasks in Chinese 用目的语完成语言任务
- Asking questions 会提问

Suggested Assignments 建议作业

- Assign listening materials: Listening.
- Copy words or characters: Reading and writing.
- Memorize some language materials, and prepare to perform during the next class: Reading and speaking.
- Produce some language materials as instructed, and prepare to perform during the next class: Writing and speaking; open-ended tasks.
- Writing on topic: Speaking and writing and task – based presentation.
- Peer editing and writing: Cooperative learning, interactive learning and discourse development.
- Create projects using oral and written presentations: All language skills.
- 听力练习。
- 读写练习。
- 记忆语言材料，准备测试：读说。
- 创造性地运用语言材料，预备课上展示：说写，语言实践任务。
- 有题目地写作：说写，语言实践任务。
- 同伴互相编辑写作：合作学习，学习交流，成段表达。
- 创作口语和书面报告：综合训练。

Suggested Assessment Focus　建议评估重点

Listening comprehension　听力理解

• Comprehension of learned words	听懂所学的词
• Comprehension of short sentences	听懂短句
• Comprehension of mini dialogues	听懂小对话

Speaking　说

• Emphasizing correct pronunciation	发音正确
• Emphasizing correct tones	声调正确
• Emphasizing fluency	流利
• Emphasizing producing correct sentences	能说句子
• Emphasizing being able to initiate and respond to interactions properly	发问并回答

Reading　阅读

• Words, sentences and short texts in *pinyin*	阅读拼音形式的词、句子、短文
• Words, sentences, and short texts in Chinese characters	阅读汉字形式的词、句子、短文
• Guess meaning with common sense and contextual clues	根据背景知识和上下文猜断语义

Writing　写

• Using correct spelling of *pinyin*	正确用拼音书写
• Writing characters correctly	正确用汉字书写
• Creating texts in *pinyin*	用拼音写作表达
• Creating texts with known characters	用已知汉字写作表达
• Writing with a Chinese word processor	会用中文处理软件

Suggested Assessment　建议测试评估形式

See page 90.

见 90 页。

Rubrics for Assessment 测试标准

Make a clear rubric specifying expectations and the required elements according to the content coverage of the day or lesson.

根据每日课堂的学习进度，制定明确、清晰的测试评分标准，以申明期待和要求。

Sample Unit Project 教学单元综合项目测试例案

Unit Three Project A: One Day in My Life

第三教学单元综合项目（一）：我的一天

Format:

Oral and written presentation

Topic:

Time and activities

Content:

- A brief self-introduction (e. g. name in English and Chinese, nationality and language, family, etc.)
- Hobby
- Know how and skill
- Routines (time, place, manner, etc.)
- Plan
- Reasoning
- Three questions for listening comprehension

Evaluation:

- Content knowledge:

  Linguistic components

  Functional use of the language

  Mechanics (grammatical and technical errors)
- Creativity in presentation:

  Overall design

  Visual aids or artistic expressions
- Delivery:

  Pronunciation, tones and fluency

Organization of information

Presentation

Reference

• Effort

Writing Sample 1　范文（一）

我的名字叫 Leo。我今年十六岁。

每天早上七点半起床。起床以后开车去上学。

我星期一和星期三上汉语课。我星期二和星期四上英语和运动课。放学以后，我开车回家。我喜欢看电影和用电脑。因为我喜欢看电影，所以常常看。我不喜欢跑步和走路。要是我喜欢走路，我就走路来上学。我常常一边吃饭，一边打电话。我妈妈说："别一边吃饭，一边打电话。"

(By Leo L. , Northside College Preparatory High School, Chinese 1)

Writing Sample 2　范文（二）

我是谁?

我不但非常好看而且有意思。我会弹吉他。虽然我的音乐难唱，可是我唱歌唱得太好听了。

我家有七个人。我有一个哥哥，他有三个女儿，Michelle 最小。虽然我爱她，可是她又不可以看我的吉他又不可以摸我的吉他。我喜欢买吉他。我没有钱不能买很多的吉他。要是我有钱，我就买很多的吉他，因为我想要很多吉他。

我会一边开会，一边弹吉他。我常常一边写信，一边弹吉他。去年四月我睡觉的时候写了一首歌。

要是我高兴，我就说"Have mercy"。因为我喜欢我的爱人，所以我常常对她说"Have mercy"。

我是谁? 我是 Jesse 叔叔*! 你认识我吗? 我还有名吗?

* A character in "Full House" — a popular TV show in the late 1980s.

(By Simon S. , Northside College Preparatory High School, Chinese 2)

Unit Three Project B: My Plan
第三教学单元综合项目（二）：我的计划

Dialogue:

Making an Appointment

Format:

Oral and written presentation

Topic:

Making plans

Content:

Use all of the below, but make it into a story with dialogue

- A brief introduction to the person (e. g. name in English and Chinese, nationality and language, family, etc.)
- Hobby
- Know how and skill
- Routines (time, place, manner)
- Plan
- Reasoning
- Three questions for listening comprehension

Evaluation:

- Content knowledge:
  - Linguistic components
  - Functional use of the language
  - Mechanics (grammatical and technical errors)
- Creativity in presentation:
  - Overall design
  - Visual aids or artistic expressions
- Delivery:
  - Pronunciation, tones and fluency
  - Organization of information
  - Presentation
  - Reference
- Effort

Writing Sample　范文

大明：明天我想和我的朋友去看电影，你想不想跟我们一起去？

小分：什么电影？有意思吗？

大明：是一个新的中国电影。

小分：在哪儿看？

大明：在芝加哥大学。我们要看晚上九点的。

小分：我也想去，可是晚上九点太晚了，有没有七点的？

大明：好，我们看七点的。看电影以后，我们去中国饭馆吃晚饭好吗？

小分：那太好了！我们怎么去？坐公共汽车还是开车？

大明：我开车。我可以去你家接你。

小分：你什么时候来我家？

大明：五点半，怎么样？

小分：好，明天下午五点半见。

大明：再见，不见不散。

Unit Four：Going Shopping
第四教学单元：买东西

Theme 主题

Going Shopping 买东西

Topics 交谈要点与话题

- Large Numbers 大数字
- Money 钱
- Colors 颜色
- Clothing 服装
- Tools 用具
- Describing things 描述
- Identifying Objects 识别
- Bargaining 讨价还价
- Comparing and Judging 比一比
- Complex Noun Phrases 复杂名词词组

Content of Teaching and Learning 教学内容

Linguistic Functions 语用功能

- Paragraph-length narration 成段表述
- Inquiring and responding in dialogues 问答对话
- Commenting 评论
- Reasoning 表述原因理由条件
- Describing things 描述
- Identifying objects 识别
- Bargaining 讨价还价
- Comparing and judging 判断比较

- Listening with comprehension to passages of increasing length 听力理解
- Reading passages with comprehension　段落的阅读理解
- Using a Chinese word processor　使用中文处理软件
- Writing in paragraphs　写作

Grammatical Patterns and Vocabulary　语法点与词汇

(Refer to *Functional and Grammatical Walk Through*)

(参照《什么篇：语用与语法走廊》(索引：B/1/2/3/8/10/11/12/13/18/20))

Vocabulary　词汇	Grammatical Points　语法点
Large numbers 大数字 (1) Money　钱 (1) Measure words 量词 (3/11) Colors　颜色 (10) Clothing　服装 (11) Tools　用具 (11) Conjunctions for complex sentences 复句连词 (12)	Formation of large numbers　大数字 (1) Units of money and conversion　钱的换算 (1) "是……的" structure (10) Adjectives as predicate　形容词谓语句 (2/10) Three levels of comparison: Adjectives　更,最(20) "比" sentence (20) "跟……一样" sentence (20) Use of modal verbs　情态动词的使用 (8) Use of complex sentences　复句 (12) Complex noun phrases　复杂名词词组(11/18) Yes/No questions　是非疑问句 (2/13) Wh-question　特殊疑问句 (1/13) Chinese characters　汉字 (B)

Cultural Studies and Connections　文化及跨学科联系

- Social and cultural variations　社会文化变异：
  - Bargaining　讨价还价
  - Sales　减价
- Social Studies　社会学：

Currency 货币

Fashion 流行款式

Advertising 广告

Consumers and consumption 消费者与消费

Family budget 家庭预算

- Mathematics 数学：

  Currency exchange 货币换算

Variations of Unit Four 第四单元的变量设置

The instructor can customize this unit design according to the needs of the class, curriculum at large, the available contact hours and schedule.

教学单元应根据课堂教学的需求、课程设置的全局情况及课时的限制酌情加减。

Variables that can be taken into consideration are:

- Number of grammatical patterns involved,
- Extensiveness of vocabulary,
- Depth of communication tasks, and
- Proficiency of language skills.

应考虑的变量如下：

- 语法点的数量，
- 词汇的覆盖面，
- 语用实践活动的深度，
- 语言技巧的水平。

Suggested Variations of the Unit by Topic 建议参考如下

Variation A: **The unit can be easily divided into three sub-units. Each unit can include an expandable, related vocabulary list.**

方案 A： **这个单元可以分成三个教学单位。每个教学单位的词汇表可增减。**

Sub-Unit One：Large numbers/Money/Objects 教学单位一：大数字/钱/物件		
Vocabulary **词汇**	**Grammatical Points** **语法点**	**Linguistic Functions** **语用**
Large numbers 大数字（1） Money　钱（1） Colors　颜色（10） Clothing　服装（11） Tools　用具（11）	Formation of large numbers 大数字（1） Units of money and conversion 钱的换算（1） Measure words for clothing 衣服的量词（11） “是……的” structure（10） Adjectives as predicate 形容词谓语句（2/10） Yes/No questions 是非疑问句（2/7/13） Wh-questions　特殊疑问句： 怎么样/多少钱（1/13）	Narration 成段表述 Describing things 描述 Identifying objects 识别

Sub-Unit Two：Compare：What is better？　教学单位二：比较		
Vocabulary **词汇**	**Grammatical Points** **语法点**	**Linguistic Functions** **语用**
Large numbers 大数字（1） Money　钱（1） Colors　颜色(10) Clothing　服装(11) Tools　用具(11)	Three levels of comparison： Adjectives/Adverbs： 更，最（20） “比” sentence（20） “跟……一样”sentence(20) Yes/No questions 是非疑问句（2/7/13） Wh-questions　特殊疑问句： 怎么样/多少钱（1/13）	Narration　成段表述 Questions and answers in dialogue 问答对话 Compare and contrast： Differences 比较不同 Identify Similarities 确认相同 Preferences　比选择 Comparing possessions 比所有

Sub-Unit Three：How well do you do it？ 教学单位三：做得怎么样		
Vocabulary 词汇	Grammatical Points 语法点	Linguistic Functions 语用
Large numbers 大数字（1） Money 钱（1） Colors 颜色(10) Clothing 服装(11) Tools 用具(11)	Use of modal verbs 情态动词的使用（8） Use of complex sentences 复句（9） Complex noun phrases 复杂名词词组（11/18） Yes/No questions 是非疑问句（2/7/13） Wh-questions 特殊疑问句： 怎么样/多少钱/ 为什么（1/13）	Narration 成段表述 Questions and answers in dialogue 问答对话 Complex noun phrases 复杂名词词组 Comments 评论 Reasoning 表述原因、理由、条件

Variation B： **The unit can be simply divided into two sub-units.**
Map vocabulary and grammatical patterns according to language use；and
Keep vocabulary and grammatical patterns to a functional minimum.

方案B： 分两个从属教学单位。把握每个教学单位的词汇量和语法点。

Sub-Unit One：Large numbers/Money/Objects 教学单位一：大数字/钱/物件		
Vocabulary 词汇	Grammatical Points 语法点	Linguistic Functions 语用
Large numbers 大数字（1） Money 钱(1) Colors 颜色（10 ） Clothing 服装（11） Tools 用具（11）	Formation of large numbers 大数字（1） Units of money and conversion 钱的换算（1） Measure words for clothing 衣服的量词（11） “是……的” structure（10） Adjective as predicate 形容词谓语句（2/10） Wh-questions 特殊疑问句： 怎么样/多少钱（1/13）	Narration 成段表述 Describing things 描述 Identifying objects 识别

Sub-Unit Two: Compare: What is better? 教学单元二：比较		
Vocabulary 词汇	**Grammatical Points 语法点**	**Linguistic Functions 语用**
Large numbers 大数字(1) Money 钱(1) Colors 颜色（10） Clothing 服装（11） Tools 用具（11）	Three levels of comparison: Adjectives/Adverbs: 更，最（20） "比" sentence（20） "跟……一样" sentence(20) Wh-questions 特殊疑问句： 怎么样/多少钱（1/13）	Narration 成段表述 Questions and answers in dialogue 问答对话 Compare and contrast: Differences 比较不同 Identify similarities 确认相同 Preferences 比选择 Comparing possessions 比所有

Variation C: **The unit retains two sub-units.**
Map vocabulary and grammar according to functional language use; and
Keep grammatical structures to a functional minimum.

方案 C： **保留两个教学单位。把握每个教学单位的词汇量和语法点，限制在最少。**

Sub-Unit One: Money/Objects 教学单位一：钱/物件		
Vocabulary 词汇	**Grammatical Points 语法点**	**Linguistic Functions 语用**
Money 钱(1) Colors 颜色(10) Clothing 服装(11) Tools 用具（11） Food 食物（22）	Units of money and conversion 钱的换算（1） Measure words for clothing/objects/food 衣服、物件和食物的量词(2) "是……的" structure（10） Adjectives as predicate 形容词谓语句（2/10） Wh-questions 特殊疑问句： 怎么样/多少钱（1/13）	Narration 成段表述 Describing things 描述 Identifying objects 识别

Sub-Unit Two: Compare: What is better? 教学单位二：比较		
Vocabulary 词汇	**Grammatical Points 语法点**	**Linguistic Functions 语用**
Money 钱(1) Colors 颜色(10) Clothing 服装(11) Tools 用具(11) Food 食物(22)	Three levels of comparison: Adjectives/Adverbs: 更，最（20） "比" sentence（20） "跟……一样"sentence（20）	Narration 成段表述 Questions and answers in dialogue 问答对话 Compare and contrast: Differences 比较不同 Identify similarities 确认相同 Preferences 比选择 Comparing possessions 比所有

Instructional Tips 教学指导策略提示

Tip 1:

Use topics with which students are most familiar to introduce new language use. Practice new learning in a variety of situations. A teacher should prepare the following to facilitate learning:

- Select relevant topics and situations that will prompt language use.
- Design appropriate activities and tasks that reinforce learning.
- Provide necessary language materials and expressions (vocabulary, sentence patterns, etc.) that allow extension of learning.

用学生熟悉的情景介绍引入新语言的学习并在不同的情景中练习扩展语言的运用。这需要老师作以下的准备：

- 挑选可以引发语用的相关话题和情景。
- 设计合适的教学活动实现并加强教学。
- 提供扩展学习的必需语言表达方式方法（包括词汇与句型等）。

Tip 2:

When designing learning activities, include sentence patterns, vocabulary as well as topics from the previous unit for continuation of learning.

新的教学应建立在已知的基础上，尽可能发挥运用已学会的语句、词汇和话题，使语言的发展有其连续性和连贯性，不断温故知新。

Tip 3:

When planning lessons, control the sequence and the pace of the learning content. The lesson should follow a logical progression: Do one thing at a time; one activity paves the way for the next. This is important for younger students.

设计教案时，控制教学进程与进度。教学活动应有其合理的进展过程，按部就班，循序渐进。学生的年龄越小，教学的进展和速度越要合理安排。

Tip 4:

Interactive activities are crucial to language learning. However, for a class of more than 20 students (a typical required class size in many public schools is 28) clear instruction and strong classroom management are a must for effective and efficient interactive activities.

互动的教学活动对语言学习至关紧要。要使互动学习有成效有效率，特别是在较大的课堂上（典型的公立学校的课堂要求 28 人一班）教学指导要清晰明确，课堂管理得精益求精。

Tip 5:

It is still important at this stage to scaffold development of proficiency by modeling language use.

示范正确的语言运用在这个阶段的学习中起支持语言能力发展的作用。

Suggested Activities　建议教学活动

Learning Large Numbers　学数字

Activity 1　　Large Numbers in Real Life　生活中的大数目

Language task: Use of large numbers in Chinese

Functions:　Inquiring and reporting numbers

Listening, speaking and reading

Use: Class activity or assessment

这个活动学习大数目，并且可以与其他学科的知识联系起来。用生活中的大数目学习：

- 地理：人口、国家领土面积。
- 经济：平均年收入、房价、物价等。

Suggested Topics:

Geography:

- Compare the population of China, U. S. A. , and Canada.
- Compare the sizes of China, U. S. A. and Canada (in square kilometers).

Economy:

- Average yearly income in big cities.
- Average real-estate values and purchase prices.

Preparation for the activity:

Research related data.

Procedure:

Step 1: Raise real-life issues that involve numbers

Step 2: Say the number in Chinese

Analysis of the activity:

- It relates to real-life knowledge.
- It connects to other subject areas of learning.
- It can be used with problem-based learning.
- It involves multiple skills.

Activity 2 Conversion of Large Numbers 大数字的转换

Language task: Create large numbers in Chinese

Functions: Write numbers in Chinese

Speaking, reading and writing

Use: Class activity, homework assignment, assessment

让学生每人在黑板上写一个大数。每人再挑一个别人写的数，大声用中文说出，大家评对错。还可让学生回家做数个类似的练习。但一定要在课上练习充分，让每人都有信心和方法正确换算。

Procedure:

Step 1: Create a large number

- Ask students to each write a large number on the board.

Step 2: The teacher says the large number in Chinese

- Ask a student to select a number on board and say it aloud in Chinese.

Follow-up:

- Homework:

  Ask the students to write ten large numbers and convert them to Chinese.

- Check homework results:

  Ask each student to read one number from the list in English.

  Translate into Chinese.

  Ask the class to listen and confirm the accuracy.

Notes:

- Our students love this activity.
- Try to make sure they can do it correctly with confidence.

Learning Vocabulary 学习词汇

Activity 3 Use Visual Aids, Live Objects or Cards: Asking "What Is This?"

看图说话：这是什么？

Language task: Identify objects

Functions: Ask about items

Listening, speaking, reading and writing

Use: Class activity or assessment

看图或卡片，立即用中文说出。也可让学生互问。还可让学生在对话后报告对话的情况。

Preparation for the activity:

- Objects
- Cards
- Other visual aids

Procedure:

Step 1: What is it?

- Present an object or card to students.
- Ask students to identify it in Chinese.

Step 2: Student's turn

- Ask students to ask one another.

Step 3: Solicit a report

- Ask students to report the results to class.
(They may report the mistakes as well in Chinese.)

Developing Discourses 对话

Activity 4 Fashion Show 时装表演
Language task: Describe what the model is wearing
Functions: Practice vocabulary related to clothing
Speaking, listening, writing
Use: Class activity, homework assignment, assessment

In this game, the students describe what a model is wearing. The description and presentation can be based on interpersonal interactions. The content of the game and activities are expandable.

做法:

- 一个学生做模特状，其他学生从头到脚描述他/她的穿戴。
- 可先对话问答以熟悉句型和词汇，还可加衣物的价钱、颜色等描述。
- 在这一活动的基础上还可以布置说、写、扩展使用等家庭作业。

Preparation for the activity:

- Vocabulary related to clothing and money
- Measure words
- “是……的” structure
- Adjectives as predicate
- Exchange rates

Procedure:

Step 1: Warm-up activity

- Describe what you are wearing today by using:

  今天我穿了一件（一条/一双）……

  我的……是……（颜色）的。

- May also add:

  我的……不太贵，很好看，又便宜又漂亮。

  我的……是在……买的。

Step 2: Have a student come to the center or front of the class (or do a cat walk if the model so desires).

Step 3: Have another student describe what the model is wearing by using the same sentence patterns above.

Follow-up: Homework

Go home and write the description down.

Elaborations:

- If you know how to describe the price of the clothing, add the price.
- Go to your closet and do a rough count: How many pieces of clothing are there?
- How much are your possessions worth in total?
- If you know the exchange rate and can do the math, how much is that in RMB?

  (Possible byproduct: Gratefulness to parents? Is it time to clean up your closet or your room?)

Activity 5　Dialogue: What do you have?　你有什么?

Language task: Ask and describe what your partner has

Functions: Practice vocabulary related to objects
Identify and describe items
Speaking, listening, writing

Use: Class activity, homework assignment, assessment

谈学生有的东西，学习词汇和有关句型。可先对话问答以熟悉句型和词汇。

还可加衣物的价钱、颜色等描述，或购买的地方、时间等。

在这一活动的基础上还可以布置说、写、扩展使用等家庭作业。

Preparation for the activity:

- Learn vocabulary related to objects and money.
- Measure words
- "是……的" structure
- Adjectives as predicate
- Exchange rates

Procedure:

Step 1: Warm-up activity

- Describe what you have by using:

  我有（一个/一张/一本）……
  我的……是……（颜色/语言）的。
  那（这）个/张/本……是……（某人）的。

- May also use:

  她/他/我的……不太贵，很好看，又便宜又漂亮。
  是在……（地点/时间）买的。

- May also use:

  我常常用……做……

Step 2: Prepare questions

- Brainstorm appropriate questions.

Step 3: Pair up

- Pair up students.

Step 4: Exchange information

- Interview your partner using the prepared questions.

Step 5: Optional

- Report your conversation to class.

Follow-up: Homework

Go home and write down the conversation.

Elaborations:

- If you know how to say the price, add the price to the written assignment.
- Go to your bedroom and do a rough count: How many things are there?
- How much are your possessions worth in total?
- If you know the exchange rate and can do the math, how much is that in RMB?

Writing Sample　范文

Clothing in my closet　我的衣柜

我有一件夹克、六件运动衫和六件衬衫。我的夹克是红的和白的。我有很多颜色的运动衫和很多颜色的衬衫。我有五条短裤、四条运动裤、两条游泳裤、三条咔叽裤、五条牛仔裤、两条西服裤和七条裤衩。我有一双皮鞋、三双运动鞋、一双跑鞋、一双凉鞋、一双拖鞋、一双靴子。我的皮鞋是黑的。我有一双运动鞋是黑的和白的。我有一双运动鞋是蓝的和白的。我有一双运动鞋是白的、红的和黑的。我的跑鞋是红的、黑的和白的。我的凉鞋是黑的。我的拖鞋是蓝的。我的靴子是棕的和黑的。

(By Calvin L., Northside College Preparatory High School, Chinese 1)

Preferences and Plans　选择和计划

Activity 6　Creative Writing: Journal "What Did I Buy During the Week?"
写作：这星期我买什么了？

Language task: Write about your life

Functions: Relating objects to prices
Developing a discourse
Writing

Elaboration: Presentational: Report

Use: Class activity, homework assignment, assessment

在谈价格的基础上，写出本周采购的情况和价格，也可加口头报告。

Procedure:

Step 1: Discuss objects and prices in class

- In combination with Activity 2 in Unit One, students discuss one or two objects and their prices with a partner and report to class.

Step 2: Take it home

- Write about the topics discussed.

Elaboration:

Include questions and answers.

Follow-up:

- This activity lays ground for presentation.
- This activity also lays ground for a peer editing and rewriting activity.
- This activity can also serve as a partial draft for a later project.

Activity 7 Creative Writing: I Have the Best! 创作：我的最好！
Language task: Make a commercial advertisement
Functions: Relate objects with prices and descriptions
Develop a discourse
Writing
Elaboration: Presentational: Report
Use: Class activity, homework assignment, assessment

做一个广告。要说明卖的物件、特点、价格及其他条件。比较。要有说服力。

可扩展成为综合项目的一部分。

Procedure:

Step 1: Discuss the prices and characteristics of objects

- Compare in class.

- In combination with Activity 2 in Unit One, students discuss one or two objects and prices with a partner and report to class.

Step 2: Take it home

- Write about the topics discussed.
- The descriptions must be in a commercial format as if they are promoting the product.

Elaboration:

Include questions and answers.

Follow-up:

- This activity lays ground for presentation.
- This activity also lays ground for a peer editing and rewriting activity.
- This activity can also serve as a partial draft for a later project.

Activity 8	Peer Editing and Rewriting: "Shopping" 同伴改稿:买东西
Language task:	Tell stories related to shopping experiences
Functions:	Relate objects with prices and descriptions
	Develop a discourse
	Writing, speaking, listening, reading
Elaboration:	Presentational: Report or presentation
Use:	Class activity, homework assignment, assessment

这个活动是以上几个写作活动的继续。也可用于综合项目的一部分。

做法:

- 同伴相互审阅初稿。各自选出对方好的句子，并提出一到两条修改建议。
- 综合两人的作文，共同创作一个对话。

Preparation for the activity:

Must have completed either of Activity 3, 4 or 5.

Procedure:

Step 1: Instructions

- Clarify tasks and lay out specific required elements.

Step 2: Form a team

- Pair up learners randomly.

Step 3: Create a dialogue

- Ask students to read each other's writing and select the best sentences to form a foundation for a dialogue or two.

Follow-up:

The result can serve as a draft for a later project (see below Activity 7).

Comprehensive Learning　综合学习

Activity 9	Project: Shopping　综合项目：买东西
Language task:	Tell a story: A shopping experience
Format:	Oral presentation and written presentation
Function:	Demonstrate language proficiency through use
Use:	Class activity, homework assignment, assessment

A task-based project must be clearly structured. The basic instructions include:

- Be clear about the topic and format.
- Lay out detailed content, specifics on sentence patterns, vocabulary, and other required elements.
- Provide examples of writing presentation and rubrics.

指导学生完成语言实践任务项目应有明确的指示。基本教学指导应包括：

- 明确话题和形式。
- 规定内容、句型、词汇及其他必要成分的使用。
- 提供范文，评估标准等。

See Part I: Teaching Tips — Best Practices, Question 13: How do I design a good project?

请参照上篇：教学小诀窍——好经验，问题13：怎么设计一个好的综合性的学习项目？

（See assessment sample below）见下范例：教学单元综合项目测试标准例案。

Critical Thinking and Comparative Study 评判和比较

Activity 10 Guessing Game — Winning Bonus 猜猜看：有奖游戏

Activity 11 Discovering Rules 找出规律

（See Unit One，Activity 6 and Activity 7）

（请参照第一教学单元活动 6 和活动 7）

Don't forget to constantly use these activities in class.

Suggested Assignment Focus 建议作业的重点

- Reading with increasing number of Chinese characters 阅读加大汉字数量
- Writing in sentences using Chinese characters 用汉字写句子
- Developing all four language skills 发展听、说、读、写技能
- Completing basic language tasks in Chinese 用目的语完成语言任务
- Asking questions 会提问

Suggested Assignments 建议作业

- Assign listening materials：Listening.
- Copy words or characters：Reading and writing.
- Memorize some language materials，and prepare to perform during the next class：Reading and speaking.
- Produce some language material as instructed，and prepare to perform during the next class：Writing and speaking；open-ended tasks.
- Writing on topic：Speaking and writing and task-based presentation.
- Peer editing and writing：Cooperative learning，interactive learning and discourse development.
- Create projects using oral and written presentations：All language skills.
- 听力练习。

- 读写练习。
- 记忆语言材料，准备测试：读说。
- 创造性地运用语言材料，预备课上展示：说写，语言实践任务。
- 有题目的写作：说写，语言实践任务。
- 同伴互相编辑写作：合作学习，学习交流，成段表达。
- 创作口语和书面报告：综合训练。

Suggested Assessment Focus 建议评估重点

Listening comprehension 听力理解

• Comprehension of short passages with pre-activity clues	在有预听活动的情况下听懂成段叙述
• Comprehension of questions	听懂提问
• Comprehension of interpersonal exchanges	听懂人际交流与对话

Speaking 说

• Emphasizing speaking in discourse	承前启后的叙述表达
• Emphasizing fluency	表达流利
• Emphasizing ability to initiate and respond properly to interactions	发问并回答

Reading 阅读

• Reading passages in Chinese characters	阅读理解汉字书写的段落
• Reading texts that have unfamiliar words	阅读理解有生词的文章
• Guessing meaning with common sense and contextual clues	根据背景知识和上下文猜断语义

Writing 写

• Using correct spelling of *pinyin* and selecting the correct characters when typing in a Chinese word processor	用电脑输入时能用拼音正确拼写并选择正确的汉字
• Handwriting Chinese characters correctly	正确手书汉字

• Developing writing skills with correct use of patterns and with logic	写作有逻辑性,语法错误较少
• Writing in paragraphs	成段写作表达
• Creating texts with known characters and using a Chinese word processor	用汉字写作,会用中文处理软件

Suggested Assessment 建议测试评估形式

See page 90.
见 90 页。

Rubrics for Assessment 测试标准

Make a clear rubric specifying expectations and the required elements according to the content coverage of the day or lesson.

根据每日课堂的学习进度,制定明确、清晰的测试评分标准,以申明期待和要求。

Sample Unit Project 教学单元综合项目测试例案

Unit Four Project A: An Advertisement

第四教学单元综合项目(一):广告

做一个广告,具体描述颜色、特点、价钱、购买条件等,要有说服力。

Format:

Oral and written presentation

Topic:

Make an advertisement for a product: My Product Is the Best!

Content:

- Brief introduction of the item
  - Identify the product
  - Items, color, price, measure words, "是……的"

- Comment on the item
  Adjectives as predicate
- Conditions of sale
  Competitive pricing, sales, comparison, reasoning
- Three questions for listening comprehension

Evaluation:

- Content knowledge:
  Linguistic components
  Functional use of the language
  Mechanics (grammatical and technical errors)
- Creativity in presentation:
  Overall design
  Visual aids or artistic expressions
- Delivery:
  Pronunciation, tones and fluency
  Organization of information
  Presentation
  Reference
- Effort

Unit Four Project B: Project: Shopping

第四教学单元综合项目（二）：买东西

买东西的对话。要讨价还价，货比三家。

Format:

Oral and written presentation

- In narration and dialogue
- With artistic display or a PowerPoint presentation

Topic:

Shopping

Content:

- Identify the product
  Items, color, price, measure words, "是……的"

- Comment on the item
  Adjectives as predicate
- Shopping experience
  Time, location, exchange with the salesperson, payment
- Three questions for listening comprehension

Requirements:

- Each presentation must contain positive and negative sentence forms.
- Each presentation must contain questions and answers.

Evaluation:

- Content knowledge:
  Linguistic components
  Functional use of the language
  Mechanics (grammatical and technical errors)
- Creativity in presentation:
  Overall design
  Visual aids or artistic expressions
- Delivery:
  Pronunciation, tones and fluency
  Organization of information
  Presentation
  Reference
- Effort

Writing Sample　范文

货比三家

我昨天去了 Foot Locker 商店，我要买一双运动鞋。我问店员有什么运动鞋。他给了我一双灰的和绿的 New Balance 的运动鞋。我不喜欢 New Balance 的运动鞋的颜色。店员又给了我一双白的和红的 Asics 的运动鞋。我不喜欢白的。他又给了我一双 Nike 的运动鞋。Nike 的运动鞋是红的和黑的，也非常好看。我问 Nike 的运动鞋多少钱，他说 Nike 的运动鞋是五十九块。我觉得这双鞋太贵了。我问他便宜一点怎么样。他卖给我五十八块九毛九分钱。我觉得很便宜，我就买了两双 Nike 的运动鞋。我一共用了一百一十七块九毛八。

(By Calvin L. , Northside College Preparatory High School, Chinese 1)

Unit Four Project C: Comparison: My Friends and Me

第四教学单元综合项目（三）比较：我跟我的朋友

比较你和你的朋友的各个方面。

Format:

Oral and written presentation

- A PowerPoint presentation or other artistic display

Topic:

Comparative studies of our life stories: My Friend and Me

Content:

- Brief introduction of the subjects
- Comparison
  - Compare people, objects, and activities
  - Compare and contrast: differences and similarities
  - Compare preferences
  - Compare possessions
- Positive and negative forms of all sentence patterns
- Complex sentences
- Questions and answers
- Three questions for listening comprehension

Evaluation:

- Content knowledge:
  - Linguistic components
  - Functional use of the language
  - Mechanics (grammatical and technical errors)
- Creativity in presentation:
  - Overall design
  - Visual aids or artistic expressions

- Delivery:
  - Pronunciation, tones and fluency
  - Organization of information
  - Presentation
  - Reference
- Effort

Writing Sample　范文

我弟弟喜欢打球

我叫D。我的生日是一九八五年×月×号。我是韩国人，也是美国人。我有爸爸妈妈，还有一个弟弟。我弟弟叫J。我弟弟的生日是一九八七年×月×号。我比弟弟大两岁。

我和我弟弟打球打得很多。因为我弟弟喜欢打球，我也喜欢打球，所以他跟我打得非常多。我还和弟弟一起玩电脑、打球、玩电动。因为我们打得很多，所以我们常打架。

要是我打篮球，弟弟就打篮球。要是我打棒球，弟弟就打棒球。要是我打橄榄球，弟弟就打橄榄球。

我弟弟说："我要跟你一样。"我说："我比你大两岁，你跟我不一样。"我弟弟说："我觉得我跟你一样大。"

虽然我说我弟弟，可是我弟弟不听。他跟我吃得一样。他跟我穿得一样。他跟我打得一样。他跟我休息得一样。他跟我一样运动、学习、唱歌和跑步。

因为我弟弟跟我打得很多，所以他打得很好。要是我接球接得好，我弟弟就接球接得好。要是我打排球打得好，我弟弟就打排球打得好。虽然今天我弟弟比我高一点，可是我比他打球打得好很多。

今天很多人问："你们是孪生兄弟吧?"我说："不。"我弟弟说："是!"

Questions　问题

1. 我弟弟叫什么?

2. 我弟弟要什么？

3. 我打球打得好吗？

（By Drew L.，Northside College Preparatory High School，Chinese 1）

Unit Five: My Stories
第五教学单元：我的故事

Theme　主题

My Stories　我的故事

Topics　交谈要点与话题

- Completion of Events and Further Inquiry of Time, Place and Manner
  已完成的一个事件及进一步询问事件发生的时间、地点及方式
- Conditions of Events　复杂状语
- Duration　时间段
- Plan　计划
- Reasons　原因和理由
- Requisites, Ability and Permission　条件、能力和许可
- Emphasizing　强调（宾语前置）

Content of Teaching and Learning　教学内容

Linguistic Functions　语用功能

- Completed event and conditions　事件完成及条件
- Planning　计划
- Commenting　评论
- Reasoning　表述原因、理由、条件
- Emphasizing　强调（宾语前置）
- Describing details　表述细节
- Seeking and exchanging information in dialogue　问答对话
- Listening with comprehension to passages of increasing length
  听力理解
- Reading passages with comprehension　段落的阅读理解

- Using a Chinese word processor　使用中文处理软件
- Writing in paragraphs　写作

Grammatical Patterns and Vocabulary　语法点与词汇

(Refer to *Functional and Grammatical Walk Through*)

(参阅《什么篇：语用与语法走廊》（索引：B/6/7/8/11/12/13/16/17/18））

Vocabulary　词汇	Grammatical Points　语法点
Verbs related to daily activities 日常活动动词（7） Time expressions　时间词（6） Locations　地点（16） Manner and means 方式与工具（17） Conjunctures for complex sentences 复句连词（12）	"了" in sentences（13） "是……的" structure（13） Duration　时间段（6） Use of modal verbs　情态动词的使用(8) Use of complex sentences　复句（12） Complex noun phrases 复杂名词词组（11/18） Wh-questions　特殊疑问句：(13) 什么时候/多长时间/在哪儿/ 怎么/为什么/是……的？ Chinese characters　汉字（B）

Cultural studies and connections　文化及跨学科联系

- Social and cultural values　社会文化观念价值

Variations of Unit Five　第五单元的变量设置

The instructor can customize this unit design according to the needs of the class, curriculum at large, the available hours and course schedule.

教学单元应根据课堂教学的需求、课程设置的全局情况及课时的限制酌情加减。

Variables that can be taken into consideration are:

- Number of grammatical patterns involved,
- Extensiveness of vocabulary,
- Depth of communication tasks, and
- Proficiency of language skills.

应考虑的变量如下：

- 语法点的数量，
- 词汇的覆盖面，
- 语用实践活动的深度，
- 语言技巧的水平。

Suggested Variations of the Unit by Topic　建议参考如下

Variation A: The unit can be easily divided into three sub-units. Each unit can include an expandable, related vocabulary list.

方案 A: 这个单元可以分成三个教学单位。每个教学单位的词汇表可增减。

Sub-Unit One: General Activities vs. Specific Events 教学单位一：日常活动与特定事件		
Vocabulary **词汇**	**Grammatical Points** **语法点**	**Linguistic Functions** **语用**
Verbs related to daily activities 日常行为动词(7) Time expressions 时间词（6） Locations 地点（16） Manner and means 方式工具（17）	“了” in sentences（13） “是……的”structure(13) Wh-questions　特殊疑问句： 什么时候/多长时间/ 在哪儿/怎么/ 为什么/是……的?(13)	Making general statements and asking about routine activities 叙述和询问日常活动 Asking and reporting about completed events and conditions 讲述和询问事件完成及条件

Sub-Unit Two：Duration 教学单位二：时间段		
Vocabulary **词汇**	**Grammatical Points** **语法点**	**Linguistic Functions** **语用**
Time expressions： The moment vs. duration 时间点与时间段(6)	Use of time expressions： The moment and duration 时间点与时间段的使用(6) Questions 询问时间及其他条件(6)	Narration 成段表述 Questions and answers in dialogue 问答对话

Sub-Unit Three：Plans, Reasons and Conditions **教学单位三：计划、理由和条件**		
Vocabulary **词汇**	**Grammatical Points** **语法点**	**Linguistic Functions** **语用**
Conjunctions for complex sentences 复句连词（12）	Use of modal verbs 情态动词的使用（8） Use of complex sentences 复句（12） Complex noun phrases 复杂名词词组(11/18)	Plans 计划 Comments 评论 Reasoning 表述原因、理由、条件

Variation B： **The unit can simply keep the first two sub-units.**
Map vocabulary and grammatical patterns according to language use；and
Keep vocabulary and grammatical patterns to a functional minimum.

方案 **B**： 保留前两个方案的从属教学单位。把握每个教学单位的词汇量和语法点。

Sub-Unit One: General Activities vs. Specific Events 教学单位一：日常活动和特定事件		
Vocabulary **词汇**	**Grammatical Points** **语法点**	**Linguistic Functions** **语用**
Verbs related to daily activities 日常行为动词(7) Time expressions 时间词（6） Locations　地点(16) Manner and means 方式工具（17）	“了” in sentences（13） “是……的” structure（13） Wh-questions　特殊疑问句： 什么时候/多长时间/ 在哪儿/怎么/ 为什么/是……的?（13）	Making general statements and asking about routine activities 叙述和询问日常活动 Asking and reporting about completed events and conditions 讲述和询问事件完成及条件

Sub-Unit Two: Duration　教学单位二：时间段		
Vocabulary **词汇**	**Grammatical Points** **语法点**	**Linguistic Functions** **语用**
Time expressions: The moment vs. duration 时间点与时间段（6）	Use of time expressions: The moment and duration 时间点与时间段的使用(6) Questions 询问时间及其他条件（6）	Narration　成段表述 Questions and answers in dialogue 问答对话

Variation C:　**The unit has two simple sub-units.**
Map vocabulary and grammar according to functional language use; and
Keep sentence patterns and vocabulary to a functional minimum.

方案 C:　**分两个简单教学单位。把握每个教学单位的词汇量和语法点，控制在最基本的使用上。**

Sub-Unit One: General Activities and Conditions 教学单位一：日常活动和条件		
Vocabulary **词汇**	**Grammatical Points** **语法点**	**Linguistic Functions** **语用**
Verbs related to daily activities 日常行为动词（7） Time expressions 时间词（6） Locations 地点(16) Manner and means 方式工具（17）	“了”in sentences(13) “是……的”structure(13) Wh-questions 特殊疑问句： 什么时候/多长时间 在哪儿/怎么（13）	Making general statements and asking about routine activities 叙述和询问日常活动

Sub-Unit Two: Specific Events and Duration 教学单位二：特定事件和时间		
Vocabulary **词汇**	**Grammatical Points** **语法点**	**Linguistic Functions** **语用**
Time expressions: The moment vs. duration 时间点与时间段（6）	“了” in sentence（13） Use of time expressions: The moment and duration 时间点与时间段的使用(6) Questions 询问时间及其他条件(6)	Narration 成段表述 Questions and answers in dialogue 问答对话

Instructional Tips 教学指导策略提示

Tip 1:

When telling a story, use of the “了” sentence is not avoidable. Chances are that some students will ask about it. If explanation is needed, use life situations to show the contrast between general activities and specific activities and select appropriate topics and situations to prompt different usages for reinforced practice.

讲述故事就会不可避免地出现“了”。十有八九会有学生询问为什么。如果解释不可避免，建议通过生活情景来显示一般日常活动与特定时间完成的对比。并且还可以选择一些非用“了”不可的话题和情景来强化练习使用。让学生有一个从感性到理性的认识并争取达到自觉地到习惯地运用。

Tip 2:

“了” is a difficult concept to command. Use contrast to show the differences in patterns for general and specific activities as suggested above.

Warning: How to explain the use of “了” is up to each teacher, but don't ever tell young English speaking learners that it indicates past tense, because “了” may suggest present or future situations and learners will be confused with these usages.

Help: Consult *Functional and Grammatical Walk Through* (13) beforehand.

“了”的使用是教学难点。对比日常和特殊行为的不同有利于理解和使用。

不管教师要如何教授“了”的使用，不要告诉学生是过去时态。

参阅《什么篇：语用与语法走廊》13 节。

Tip 3:

When telling stories that involve specific events, review verbs, time expressions and other conditions of general activities as preparation.

讲述一件事的发生以前，建议充分复习日常活动及条件的描述。

Tip 4:

Keep in mind when designing lessons that some young students, even some high school students, are still in developmental stages of logical thinking. Learning a foreign language helps them to improve communicative level step by step. They learn to give a complete account of an event, to describe the process, the conditions and the conclusion of the event, to express their comments and personal feelings about the event.

有些年龄小的学生，甚至高中的学生成段表达叙述及逻辑思维的能力并不是很强。外语学习也是帮助他们提高这种交际表达水平。帮助学生一步步地学会描述一个事件的过程、条件、结果及对事件的评论感受。

Tip 5：

Set a special time slot to introduce Chinese culture as necessary. Still don't forget that culture penetrates all language use, and cultural comparison can be constant in language learning. Emphasize cultural differences as well as similarities during language teaching and learning. Students will learn to be observant and appreciative of the variations and diversity of languages and cultures.

拿出时间介绍中国文化是有必要的。同时不要忘记文化渗透于语言运用中。文化对比随处可见。在汉语课堂教学过程中随时强调文化的不同与相同。学生就会学会观察思考和鉴别欣赏文化与语言的多样性和多元化。

Tip 6：

Classroom instruction must have structure as well as flexibility and variety. With a set structure and rules to follow, students know what to expect and what to do; learning becomes efficient with routines. With flexibility and variety, lessons are more lively and students are more engaged and active. More importantly, flexibility and variety provide conditions and room for different learning styles.

课堂教学既要有规律又要有灵活多样性。有了规律和常规课堂管理就有序可循，学生对常规心中有数，学习可以按部就班。灵活多样能使教学生动，学习不至于枯燥乏味，学生能保持精力集中、从而积极参与课堂活动。另外多样化为不同的学习风格提供发挥的条件和余地。

Suggested Activities 建议教学活动

Activity 1 My Journal 我的日记/周记

Language task： Keep a weekly journal

Functions： Record life stories

Writing, reading, listening and speaking

Use: Class activity, homework assignment, assessment

记周记不失为一个有意义的家庭作业。日记/周记的内容跟语言学习的积累增长。在学了表达描述具体事件后可以让学生记周记。先给学生周记的基本要求。每周，要求在日记里加一个语法点或语用功能。在一段时间后，特别是一个教学单元结束时，老师可以让学生把几周的日记摘选组成一个展示，既复习又提高。

Preparation for the activity:

Designate a small notebook to use as a journal.

Get started:

Introduce the required journal writing format and its expected elements.

Homework:

- Define it as a weekly assignment.
- Make sure to collect it weekly and return it in time for future use.

Progression in writing:

Add new requirements as learning progresses.

Elaboration:

- Exchange journal stories in class for speaking and listening practice.
- Assemble journal entries into a collection as a project.

Suggested format and content for journal writing

对日记格式与内容的建议

Date　日期

Weather　天气

General statement: Your mood in general for the day　当天的心情

Record of activity　记录活动:

Everyday activities and routines　常规活动

Specific Events　特殊事件

To Add as learning progresses　可增添内容

Plan　计划

Conditions of the activity：Time，place，how　常规活动发生的条件

Recount：Conditions of the event（s）：Time，place，how，duration

事件发生的情况

Reasoning，comparison，weather of the day in detail，etc.

评论、比较及其他细节

Activity 2　A "Before" Story and an "After" Story
之前的故事和之后的故事

Language task：Telling and retelling a story

Functions：Recount events
Listening and speaking，reading and writing

Use：Class activity，homework assignment，assessment

做法：

- 老师讲个小故事并提问检查听力理解。
- 阅读一篇与故事一相似的故事并提问检查阅读理解。
- 在阅读基础上会话。
- 模仿阅读写作。
- 还可给一系列问题让学生口头报告。

Preparation for the activity：

Prepare at least two stories. One for listening and the other for reading.

Procedure：

Step 1：Listening comprehension and response to questions

- Teacher tells a story.
- Ask the students questions to verify comprehension. Students answer.

Step 2：Reading comprehension

- Give a written story with a similar level of difficulty.

- Ask a student to read briefly.
- Ask questions to verify comprehension.

Step 3: Reinforce reading

- Ask a student to read a sentence and another to translate out aloud.

Follow-up: Homework

Write a story by modeling the reading.

Elaboration:

List questions in writing for group presentation

Activity 3　Sharing Stories　分享故事

Language task: Telling and retelling a story

Functions: Recount events

Listening and speaking (possibly reading)

Use: Class activity, homework assignment, assessment

This activity is a follow-up on Activity 2 above.

这是上面的活动的延续。

做法:

- 分成3~4人的小组。
- 小组分享每人的故事。
- 小组汇报：每人用2~3个句子讲述另一个人的故事梗概。

Preparation for the activity:

Finished stories for presentation

Procedure:

Step 1: Form a group

- Divide class into groups of three or four.
- Designate a group leader.
- Make instructions and expectations clear.

Step 2：Share stories

- Each student tells a story that was prepared as a homework assignment.

Step 3：Group summary

- By group：Each gives a brief recount（two to three sentences）of another person's story.

Activity 4 Timed Speeches 计时快说

（Please see Example 8 in Part Ⅰ "Timed Speeches" for more details.）

（请参照上篇课堂活动案例 8 "计时快说"）

Activity 5 Fashion Show 时装表演

（See Unit Four or Example 10 in Part Ⅰ for more details.）

（参照第四教学单元或上篇课堂活动案例 10）

Critical Thinking and Comparative Study 评判和比较

Activity 6 Guessing Game — Winning Bonus 猜猜看：有奖游戏

Activity 7 Discovering Rules 找出规律

（See Unit One，Activity 6 and Activity 7）

（请参照第一教学单元活动 6 和活动 7）

Don't forget to constantly use these activities in class.

Suggested Assignment Focus 建议作业的重点

• Speaking with fluency	增强说话的流利程度
• Reading with increasing number of Chinese characters	阅读加大汉字数量
• Writing in sentences and paragraphs，using an increasing number of Chinese characters，and using a Chinese word processor	汉字写作，写作加大汉字用量，会用中文处理软件

- Developing all four language skills　发展听、说、读、写技能
- Completing basic language tasks in Chinese　用目的语完成语言任务
- Asking questions and exchanging information　提问并交换信息
- Using authentic materials　使用真实语言材料
- Integrating information technology and research methods　查阅资料

Suggested Assignments　建议作业

- Assign listening materials: Listening.
- Copy words or characters: Reading and writing.
- Memorize some language materials, and prepare to perform during the next class: Reading and speaking.
- Produce some language materials as instructed, and prepare to perform during the next class: Writing and speaking; open-ended tasks.
- Writing on topic: Speaking and writing and task-based presentation.
- Peer editing and writing: Cooperative learning, interactive learning and discourse development.
- Create projects using oral and written presentations: All language skills.
- 听力练习。
- 读写练习。
- 记忆语言材料，准备测试：读说。
- 创造性地运用语言材料，预备课上展示：说写，语言实践任务。
- 有题目的写作：说写，语言实践任务。
- 同伴互相编辑写作：合作学习，学习交流，成段表达。
- 创作口语和书面报告：综合训练。

Suggested Assessment Focus　建议评估重点

Listening comprehension　听力理解

- Comprehension of short passages with pre-activity clues　在有预听活动的情况下听懂成段叙述

• Comprehension of questions	听懂提问
• Comprehension of interpersonal exchanges	听懂人际交流与对话
Speaking 说	
• Emphasizing speaking in discourse	承前启后的叙述表达
• Emphasizing fluency	表达流利
• Emphasizing ability to initiate and respond properly to interactions	发问并回答
Reading 阅读	
• Reading passages in Chinese characters	阅读理解汉字书写的段落
• Reading texts that have unfamiliar words	阅读理解有生词的文章
• Guessing meaning with common sense and contextual clues	根据背景知识和上下文猜断语义
Writing 写	
• Using correct spelling of *pinyin* and selecting the correct characters when typing in a Chinese word processor	用电脑输入时能用拼音正确拼写并选择正确的汉字
• Handwriting Chinese characters correctly	正确手书汉字
• Developing writing skills with correct use of patterns and with logic	写作有逻辑性，语法错误较少
• Writing in paragraphs	成段写作表达
• Creating texts with known characters and using a Chinese word processor	用汉字写作，会用中文处理软件

Suggested Assessment 建议测试评估形式

See page 90.

见 90 页。

Rubrics for Assessment　测试标准

Make a clear rubric specifying expectations and the required elements according to the content coverage of the day or lesson.

根据每日课堂的学习进度，制定明确、清晰的测试评分标准，以申明期待和要求。

Sample Unit Project　教学单元综合项目测试例案

Unit Five Project A: My Journal

第五教学单元综合项目（一）：我的日记

Format:

Oral and written presentations

- PowerPoint presentation

Topic:

Stories of a Person's Daily Life — A Collection of Three Stories

Content:

- Statements about general activities
  Including: time/place/how
- Accounts of specific events
  Use of "了", "是……的"
- Comments on events and evaluation of actions
  Complements of degree/Comparisons/Reasoning
- Positive and negative forms of all sentence patterns
- Complex sentences
- Questions and answers
- Three questions for listening comprehension

Evaluation:

- Content knowledge:
  Linguistic components
  Functional use of the language
  Mechanics (grammatical and technical errors)
- Creativity in presentation:
  Overall design

Visual aids or artistic expressions

- Delivery:

  Pronunciation, tones and fluency

  Organization of information

  Presentation

  Reference

- Effort

Sample Journal　日记范文

二零零五年十月十三号

今天是星期四。我八点才起床。因为我病了，我就没上学。我在家看电视了，我是九点半看的。因为我没吃早饭我就吃中饭了，我是中午吃的。我也给老师写信了，我是用电脑写的。我有很多功课，因为我三天没上学了。我还听音乐了。我给我妈妈打了一个电话，我是下午三点打的。

二零零五年十月二十四号

今天是星期一。我六点半就起床了。我去上学了。今天我有世界文学课。这个课没意思，我看了书就睡觉了，我的老师不高兴。我说："对不起，可是我不喜欢那本书。"我也上汉语课了。上课的时候，我练习写汉字了。吃中饭的时候，我跟我的朋友说话了。因为我们有很多时间，所以我们说了半天。我三点一刻放学。今天我有很多功课，所以没有很多时间做别的事。我做功课做了三个小时。我吃晚饭以后，看电影看了两个小时。我看了电影就睡觉了。

二零零五年十月二十八号

今天是星期五。我七点四十分起床。因为我没有时间，所以我没吃早饭。今天我们有做饭课。我们坐公共汽车去博物馆了，我们看了很多墨西哥的画儿。我们从博物馆出来以后，我们就去饭馆了。我吃中饭了，我是中午一点吃的。我是跟我的朋友吃的。我们一边吃饭一边说。我是在饭馆吃的。我们吃饭从一点吃到两点。我两点半放学，可是我四点才回家。要是我不用接我妹妹，我就能三点回家。

Questions　问题

1. 我星期四做什么了？
2. 我星期四吃早饭了吗？
3. 星期一我跟谁说话了？
4. 星期一我有没有时间？
5. 星期五我是几点回家的？
6. 星期三我去公园了还是博物馆了？

(By Stephanie G., Northside College Preparatory High School, Chinese 2)

Unit Five Project B: A Story
第五教学单元综合项目（二）：小故事

写一个小故事介绍一个人和一件事。

Format:

Oral and written presentation

- A story book or PowerPoint presentation

Topic:

Someone's Story

Content:

- A brief introduction of a family or a person
- Statements of general activities
  Including time/place/how
- Accounts of specific events
  Use of "了", "是……的"
- Comments on events and evaluation of actions
  Complements of degree, comparisons, reasoning
- Positive and negative forms of all sentence patterns
- Complex sentences
- Questions and answers
- Three questions for listening comprehension

Evaluation:

- Content knowledge:

Linguistic components
Functional use of the language
Mechanics (grammatical and technical errors)

- Creativity in presentation:
  Overall design
  Visual aids or artistic expressions
- Delivery:
  Pronunciation, tones and fluency
  Organization of information
  Presentations
  Reference
- Effort

Unit Five Project C: A Before and After Story

第五教学单元综合项目（三）：之前和之后的故事

写一个故事：事件发生前的计划，事情的经过和与之有关的对话。

Format:

Oral and written presentation

- A dialogue and a narration
- A PowerPoint presentation or other artistic displays

Topics:

- A Before and After Story
- A plan and execution of the plan

Content:

- Brief introduction of the people involved in the story
- Statements of general activities:
  Including time, place, how
- Recounts of specific events
  Use of "了", "是……的" /Time Duration
- Comments on events and evaluation of actions
  Complements of degree, comparisons, reasoning
- Positive and negative forms of all sentence patterns

- Complex sentences
- Questions and answers
- Three questions for listening comprehension

Evaluation:

- Content knowledge:
  Linguistic components
  Functional use of the language
  Mechanics (grammatical and technical errors)
- Creativity in presentation:
  Overall design
  Visual aids or artistic expressions
- Delivery:
  Pronunciation, tones and fluency
  Organization of information
  Presentation
  Reference
- Effort

Unit Six: I Love Spring in Chicago
第六教学单元：我爱芝加哥的春天

Theme 主题

I Love Spring in Chicago 我爱芝加哥的春天

Topics 交谈要点与话题

- A City — My Hometown 城市——我的家
- Life in the City 城市生活
- Seasonal Changes 季节变化
- Weather Phenomenon 天气

Content of Teaching and Learning 教学内容

Linguistic Functions 语用

- Identifying a geographic location 确认地理位置
- Describing weather conditions by season 按季节描述天气
- Commenting 评论
- Reasoning 表述原因、理由、条件
- Comparisons 比较
- Emphasizing 强调（宾语前置）
- Narrating in paragraph-length passages 成段表述
- Seeking and exchanging information through interactions 问答对话
- Listening with comprehension to passages of increasing length 听力理解
- Reading passages with comprehension 段落阅读理解
- Using a Chinese word processor 使用中文处理软件
- Writing in paragraphs 写作

Grammatical Patterns and Vocabulary　语法点与词汇

(Refer to *Functional and Grammatical Walk Through*)

(《什么篇：语用与语法走廊》(索引：B/6/7/11/12/13/15/16/17/18/20/23))

Vocabulary　词汇	Grammatical Points　语法点
Verbs related to daily activities 日常行为动词（7） Time expressions　时间词（6） Locations and positions 地点位置（15） Manner and means 方式工具（17） Conjunctions for complex sentences 复句连词（12） Seasons and the weather 季节与天气（23）	"是/在/有" indicates location（15） "了" indicates change and other usages(13) Duration　时间段（6） Use of modal verb　情态动词的使用（8） Use of complex sentences　复句（12） Complex noun phrases 复杂名词词组（11/18） Comparisons　比较（20） Wh-questions　特殊疑问句： 什么时候/多长时间/在哪儿/怎么/怎么样/多少/为什么/是……的?(6/13) Chinese characters　汉字（B）

Cultural Studies and Connections　文化及跨学科联系

- Social Studies　社会学
  - Geography　地理
  - Community　社区
  - Cultural comparisons　文化对比
- Research and Gather Information　收集研究资料

Variations of Unit Six　第六单元的变量设置

The instructor can customize this unit design according to the needs of the class, curriculum at large, the available instructional hours and course schedule.

教学单元应根据课堂教学的需求、课程设置的全局情况及课时的限制酌情加减。

Variables that can be taken into consideration are:

- Number of grammatical patterns involved,
- Extensiveness of vocabulary,
- Depth of communication tasks, and
- Proficiency of language skills.

应考虑的变量如下：

- 语法点的数量，
- 词汇的覆盖面，
- 语用实践活动的深度，
- 语言技巧的水平。

Suggested Variations of the Unit by Topic　建议参考如下

Variation A:　**The unit can be easily divided into three sub-units. Each unit can include an expandable, related vocabulary list.**

方案 A:　**这个单元可以分成三个教学单位。每个教学单位的词汇表可增减。**

Sub-Unit One: A City and Its Geographic Location/Life in the City 教学单位一：城市地理位置/城市生活		
Vocabulary 词汇	**Grammatical Points 语法点**	**Linguistic Functions 语用**
Locations and positions 地点与位置（15） Verbs related to daily activities 日常生活行为动词（7） Time expressions 时间词(6) Locations 地点（16） Manner and means 方式/工具（17）	“是/在/有” indicates location（15） Wh-questions 特殊疑问句：在哪儿（13）	Identifying a geographic location 确认地理位置

Sub-Unit Two: Seasons and the Weather　教学单位二：季节与天气		
Vocabulary 词汇	**Grammatical Points 语法点**	**Linguistic Functions 语用**
Seasons and the weather 季节与天气（23） Time expressions: The moment vs. duration 时间点与时间段(6)	"了" indicates change and other usages(13) Duration　时间段(6)	Describing weather conditions by season 按季节描述天气 Comments　评论 Reasoning 表述原因、理由、条件 Comparison　比较

Sub-Unit Three: Comparing Cities/Weather/Life 教学单位三：比较城市/天气/日常生活		
Vocabulary 词汇	**Grammatical Points 语法点**	**Linguistic Functions 语用**
Conjunctions used for complex sentences 复句连词（12）	Use of modal verbs 情态动词的使用(8) Use of complex sentences 复句（12） Complex noun phrases 复杂名词词组（11/18）	Plan　计划 Comments　评论 Reasoning 表述原因、理由、条件 Comparison　比较

Variation B:　**The unit can simply keep the first two sub-units.**
Map vocabulary and grammatical patterns according to language use; and
Keep vocabulary and grammatical patterns to a functional minimum.

方案 B:　**保持头两个从属教学单位。把握每个教学单位的词汇量和语法点。**

Sub-Unit One：A City and Its Geographic Location/Life in the City 教学单位一：城市地理位置/城市生活		
Vocabulary 词汇	**Grammatical Points 语法点**	**Linguistic Functions 语用**
Locations and positions 地点与位置（15） Verbs related to daily activities 日常生活行为动词（7） Time expressions 时间词(6) Locations 地点（16） Manner and Means 方式/工具（17）	"是/在/有" indicates location（15） Wh-questions 特殊疑问句：在哪儿（13）	Identifying a geographic location 确认地理位置

Sub-Unit Two：Seasons and the Weather 教学单位二：季节与天气		
Vocabulary 词汇	**Grammatical Points 语法点**	**Linguistic Functions 语用**
Seasons and the weather 季节与天气（23） Time expressions：The moment vs. duration 时间点与时间段(6)	"了" indicates change and other usages（13） Duration 时间段（6）	Describing weather conditions by season 按季节描述天气 Comments 评论 Reasoning 表述原因、理由、条件 Comparison 比较

Variation C： **The unit uses the simplified versions of Variation A's Sub-Units Two and Three.**

Map vocabulary and grammar according to language function; and

Keep sentence patterns and vocabulary to a functional minimum.

方案 C： **保留方案 A 的教学单位二和教学单位三，简化教学内容。把握每个教学单位的词汇量和语法点，限制在最少。**

Sub-Unit One: Seasons and the Weather　教学单位一：季节与天气		
Vocabulary 词汇	**Grammatical Points 语法点**	**Linguistic Functions 语用**
Seasons and the weather 季节与天气（23） Time expressions: The moment vs. duration 时间点与时间段(6) Verbs related to daily activities 日常生活动词（7）	“了”indicates change and other usages(13) Duration 时间段（6）	Describing weather conditions by season 按季节描述天气 Describing people's activities by season 按季节描述活动

Sub-Unit Two: Comparing Weather　教学单位二：比较天气	
Grammatical Points　语法点	**Linguistic Functions　语用**
Comparisons　比较（20）	Description　描述 Comments　评论 Comparisons　比较

Instructional Tips　教学指导策略提示

Tip 1:

Seasons and the weather are, for the most part, about vocabulary.

季节和天气话题的教学重点是学习词汇。

Tip 2:

There are many ways to spice up this topic:

- Use a rhyme or a song to teach seasons and the weather to make it fun.
- Use the life experiences of the students to make it more interesting.

有很多种办法能让这个话题的教学生动活泼：童谣、歌曲或学生自己的生活经历和故事。

Tip 3:

It is a good idea to review verbs, time expressions and the conditions of general activities before teaching about the weather. Seasons and the weather are constantly changing. This is a good topic for practicing comparisons.

谈一个城市的季节和气候之前可以先谈活动，谈与活动有关的时间等条件，既作铺垫又自然引出话题。季节和气候的变化也是谈比较的一个好机会。

Tip 4:

There are many authentic materials available online and in daily newspapers. Use them as supplementary materials.

与现实生活相似的语言实践活动能刺激新语言的学习；这个题目的活材料很多：网上、报刊上等都有，都可用来做补充教材。

Tip 5:

Remember always:

- Scaffold new learning with previous materials.
- Support development of proficiency through activities needing multiple skills.
- Deliver instructions one step at a time.
- Reinforce learning with pre-activity for warm-up, activity to engage, and post-activity to follow-up.

教学中要用已知带不知；通过各种技能的活动支持语言能力的发展；教学指导要稳扎稳打，按部就班。

Tip 6:

Discussing seasons and the weather can also be used in connection with other subjects, such as geography, economy, social studies, travel, international studies, etc.

季节与天气还可以跟其他科目的学习联系起来。例如，学习社会学的地理、经济等题目或旅游及国际知识的学习等。

Tip 7:

This can also be a cultural exchange topic. Allow students to bring in information about other countries or places they know or are familiar with to share with the class in Chinese.

这个题目也可以引进文化交流，让学生给全班介绍他们所想介绍或熟悉的国家和地区，但必须用汉语。

Suggested Activities　建议教学活动

Activity 1　My Journal　我的日记/周记

Keeping a weekly journal is a meaningful homework assignment. Journals can be developed gradually as language use grows. We use a weekly journal after the class begins focusing on specific events. Each week, add new linguistic functional elements to the journal entry requirements.

记周记不失为一个有意义的家庭作业。日记或周记的内容跟语言的学习积累同步。在学了表达描述具体事件后让学生记周记。每周，要求在日记里加一个语法点或语用的功能。

At the end of the unit, the teacher may ask students to assemble all journal entries into a presentation.

在一段时间后，特别是一个教学单元结束时，老师可以让学生把几周的日记摘选组成一个展示，既复习又提高。

(See Unit Five, Activity 1 or Example 20 in Part I for more details.)

(参照第五教学单元活动 1 或上篇课堂活动案例 20。)

Activity 2　Snowball Rolling: Identify These Cities!
加长叙述：找出这些地方来

Language task: Identify a city location — Where do your relatives and friends live?

Functions: Describe cities
Listening and speaking, reading and writing

Use: Class activity, homework assignment, assessment

这个活动谈城市的所在地及其他有关的情况，主要练习听说。是这样开展进行的：老师说一个句子，然后用问答的方式让学生逐个说会。一句一句地加内容：学生的回答叙述不断加长（语速可以不断加快），每次有数个学生回答，直到故事讲完。

还可在会话的基础上进行阅读：阅读另一相似故事，问答检查理解。还可加模仿的写作活动。

Preparation for the activity:

List of cities and states

Procedure:

Step 1: Start a snowball

- Teacher makes a statement about a city and asks questions.
- Select students to answer in turn.

Step 2: Get rolling

- Teacher continues to add a sentence at a time.
- Select students to repeat the growing passage in turn.

Step 3: Reading sample

- Read a sample passage that uses all previously recited sentences.

Step 4: Work in class

- Jot down the information about cities in which relatives or friends live.
- Model the recited example to orally describe one city (to a partner or to class depending on time).

Step 5: Homework time

- Write several similar passages about different cities.

Follow-up:

- Peer editing
- Report to class

Activity 3	Sharing Stories 分享你的故事
Language task:	Peer editing, telling and retelling a story
Functions:	Cooperative learning: Assistant writing and speaking Reading, listening, and speaking
Use:	Class activity

This activity is a follow-up to Activity 2 above.

这个活动是在前一活动的基础上开展的合作学习活动。

做法：

- 同伴相互修改作文：要先阅读同伴的文章；找出好句子，指出错误；提出修改建议。
- 分成 3～4 人小组，讲述自己的故事。
- 每人用 2～4 句话总结另一人的故事。

Preparation for the activity:

Complete stories for peer editing and presentation.

Procedure:

Step 1: Pair up

Pair up students to do a peer editing:

- Read your partner's writing,
- Identify good sentences and mistakes, and
- Suggest revisions.

Step 2: Team up

- Divide class into groups of three to four.
- Designate a group leader.
- Make instructions and expectations clear.

Step 3: Share stories

- Each student tells a story prepared as homework and edited in class.

Step 4: Group summary

- By group: Each gives a brief recount (two to three sentences) of another's story.

Activity 4　Timed Speeches　计时快说

(Please see Example 8 in Part I "Timed Speeches" for more details.)

(请参照上篇课堂活动案例 8 "计时快说")

Activity 5 Quiz Show 智力竞赛
Language task: Answer questions on the spot
Functions: Quiz your knowledge and vocabulary
Use: Class activity, homework assignment, assessment

This game can use many topics for language learning. The example here uses weather conditions and locations of cities. Participants ask and answer on the spot questions to quiz each other on vocabulary and knowledge.

这个游戏可以用来辅助各种话题的语言学习。下面的例案是有关城市地理和天气的。参赛者当场发问或回答，测试有关的词汇与地理等方面的知识。

This game consists of preparation and execution phases. It is recommended that preparation and execution are done during separate class periods.

这个游戏分两部分。建议用不同的课堂时间来进行。

准备：

- 分成 3 ~4 个队。
- 每队准备有关若干城市的测试问题，写在卡片上（用所学句型和词汇）。
- 讨论后可分头回家准备卡片。

执行：

- 集中本队卡片，检查是否正确。
- 比赛开始：各队轮流参赛提问，其余队接受挑战。每次有一选手回答问题，答对得分。

得分：

- 一轮三分钟。得分多的队得胜。

Preparation:

Index cards

Procedure:

Step 1: Team up

- Divide the class into teams of three to four.

- Specify rules and expectations.

Step 2: Prepare for a quiz show (can be a part of a homework assignment)

- Each group is given a number of cities.
- Teams brainstorm questions related to these cities using previously patterns and words.
- Teams write questions on index cards.

Step 3: Double-check questions

- Teams meet to ensure that all questions are correct.

Step 4: Quiz begins!

- Each team goes on stage in turn as hosts.
- Hosts take turns asking questions.
- Select other teams to answer questions.
- One player answers one question at a time.

Scoring:

- Each round lasts three minutes.
- The team that answers the most questions within the time frame wins.

Activity 6　Using Pictures to Tell a Story　看图讲故事
Language task: Discuss a city
Functions: Integrated language use
Connect language learning with cultural learning
Use: Class activity, homework assignment, assessment

Provide pictures. Students contribute sentences to describe the pictures. Make up a class story emphasizing cultural characteristics and cultural comparisons in addition to geographical ones.

这个活动顾名思义，用图画来激发对一个城市的讨论。学生贡献句子，全班编出一个完整的故事。除描述季节、天气等外，注意引导对文化特征和文化比较的讨论。

Activity 7 Research Project: Introduce a City
研究项目：介绍一个城市

Language task: Introduce a city

Functions: Integrated language use
Connect language learning with cultural learning
Research

Use: Class activity, homework assignment, assessment

选一个理想的或喜欢的城市，收集有关这个城市的资料。整合并修改与这个话题有关的作业，加入合适的内容，写成一篇介绍文章。加图片或其他视觉资料。准备口头和笔头报告。

注意：若采用其他人的资料必须注明出处。

Procedure:

Step 1: The city of your dreams
- Select city and gather information through research.

Step 2: Review and draft
- Pull all work that has been done in class as a resource (class materials and previously completed homework).
- Students check with instructor for required elements to be included in the project.

Step 3: Edit and revise
- Edit and rewrite drafts and finalize the writing.

Step 4: Visual and artistic support
- Design a display with visuals and artwork.

Step 5: Memorize research
- Prepare for an oral presentation with the display.

Follow-up:

- Present it to class.
- Can be used as a quarterly or term assessment.

Caution：

- Don't forget to cite sources correctly.
- Plagiarism is using other people's work without proper acknowledgement.
- Plagiarism is also cheating.

Critical Thinking and Comparative Study 评判和比较

Activity 8 Guessing Game — Winning Bonus 猜猜看：有奖游戏

Activity 9 Discovering Rules 找出规律

(See Unit One, Activity 6 and Activity 7)

（请参照第一教学单元活动 6 和活动 7）

Don't forget to constantly use these activities in class.

Suggested Assignment Focus 建议作业的重点

- Speaking with fluency 增强说话的流利程度
- Reading with increasing number of Chinese characters 阅读加大汉字数量
- Writing in sentences and paragraphs using an increasing number of Chinese characters, and using a Chinese word processor 用汉字写作，写作加大汉字量，会用中文处理软件
- Developing all four language skills 发展听、说、读、写技能
- Completing basic language tasks in Chinese 用目的语完成语言任务
- Asking questions and exchanging information 提问并交换信息
- Using authentic materials 使用真实语言材料
- Integrating information technology and research methods 查阅资料

Suggested Assignments 建议作业

- Assign listening materials：Listening.
- Copy words or characters：Reading and writing.

- Memorize some language materials, and prepare to perform during the next class: Reading and speaking.
- Produce some language materials as instructed, and prepare to perform during the next class: Writing and speaking; open-ended tasks.
- Writing on topic: Speaking and writing and task-based presentation.
- Peer editing and writing: Cooperative learning, interactive learning and discourse development.
- Create projects using oral and written presentations: All language skills.
- 听力练习。
- 读写练习。
- 记忆语言材料，准备测试：读说。
- 创造性地运用语言材料，预备课上展示：说写，语言实践任务。
- 有题目的写作：说写，语言实践任务。
- 同伴互相编辑写作：合作学习，学习交流，成段表达。
- 创作口语和书面报告：综合训练。

Suggested Assessment Focus　建议评估重点

Listening comprehension　听力理解

• Comprehension of short passages with pre-activity clues	在有预听活动的情况下听懂成段叙述
• Comprehension of questions	听懂提问
• Comprehension of interpersonal exchanges	听懂人际交流与对话

Speaking　说

• Emphasizing speaking in discourse	承前启后的叙述表达
• Emphasizing fluency	表达流利
• Emphasizing ability to initiate and respond properly to interactions	发问并回答

Reading　阅读

• Reading passages in Chinese characters	阅读理解汉字书写的段落

• Reading texts that have unfamiliar words	阅读理解有生词的文章
• Guessing meaning with common sense and contextual clues	根据背景知识和上下文猜断语义

Writing　写

• Using correct spelling of *pinyin* and selecting the correct characters when using a Chinese word processor	用电脑输入时能用拼音正确拼写并选择正确的汉字
• Handwriting Chinese characters correctly	正确手书汉字
• Developing writing skills with correct use of patterns and with logic	写作有逻辑性，语法错误较少
• Writing in paragraphs	成段写作表达
• Creating texts with known characters and using a Chinese word processor	用汉字写作会用中文处理软件

Suggested Assessment　建议测试评估形式

See page 90.

见 90 页。

Rubrics for Assessment　测试标准

Make a clear rubric specifying expectations and the required elements according to the content coverage of the day or lesson.

根据每日课堂的学习进度，制定明确、清晰的测试评分标准，以申明期待和要求。

Sample Unit Project　教学单元综合项目测试例案

Unit Six Project A: Introduce a City

第六教学单元综合项目（一）：介绍一个地方

介绍一个城市：季节气候、人文地理、文化习俗。

Format:

Oral and written presentation

- A PowerPoint presentation or other visual and artistic displays

Topic:

Seasons and the weather in a city

Content:

- General introduction to the city:
  Size, location, who lives in the city, etc.
- Seasons
  Changes, duration, comparisons
- Weather
  Temperature, other atmospheric phenomenon
- Activities
  Activities by age groups, reasoning, comments
- Positive and negative forms of all sentence patterns
- Complex sentences
- Questions and answers
- Three questions for listening comprehension

Evaluation:

- Content knowledge:
  Linguistic components
  Functional use of the language
  Mechanics (grammatical and technical errors)
- Creativity in presentation:
  Overall design
  Visual aids or artistic expressions
- Delivery:
  Pronunciation, tones and fluency
  Organization of information
  Presentation
  Reference
- Effort

Unit Six Project B: A Tale of Two Cities

第六教学单元综合项目（二）：双城记

比较两个城市的季节和天气及人们的爱好和活动。

Format:

Oral and written presentation

- A story book or a PowerPoint presentation

Topic:

Compare two cities

Content:

- Brief introduction to the two cities
- Comparison
  Seasons/Weather/Activities
- Tell a story
- Conclusion and comments
- Positive and negative forms of all sentence patterns
- Complex sentences
- Questions and answers
- Three questions for listening comprehension

Evaluation:

- Content knowledge:
  Linguistic components
  Functional use of the language
  Mechanics (grammatical and technical errors)
- Creativity in presentation:
  Overall design
  Visual aids or artistic expressions
- Delivery:
  Pronunciation, tones and fluency
  Organization of information
  Presentation
  Reference
- Effort

Unit Six Project C: I Live in Chicago

第六教学单元综合项目（三）：我家住在芝加哥

介绍自己和自己居住的城市。请朋友来访。

Format:

Oral and written presentation

- A dialogue, a narration, a PowerPoint presentation or other artistic displays

Topic:

Life in Chicago

Content:

- A brief self-introduction
- Introduction to Chicago
  - Location, size, importance, etc.
  - Seasons and the weather
- Narration: Life in Chicago
  - Activities in general including: Time/Place/How
  - Personal stories
- Dialogue:
  - Invite friends to visit Chicago
  - Plan activities, comparisons, comments
- Positive and negative of all sentence patterns
- Complex sentences
- Questions and answers
- Three questions for listening comprehension

Evaluation:

- Content knowledge:
  - Linguistic components
  - Functional use of the language
  - Mechanics (grammatical and technical errors)
- Creativity in presentation:
  - Overall design
  - Visual aids or artistic expressions

- Delivery:
  - Pronunciation, tones and fluency
  - Organization of information
  - Presentation
  - Reference
- Effort

Writing Sample　范文

巴　黎

巴黎是法国的首都。巴黎在法国的北方。一年四季不分明。巴黎的天气有时候好有时候坏。巴黎的天气不冷也不热。

巴黎的春天是从四月到六月。春天常常下雨或者下毛毛雨。春天天气一天比一天潮湿。最低温度是摄氏九度。树绿了，花开了，小鸟唱歌了。法国人喜欢看朋友，去咖啡馆。外国人喜欢在公园走路。

夏天不长，是从七月到八月。天气一天比一天暖和。可是巴黎的夏天天气比芝加哥夏天的天气凉快。最高温度是摄氏十七度。很多法国人在海边游泳、滑水、骑车、航海、打球或者去别的地方旅游。他们跟家人或朋友去。我的朋友喜欢去巴黎因为她喜欢买东西。因为巴黎有很多商店，所以她逛商店。

秋天是巴黎最好的季节。秋天的天气十分凉快。秋天是从九月到十一月。秋天天气跟春天天气一样，有时下毛毛雨。法国人非常忙，因为他们又回去工作又回学校上学。秋天法国人看网球赛。

冬天是从十二月到三月。冬天天气冷可是没有芝加哥那么冷。虽然巴黎的天气冷可是下雪下得不大。冬天温度最低是摄氏零下三度。法国人比芝加哥人穿衣服穿得少。我不喜欢巴黎的冬天因为我喜欢雪。巴黎有名是因为有艾菲尔铁塔。要是我有很多钱，我就去看艾菲尔铁塔、卢浮宫和圣母院。

Sample Questions　问题

1. 巴黎什么季节最好？
2. 巴黎春天的天气怎么样？

3. 五月是不是冬天？
4. 巴黎的夏天是从几月到几月？
5. 巴黎人春天做什么？
6. 外国人在哪儿走路？
7. 他们跟谁去别的地方旅游？
8. 你最喜欢什么季节？

（By Stephanie G. , Northside College Preparatory High School，Chinese 2）

Unit Seven: My Life at School
第七教学单元：我的校园生活

Theme　主题

My Life at School　我的校园生活

Topics　交谈要点与话题

- Directions and Positions　方位
- Campus　校园
- School Surroundings　学校的四周
- School Life　学校的生活
  - Curriculum and Subjects　课程科目
  - Extra-curricular Activities　课外活动
  - Manner and Location　活动方式和地点

Content of Teaching and Learning　教学内容

Linguistic Functions　语用

- Identifying a geographic location and position　确认地理位置和方位
- Relating actions with locations and means and manner
  明确行为与地点、方式
- Describing scenes and events　描述场景与事件
- Asking and exchanging information in interactions　问答对话
- Listening with comprehension to passages of increasing length
  听力理解
- Reading passages with comprehension　段落的阅读理解
- Using a Chinese word processor　使用中文处理软件
- Writing in paragraphs　写作

Grammatical Patterns and Vocabulary 语法点与词汇

（Refer to *Functional and Grammatical Walk Through*）

（《什么篇：语用与语法走廊》（索引：B/6/7/13/15/16/17））

Vocabulary 词汇	Grammatical Points 语法点
Verbs related to daily activities 日常活动（7） Time expressions 时间词（6） Locations and positions 地点方位(15) Places 地方设施（16） Manner and means 方式（17） Off-campus facilities 校外的设施(16) On-campus facilities 学校校园与设施（15） Subjects of learning 学习课程与科目（15）	"是/在/有" indicates location and position "是/在/有"表述地点方位(15) "……了……就"（13） Duration 时间段（6） Yes/No questions 是非疑问句（13） Wh-questions 特殊疑问句（13） Chinese characters 汉字（B）

Cultural Studies and Connections 文化及跨学科联系

- Geographic locations 地理位置与联系
- Social Studies 社会学

  School life and adolescence 学校生活和青少年

  Community 社区

  Comparing educational systems and learning environments

  对比教育体制与学习环境

Variations of Unit Seven 第七单元的变量设置

The instructor can customize this unit design according to the needs of the class, curriculum at large, the available instructional hours and course schedule.

教学单元应根据课堂教学的需求、课程设置的全局情况及课时的限制酌情加减。

Variables that can be taken into consideration are:

- Number of grammatical patterns involved,
- Extensiveness of vocabulary,
- Depth of communication tasks, and
- Proficiency of language skills.

应考虑的变量如下：

- 语法点的数量，
- 词汇的覆盖面，
- 语用实践活动的深度，
- 语言技巧的水平。

Suggested Variations of the Unit by Topic　建议参考如下

Variation A:　**The unit can be easily divided into three sub-units. Each unit can include an expandable, related vocabulary list.**

方案 A:　**这个单元可以分成三个教学单位。每个教学单位的词汇表可增减。**

Sub-Unit One: Geographic Locations and Positions 教学单位一：地点方位		
Vocabulary 词汇	**Grammatical Points 语法点**	**Linguistic Functions 语用**
Locations and positions 地点方位（15） Places　地点设施(16) Manner and means 方式（17）	“是/在/有” indicates locations and positions “是/在/有” 表述地点方位（15）	Identifying a geographic location and position 确认地点方位 Relating actions with location and means 明确行为与地点、方式

Sub-Unit Two：School 教学单位二：学校		
Vocabulary 词汇	Grammatical Points 语法点	Linguistic Functions 语用
On-campus facilities 学校校园与设施(15) Subjects of learning 学习课程与科目(15)	“是/在/有” indicates locations and positions “是/在/有” 表述 地点方位（15） “……了……就”（13）	Identifying a geographic location and position 确认地点方位 Relating actions with locations and means 明确行为与地点、方式

Sub-Unit Three：School Life 教学单位三：学校生活
Connect Sub-Unit One and Sub-Unit Two 融会教学单位一与二。
Group Project 小组活动项目 Emphasis 强调：Functional use of language 融会贯通地使用

Variation B： **The unit can simply keep the first two sub-units.**
Map vocabulary and grammatical patterns according to language use；and
Keep vocabulary and grammatical patterns to a functional minimum.

方案 B： **保持方案的头两个从属教学单位。把握每个教学单位的词汇量和语法点。**

Sub-Unit One：Geographic Locations and Positions 教学单位一：地点方位		
Vocabulary 词汇	Grammatical Points 语法点	Linguistic Functions 语用
Locations and positions 地点方位（15） Places 地点设施(16) Manner and means 方式（17）	“是/在/有” indicates locations and positions “是/在/有” 表述 地点方位（15）	Identifying a geographic location and position 确认地点方位 Relating actions with location and means 明确行为与地点和方式

Sub-Unit Two: School　教学单位二：学校		
Vocabulary 词汇	Grammatical Points 语法点	Linguistic Functions 语用
On-campus facilities 学校校园与设施(15) Subjects of learning 学习课程与科目(15)	"是/在/有" indicates locations and positions "是/在/有"表述地点方位 (15) "……了……就" (13)	Identifying a geographic location and position 确认地点方位 Relating actions with locations and means 明确行为与地点、方式

Variation C:　The unit has two different and simpler sub-units.
Map vocabulary and grammar according to language function; and
Keep sentence patterns and vocabulary to a functional minimum.

方案 C:　分两个不同的简单教学单位。把握每个教学单位的词汇量和语法点，限制在最少。

Sub-Unit One: Chicago and Its Geographic Location 教学单位一：芝加哥的地理位置		
Vocabulary 词汇	Grammatical Points 语法点	Linguistic Functions 语用
Locations and positions 地点方位 (15) Places　地点设施(16)	"是/在/有" indicates locations and positions "是/在/有"表述地点方位(15)	Identifying a geographic location and position 确认地点方位

Sub-Unit Two: My Life in Chicago　教学单位二：我在芝加哥		
Vocabulary 词汇	Grammatical Points 语法点	Linguistic Functions 语用
School　学校 (15) Activities　活动(7)	Location for activities 行为地点 (16) Means/Manner for activities 行为方式 (17)	Relating actions with locations and means 明确行为与地点、方式

Instructional Tips 教学指导策略提示

Tip 1:

Closely relating the content of learning to the lives of the students will promote interest in learning and leave room for expansion.

把教学与学生的生活联系起来能提高学习兴趣。

Tip 2:

The outlines of grammatical difficulties and simple explanations are found in *Functional and Grammatical Walk Through*, and the vocabulary list in chapters 16 and 17 might be helpful, too.

《什么篇：语用与语法走廊》的有关章节和16、17节的词汇对这个话题的学习有用。

Tip 3:

It is a good idea to review verbs, time expressions and conditions of general activities before talking about life in a city or school.

谈城市或学校生活之前可以先谈活动，与活动有关的时间等条件。既作铺垫又自然引出话题。

Tip 4:

Connect this unit with Unit Six for continuity in language use and topics of discussion.

这个单元的话题与第六单元承上启下。

Tip 5:

A teacher simply lecturing is not always a good practice in grades 6 ~ 12 classrooms. Letting the students teach for a change is one effective way to motivate and engage them. Students may share information, critique one another, or explore learning together. The key is good planning and organization. Make sure that the activity is relevant and purposeful, the requirements are clear and resources are available, and every student takes responsibility so that everyone is contributing to the process and the learning content. If a student presentation is involved, give clear instruction and time for preparation. When the students are confident, they will perform better.

在中小学课堂上，老师授课学生听并不总是一个好办法。让学生也当当老师，互教互学。既调动了学生的学习热情与积极性，又让学生集中精力，提高学习效果。可做的活动有很多：学生可以互相交流信息，对别人的作业提出批评建议，或一起探讨新的知识共同学习。做好这样的合作学习活动的关键是要计划好、组织好。活动要有的放矢，与课堂教学紧密相关。活动要求要明确，所需设备或资料要齐备；让每个学生都能参与其中并有所贡献。如果需要学生讲演报告，要给予时间和指导，让学生作好充分准备，以增强信心、取得最佳效果。

Suggested Activities　建议教学活动

Activity 1　　Game: Guess Who Is on Your Right?
猜一猜：谁在你的旁边?

Language task: Identifying the location of a person

Functions: Learning vocabulary
Listening comprehension and speaking correctly with clarity

Use: Class activity or assessment

This game has two versions: a simple version and a complex version.

这个游戏有简和繁两种版本。

简本：

- 准备一条蒙眼布。
- 分两队，各队占教室的一边。
- 1 队派一人 Player 1A 去 2 队，用围巾蒙住一人 Player 2A 的眼睛。1 队另一人 Player 1B 轻轻走到离蒙眼人 Player 2A 很近的地方。Player 2B 用一个句子描述 Player 1B 的方位。蒙眼人 Player 2A 必须马上辨出方位抓住 Player 1B。只可一次成功。

• 描述人和被蒙眼人各得一分。各队累计分数。

Simple Version:

Preparation for the game:

• Vocabulary relating to position, sentence patterns used in identifying positions.

• A scarf for blindfolding.

Procedure:

Part 1: Team up

• Divide the class into two teams.

• Each team takes a side of the classroom.

• Players from Team 1 are labelled as: Player 1A, 1B, etc.

• Players from Team 2 are labelled as: Player 2A, 2B, etc.

Part 2: Play the game

Step 1: Player 1A goes to Team 2, blindfolds Player 2A's eyes with a scarf.

Step 2: Player 1B stands near the blindfolded Player 2A.

Step 3: Player 2B describes the position of Player 1B to Player 2A by saying:

……在你的右边。

你的右边是……

Step 4: Player 2A gets one attempt to tag Player 1B.

Rules:

• Take turns until all players have played.

• Each blindfolded player is only allowed one try to identify the position of the target.

Scoring:

• Correctly describing the position of the opposing player 1 point

• Successfully tagging the opposing player 1 point

• The team that earns the most points wins.

繁本:

• 是在简本的基础上加对 Player 1B 的外表描述，被蒙眼人 Player 2A

必须在抓住 Player 1B 时，说出他/她是谁。得分由此加倍。

- 玩游戏前提醒注意对方队员的穿戴。

Complex Version:

Preparation for the game:

- Vocabulary relating to positions and vocabulary describing clothing.
- Sentence patterns used in identifying positions.
- Sentence patterns used in identifying clothing.
- A scarf for blindfolding.

Procedure:

Part 1: Team up

- Divide the class into two teams with each taking a side of the classroom.
- Players from Team 1 are labelled as: Player 1A, 1B, etc.
- Players from Team 2 are labelled as: Player 2A, 2B, etc.

Part 2: Play the game

Step 1: Player 1A goes to Team 2, and blindfolds Player 2A with a scarf.

Step 2: Player 1B goes to stand near the blindfolded Player 2A.

Step 3: Player 2B describes the position of Player 1B to Player 2A by saying:

……在你的右边。

你的右边是……

Step 4: Player 2A gets one attempt to tag Player 1B.

Step 5: Player 2B describes Player 1B to Player 2A by saying:

今天他/她穿了一件红上衣和一条牛仔裤。

他/她戴/没戴眼镜。

Step 6: Player 2A tries to identify Player 1B by name.

Rules:

- Take turns playing until all players have played.
- Each blindfolded player is only allowed one try to identify the position of the target.

Scoring：

• Correct description of location	1 point
• Correct description of person	1 point
• Success in identifying the position	1 point
• Success in identify the person	1 point

- The team that earns most points wins.

Note：

Before the game, remind the players to pay attention and remember the appearance of the other team's members.

Activity 2 Who Are Our Neighbours? 谁是我们的邻居？

Language task：Identify locations of our neighbouring schools and other facilities

Functions： Learning vocabulary and new sentence patterns
Listening, speaking and writing

Use： Class activity, homework assignment, assessment

这个活动用来描述学校所在的社区。画一张学校所在社区的地图；描述学校四周的建筑设施。用以下的句子：

我们学校的周围有……

我们学校的前边是……

……在学校的后边。

学生还可以互相提问，或用来介绍其他与学生生活有关的地区。

Procedure：

Step 1：Map out our neighbourhood

- Identify all the buildings in the neighbourhood.
(Targets may be limited according to the intended learning objectives; use list of places (16) if needed.)

Step 2：Spell it out

- Identify our neighbours by using these sentence patterns：
我们学校周围有……
我们学校前边是……

……在学校后边。

- Each student must use all three sentence patterns.

Elaboration:

- Interpersonal: Have students pair up to ask each other questions.
- Presentational: Have students report their conversations to the class.

Follow-up:

- Homework:

  Write about the neighbourhood.

- A Twist:

  Write about your downtown or about your house.

Activity 3	Snowball Rolling: Who Are Our Neighbours?
	加长叙述：我们的社区
Language task:	Identify the locations of identified places
Functions:	Learning vocabulary and sentence patterns
	Listening and speaking, reading and writing
Use:	Class activity, homework assignment, assessment

这个活动谈城市的所在地及其他有关情况，主要练习听说。是这样开展进行的：

老师说一个句子，然后用问答的方式让学生逐个说会。一句一句地加内容：学生的回答叙述不断加长（语速可以不断加快），每次有数个学生回答，直到故事讲完。还可在会话的基础上进行阅读：阅读另一相似故事，问答检查理解。还可加模仿的写作活动。

Procedure:

Step 1: Start a snowball

- Teacher makes a statement about a city and asks questions.
- Select students in turn to answer.

Step 2: Get rolling

- Teacher continues to add a sentences at a time.

- Select students to repeat the growing passage in turn.

Step 3: Reading sample

- Read a sample passage that bears all sentence previously recited.

Step 4: Work in class

- Jot down the information about cities in which relatives or friends live.
- Model the recited example to describe one city orally. (to a partner or to class depending on time).

Step 5: Homework time

- Write several similar passages about different cities.

Follow-up:

- Peer editing/Report to class
- Preparation for the activity
  List of places (16)

Activity 4 Sharing Stories 分享你的故事
Language task: Peer editing, telling and retelling a story
Functions: Cooperative learning: Assisted writing and speaking
Reading, listening, and speaking
Use: Class activity

This activity is a follow-up to Activity 2 above.

这个活动是在前一活动的基础上开展的合作学习活动。

做法：

- 同伴相互修改作文：要先阅读同班的文章；找出好句子，指出错误；提出修改建议。
- 分成3～4人小组，讲述自己的故事。
- 每人用2～3句话总结另一人的故事。

Preparation for the activity

Complete stories for peer editing and presentation.

Procedure:

Step 1: Pair up

Pair up students to do a peer editing:

- Read your partner's writing,
- Identify good sentences and mistakes, and
- Suggest revisions.

Step 2: Team up

- Divide class into groups of three to four.
- Designate a group leader.
- Make instructions and expectations clear.

Step 3: Share stories

- Each student tells a story prepared as homework and edited in class.

Step 4: Group summary

- By group: Each gives a brief recount (two to three sentences) of another's story.

Activity 5　　Tell the Story in a Two-Minute Timed Speech　计时快说

(Please see Example 8 in Part Ⅰ "Timed Speeches" for more details.)

(请参照上篇课堂活动案例 8 "计时快说")

Activity 6　　Quiz Show: Identify Location and Means of Getting There

智力游戏：去哪儿？怎么去？

Language task: Identify and inquire locations and means

Functions: Quiz your knowledge and vocabulary

Use: Class activity, homework assignment, assessment

This game consists of a preparation part and an execution part. It is recommended to play the game during separate class periods.

这个游戏分“准备”和“执行”两个步骤进行，可分别在不同课时展开。

准备：

- 分3~4人一队。
- 每队按词汇表（《什么篇：语用与语法走廊》（16/17））做小卡片，可用图画表示交通工具和地点。

执行：

- 逐队当主持人。主持队抽卡，依次选参赛队看卡，按图说话并提问。
- 一次只能有一人说话。参赛队机会等同。一句话或一个问题各得一分。
- 每轮三分钟。得分最多的队获胜。

Preparation:

- Index cards
- Reference may also include *Functional and Grammatical Walk Through* (16/17): List of places and list of means/manner

Procedure:

Step 1: Team up

- Divide the class into teams of three to four.
- Specify rules and expectations.

Step 2: Prepare for a quiz show (can be a part of a homework assignment)

- Each group is given a number of cities.
- Teams brainstorm questions related to these cities using learned patterns and words.
- Teams write questions on index cards.

Step 3: Double-check questions

- Teams meet to ensure that all questions are correct.

Step 4: Quiz begins!

- Each team goes on stage in turn as hosts.
- Hosts take turn asking questions.
- Select other teams to answer questions.

Step 5: One player answers one question at a time:

- Say a sentence according to the drawing, such as:

  图书馆在学校的东边。

- Ask a question according to the drawing, such as:
  怎么去图书馆？图书馆在哪儿？

Scoring:

- Each correct statement　1 point
- Each correct question　1 point
- Each round last three minutes
- The team that answers the most questions within the time frame wins

Activity 7	Developing Narration Skills through Dialogue: My Life at School 通过对话提高表达能力：我的校园生活
Language task:	Discuss school work and activities
Functions:	Learning vocabulary and sentence patterns Speaking and listening, reading and writing
Use:	Class activity, homework assignment, assessment

这个活动练习听力理解、对话和成段表达能力。

课上老师提问，学生逐个回答。逐渐加快语速，加长内容，直至学生可以熟练成段表达。

课后，学生根据课上的活动把叙述写下来，还可跟阅读结合。

Procedure:

Step 1: Questions and answers

- Teacher poses questions one at a time.
- Student answers in turn.

Step 2: Snowball rolling interactions

- Teacher increases the number of questions each time.
- Student gives more comprehensive answers.

Step 3: Telling it all

- Students gradually develop answers into oral narrations.

Step 4: Homework

- Write down the narration to be presented orally.

- Write down all questions related to the content of the narration.

Sample Questions:

1. 你是几年级的学生？
2. 你在哪儿上学？
3. 你学习什么？
4. 学校在哪儿？
5. 你最喜欢什么课？
6. 你的……课的老师是谁？
7. 你的教室在哪儿？
8. 你每天几点上课？几点下课？
9. 下课以后你去哪儿？
10. 你做什么？
11. 你怎么去？
12. 跟谁一起做？
13. 你做得怎么样？

Notes:

- Questions can be grouped in segments (two to three each time) or by specific topics.
- This activity can be repeated for a few consecutive class periods.

Elaboration:

It can be elaborated using Activity 3, Activity 4 and Activity 5 listed above for further learning.

Follow-up:

It can form the basis for a larger project.

Activity 8	My Life in My Neighborhood 我的社区生活
Language task:	Introduce your life in your neighborhood
Functions:	Integrated language use
	Listening, speaking, writing
Use:	Class activity, homework assignment, assessment

这是一个综合项目。制作一个社区的地图，标定你家所在地。描述你家周围的建筑设施、方位和活动等。写下来。报告展示或与同伴展开对话。

也可与上面的几个活动结合起来或加同伴修改文稿活动。

Procedure:

Step 1: Get a map

- Draw or print out a map of your neighborhood.

Step 2: Find the center

- Locate your house.
- Identify other buildings in the neighborhood in reference to your house.

Step 3: Describe your neighborhood

- Write the descriptions down (better as homework).

Step 4: Share information

- Can be elaborated with Activity 3, Activity 4, and Activity 5 or pair up with a partner for an interactive interview.

Follow-up:

- Edit and revise: Edit and rewrite your drafts to finalize the writing.
- Add visual support: Design your display with visuals or artwork.
- Memorize the research: Prepare an oral presentation to go along with the display.
- Present it to class.
- Can be used as a quarterly or term assessment.

Caution:

- Don't forget to cite sources correctly.
- Plagiarism is using other people's work without proper acknowledgement.
- Plagiarism is also cheating.

Activity 9　Group Project: Introducing Our School
小组项目：介绍我们的学校

Language task: Make a promotional display for our school

Functions: Comprehensive use of language
Task-based learning
Cooperative learning

Use: Class activity, homework assignment, assessment

见下 Sample Rubric for Unit Projects　教学单元综合项目测试标准例案

Unit Seven Project A: My Life at School　我的校园生活

Critical Thinking and Comparative Study　评判和比较

Activity 10　Guessing Game — Winning Bonus　猜猜看：有奖游戏

Activity 11　Discovering Rules　找出规律

(See Unit One, Activity 6 and Activity 7)

（请参照第一教学单元活动 6 和活动 7）

Don't forget to constantly use these activities in class.

Suggested Assignment Focus　建议作业的重点

- Speaking with fluency　增强说话的流利程度
- Reading with increasing number of Chinese characters　阅读加大汉字数量
- Writing in sentences and paragraphs, using an increasing number of Chinese characters, and using a Chinese word processor　用汉字写作，写作加大汉字量，会用中文处理软件
- Developing all four language skills　发展听、说、读、写技能
- Completing basic language tasks in Chinese　用目的语完成语言任务
- Asking questions and exchanging information　提问并交换信息
- Using authentic materials　使用真实语言材料
- Integrating information technology and research methods　查阅资料

Suggested Assignments 建议作业

- Assign listening materials: Listening.
- Copy words or characters: Reading and writing.
- Memorize some language materials, and prepare to perform during the next class: Reading and speaking.
- Produce language materials as instructed, and prepare to perform during the next class: Writing and speaking; open-ended tasks.
- Writing on topic: Speaking and writing and task-based presentation.
- Peer editing and writing: Cooperative learning, interactive learning and discourse development.
- Create projects using oral and written presentations: All language skills.
- 听力练习。
- 读写练习。
- 记忆语言材料，准备测试：读说。
- 创造性地运用语言材料，预备课上展示：说写，语言实践任务。
- 有题目的写作：说写，语言实践任务。
- 同伴互相编辑写作：合作学习，学习交流，成段表达。
- 创作口语和书面报告：综合训练。

Suggested Assessment Focus 建议评估重点

Listening Comprehension 听力理解

- Comprehension of short passages with pre-activity clues 在有预听活动的情况下听懂成段叙述
- Comprehension of questions 听懂提问
- Comprehension of interpersonal exchanges 听懂人际交流与对话

Speaking 说

- Emphasizing speaking in discourse 承前启后的叙述表达
- Emphasizing fluency 表达流利
- Emphasizing ability to initiate and respond properly to interactions 发问并回答

Reading 阅读

• Reading passages in Chinese characters	阅读理解汉字书写的段落
• Reading texts that have unfamiliar words	阅读理解有生词的文章
• Guessing meaning with common sense and contextual clues	根据背景知识和上下文猜断语义

Writing 写

• Using correct spelling of *pinyin* and selecting the correct characters when using a Chinese word processor	用电脑输入时能用拼音正确拼写并选择正确的汉字
• Handwriting Chinese characters correctly	正确手书汉字
• Developing writing skills with correct use of patterns and with logic	写作有逻辑性，语法错误较少
• Writing in paragraphs	成段写作表达
• Creating texts with known Chinese characters and using a Chinese word processor	用汉字写作，会用中文处理软件

Suggested Assessment 建议测试评估形式

See page 90.

见 90 页。

Rubrics for Assessment 测试标准

Make a clear rubric to specify expectations and the required elements according to the content coverage of the day or lesson.

根据每日课堂的学习进度，制定明确、清晰的测试评分标准，以申明期待和要求。

Sample Unit Project　教学单元综合项目测试例案

Unit Seven Project A: My Life at School

第七教学单元综合项目（一）：我的校园生活

描写学校的生活：介绍学校内外学习课程和校外活动。

Format:

Oral and written presentation

- PowerPoint presentation or visual display

Topic:

Life at school

Content:

- General introduction of school
  Location, campus, departments, students
- General self-introduction
  Program of study, daily schedule
- Favorite things to do
  Teachers, favorite classes, friends
  Extra-curricular activities (when, where, how)
- Positive and negative forms of all sentence patterns
- Complex sentences
- Questions and answers
- Three questions for listening comprehension

Evaluation:

- Content knowledge:
  Linguistic components
  Functional use of the language
  Mechanics (grammatical and technical errors)
- Creativity in presentation:
  Overall design
  Visual aids or artistic expressions
- Delivery:
  Pronunciation, tones and fluency
  Organization of information

Presentation

Reference

- Effort

Unit Seven Project B: My Community and Life in My Neighborhood

第七教学单元综合项目（二）：我的社区和社区生活

对话与描述：我的社区和社区生活。

Format:

Oral and written presentation

- A dialogue, a narration, a PowerPoint presentation or other artistic displays

Topic:

My community and life in my neighborhood

Content:

- A brief self-introduction
  Family and other related information
- Introduction to the neighborhood
  Map: Location
  Facilities in reference to your house
  People's activities
- Personal life
  Daily routines, special events, etc.
- Positive and negative forms of all sentence patterns
- Complex sentences
- Questions and answers
- Three questions forms for listening comprehension

Evaluation:

- Content knowledge:
  Linguistic components
  Functional use of the language
  Mechanics (grammatical and technical errors)
- Creativity in presentation:

Overall design

Visual aids or artistic expressions

- Delivery:

  Pronunciation, tones and fluency

  Organization of information

  Presentation

  Reference

- Effort

Unit Seven Project C: My School

第七教学单元综合项目（三）：我的学校

小组项目：

编写一个学校介绍：介绍学校，描述学校内外、日常活动等。

Format:

Oral and written presentation

- Printed brochure, PowerPoint presentation or video production

Topic:

Promotional marketing material: My school

Content:

- General information about the school

  Faculty, students, classes, extra-curricular activities

- Campus

  Each floor: floor plan, departments, activities

  Administration and offices, facilities outside the building

- Surroundings:

  Immediate surroundings: front, back, left, right

  Community

- Positive and negative forms of all sentence patterns
- Complex sentences
- Questions and answers
- Three questions for listening comprehension

Evaluation:

- Group:
  - Originality in design
  - Artistic design
  - Coordination and organization
  - Completed on schedule
- Individual:
  - Content knowledge:
    - Linguistic components
    - Functional use of the language
    - Mechanics (grammatical and technical errors)
  - Delivery:
    - Pronunciation, tones and fluency
    - Organization of information
    - Presentation
    - Reference
  - Contribution to the group

Writing Sample 1 范文（一）

学校的三楼

我们学校的三楼有楼梯。很多人上下楼梯。芝北预科的中学生常常走过大厅去上课。芝北预科的大厅明亮和好看。你可以在那儿跑步，因为我们的大厅非常大。

大厅的左边是数学系。在大厅的墙上，数学系有很多的挂图。没人爱数学。每个数学系的教室有学生和老师、电脑、椅子、课桌和投影机。Mulligan 老师在 323 教室教几何。虽然三楼的左边都是数学系的教室，可是也有语言实验室。实验室在 327 房间。在三楼右边的另一个系是科学系。Coy 老师在 305 教室上课。这个是我最喜欢的实验室。这个实验室有高的桌子和高的椅子。我在这用火烧过我的手。三楼的这边还有一个计算机室。

图书馆的二层也在三楼。从图书馆的二层就不能去三楼的大厅。可是因为我们的中学有很多的窗户，所以你能在图书馆二层看到三楼的大厅。

为什么我们学校里有这么多的窗户？我不知道。可是我最喜欢从窗户看我们的学校的外边。

三楼有四个厕所：两个男厕所和两个女厕所。

Writing Sample 2　范文（二）

学校的四周

学校的四周有公园、停车场、工厂、河、桥和公寓。饭馆、车站和老人院离学校远一点。

公园绿，明亮。人人喜欢去公园。有人吃中饭的时候或者放学以后在公园打球。我不常去那儿，因为公园有很多的泥。

我的车现在在停车场。要是你常常骑车上学，你就想用我们的停车场。这个太有用了。可是我的车比其他的都酷。

有一个工厂在学校的附近。工厂的工人不喜欢芝北预科的中学生，他们觉得我们太讨厌了。我不觉得，我觉得工厂的人太苦了也太老了。

学校的后边是芝加哥河。河里有水，可是也有很多的其他的东西。别喝河水，河水不太好喝。

我每天从 Bryn Mawr 桥上走过，这是我最喜欢的桥。这个桥又宽又漂亮。Bryn Mawr 桥在林子旁边。

学校的对面有很多公寓。现在，还正在盖新公寓。我不想住在中学旁边。中学生很累和难看，我不喜欢起床的时候看见难看的中学生。

学校的两边都有麦当劳。很多的中学生放学以后在麦当劳吃饭。虽然我不喜欢吃麦当劳的饭，我第一年在芝北预科的时候常去这两个饭馆。这两个饭馆漂亮，色彩分明。

虽然每天下午三点有三辆公共汽车来芝北预科接学生，可是很多学生不坐这些车。有三个车站不太远，学生可以走路去车站坐其他的公共汽车。

芝北预科和麦当劳的中间是一个老人院。我没看见过住在那儿的老人，可是我知道他们喜欢芝北预科中学生，他们给我们礼物。

（By Simon S.，Northside College Preparatory High School，Chinese 2）

Unit Eight：I Live in Chicago
第八教学单元：我家住在芝加哥

Theme 主题

I Live in Chicago 我家住在芝加哥

Topics 交谈要点与话题

- Buildings 建筑
- Neighborhood 邻里
- My House 我家
  Rooms and Furniture 房间与家具
  Arrangement of Objects 摆设（有“着”“在”做补语）
- Visit My House 请你来我家

Content of Teaching and Learning 教学内容

Linguistic Functions 语用

- Describing arrangement of objects 描述室内摆设
- Giving general statements and asking about living arrangements and conditions 叙述和询问日常生活起居
- Identifying a geographic location 确认地理位置
- Asking and giving directions 问路指路
- Recognizing authentic road signs 辨认实用交通路标
- Narrating in paragraph-length passages 成段表述
- Asking about and exchanging information in interactions 问答对话
- Listening with comprehension to passages of increasing length 听力理解
- Reading passages with comprehension 段落阅读理解
- Using a Chinese word processor 使用中文处理软件

- Writing in paragraphs　写作

Grammatical Patterns and Vocabulary　语法点与词汇

(Refer to *Functional and Grammatical Walk Through*)

(《什么篇：语用与语法走廊》(索引：B/15/16/17/21))

Vocabulary　词汇	Grammatical Points　语法点
Buildings　建筑（15） Neighborhood　邻里(16) Rooms　房间（15） Furniture　家具（15） Transportation 交通工具（17） Traffic　交通运行（21） Directions　方向（21）	"是/有/在" indicates locations and positions "是/有/在" 表述地点方位（15） "有/着" indicates existence and manner of doing "有/着" 表述存在及状态（17） "在" as complement　"在" 做补语（21） Resultative complements　结果补语（21） Directional complements　趋向补语（21） Chinese characters　汉字（B）

Cultural Studies and Connections　文化及跨学科联系

- Community and life　社区与生活
- Changes in community　社区的变化
- Transportation, traffic and road signs　交通
- International travel　国际旅行

Variations of Unit Eight　第八单元的变量设置

The instructor can customize this unit design according to the needs of the class, curriculum at large, the available instructional hours and course schedule.

教学单元应根据课堂教学的需求、课程设置的全局情况及课时的限制酌情加减。

Variables that can be taken into consideration are:

- Number of grammatical patterns involved,
- Extensiveness of vocabulary,
- Depth of communication tasks, and

• Proficiency of language skills.

应考虑的变量如下：

• 语法点的数量，
• 词汇的覆盖面，
• 语用实践活动的深度，
• 语言技巧的水平。

Suggested Variations of the Unit by Topic　建议参考如下

Variation A:　**The unit can be easily divided into three sub-units. Each unit can include an expandable, related vocabulary list.**

方案 A:　**这个单元可以分成三个教学单位。每个教学单位的词汇表可增减。**

Sub-Unit One: Community and Neighborhood　教学单位一：社区邻里		
Vocabulary 词汇	**Grammatical Points 语法点**	**Linguistic Functions 语用**
Buildings　建筑（15） Neighborhood 邻里（16） Positions　方位（15）	"是/有/在" indicates locations and positions "是/有/在" 表述地点方位（15）	Identifying a geographic location 确认地理位置

Sub-Unit Two: Family Life　教学单位二：日常起居		
Vocabulary 词汇	**Grammatical Points 语法点**	**Linguistic Functions 语用**
Rooms　房间（15） Furniture　家具（15） Verbs related to daily activities 日常行为动词（7） Locations　地点（16） Manner and means 方式工具（17）	"有/着" indicates existence and manner "有/着"表述存在及状态（17） "在" as complement "在"做补语(21)	Making general statements and asking about living arrangements and conditions 叙述和询问日常生活起居

Sub-Unit Three: Transportation 教学单位三：交通		
Vocabulary 词汇	**Grammatical Points 语法点**	**Linguistic Functions 语用**
Transportation 交通工具（17） Traffic 交通运行（21） Directions 方向（21） Time expressions 时间词（6） Locations 地点（16）	Resultative complements 结果补语（21） Directional complements 趋向补语（21）	Identifying a geographic location 确认地理位置 Asking and giving directions 指路

Variation B: **The unit can simply keep the first Sub-Units** 1 **and** 3 **of Variation A.**
Map vocabulary and grammatical patterns according to language use; and
Keep vocabulary and grammatical patterns to a functional minimum.

方案 B: **保留方案 A 的教学单位一和教学单位三。把握词汇和语法点的难度，控制使用。**

Sub-Unit One: Neighborhood 教学单位一：邻里		
Vocabulary 词汇	**Grammatical Points 语法点**	**Linguistic Functions 语用**
Buildings 建筑（15） Neighborhood 邻里（16） Positions 方位（15）	"是/有/在" indicates locations/positions "是/有/在" 表述地点方位（15）	Identifying a geographic location 确认地理位置

Sub-Unit Two：Transportation 教学单位二：交通		
Vocabulary 词汇	**Grammatical Points 语法点**	**Linguistic Functions 语用**
Transportation 交通工具(17) Traffic 交通运行(21) Directions 方向（21） Time expressions 时间词(6) Locations 地点（16）	Resultative complements 结果补语（21） Directional complements 趋向补语（21）	Identifying a geographic location 确认地理位置 Asking and giving directions 指路

Variation C： **The unit can be a simplified version of a combined Sub-Units 1 and 2 of Variation B.**

Map vocabulary and grammatical patterns according to language use；and

Keep vocabulary and grammatical patterns to a functional minimum.

方案 C： **简化方案 A 的教学单位一和教学单位二。把握词汇和语法点的难度，控制使用。**

Vocabulary 词汇	**Grammatical Points 语法点**	**Linguistic Functions 语用**
Buildings 建筑（15） Neighborhood 邻里（16） Positions 方位（15） Transportation 交通工具（17） Traffic 交通运行(21) Directions 方向（21）	“是/有/在” indicates locations/positions “是/有/在” 表述地点方位（15） Simple patterns for giving directions 指路的简单模式(21)	Identifying a geographic location 确认地理位置 Asking and giving directions 指路

Variation D：　A simpler version of any of the above unit or sub-unit designs.

方案 D：　简化以上任何一个方案。

Instructional Tips　教学指导策略提示

Tip 1：

If this unit is taught after Unit Seven in this book, use the vocabulary and descriptions of larger communities to introduce vocabularies relating to specific buildings or structures.

如果在第七教学单元之后教这个单元，不妨利用前面教学单元有关大社区环境作铺垫引出或结合新的学习内容。

Tip 2：

There are many visual aids that can help when describing a house or a neighbourhood：

- Drawings and artwork about architecture,
- Photos of the family home,
- Satellite photos from the internet, and
- Student-made floor plans of their homes.

可用来谈房屋、建筑、街道、社区的视觉辅助教材教具很多。例如：图画图片、家庭照片、网上鸟瞰图或学生自己画的房屋蓝图等。

Tip 3：

This topic in this unit gives a good opportunity to review and expand learning of verbs and adverbial phrases. Make buildings, rooms, and the neighborhood alive with real-life activities.

这又是一个复习和扩展学习活动和与活动有关的时间地点方式等条件的机会。让建筑物充满生活气息。

Tip 4：

Connect this unit with Unit Six and Unit Seven for continuity in topics of discussion and language use.

这个单元的话题也与第六单元和第七单元承上启下。

Tip 5：

Accountability for teaching and learning is a big issue in K-12 classroom practice. Administrators want to supervise what is going on every minute in the classroom. Parents want to monitor their children's progress. More importantly, both teachers and students need to know how effective teaching and learning is achieved and where there is room for improvement. Everyone wants tangible results. Having clear and understandable rubrics for classroom performance, homework assignments, and assessments will make communication among all parties much easier and teaching and learning more effective. There are many online assessment tools — rubric banks that provide generic rubrics for specific areas of learning or a wide range of modalities. Teachers can borrow and modify ready-made rubrics for specific class use.

在中小学的课堂教学上，教与学的责任与效果必须能明确解释与测量。因为校方管理人员要知道以便监督管理教学；家长在乎学生的表现与成绩；更重要的是，老师和学生都要随时明确地了解课堂教与学的效率和需要改进之处。谁都想要一个“看得见、摸得着”的具体结果。空口无凭，不易理喻。要是有一个可以用来评估课堂表现、家庭作业和考试成绩的明确的评分标准细则要求，那各方之间的交流就容易多了，教与学也就有效多了。网上有很多评估工具库，老师们可以根据教学需要，下载有关的标准与细则，加以修改，用于自己的课堂。

Suggested Activities 建议教学活动

Activity 1 What Is in Our Neighborhood? 社区概况
Language task: Create a glossary in class
Functions: Learning vocabulary
Cooperative learning
Use: Class activity

用这个活动来做一个社区建筑设施的词汇表。分成3～4人的小组。每人给一个词汇表。按照所给的词汇表，小组讨论社区里都有什么建筑设施。表上没有的加上（5～10 个新词）。全班在一起互相交流，做出一个完整的词汇表。可用电脑打出一个词汇表。

课后继续这个活动，准备词汇考试。这个活动还可以用来描述家居及家具词汇。

Preparation of the activity:

A list of the vocabulary to be learned

Procedure:

Step 1: Form teams

- Divide the class into groups of three to four.
- Teams are given a list of Chinese vocabulary. (Each student must have a copy.)

Step 2: Brainstorm

- Teams are instructed to study the vocabulary related to the current topic.
- Today's topic is housing and buildings.
- The goal is to discover vocabulary words that can be added to the list.

Step 3: Create a better vocabulary list

- Each team must come up with five to ten needed words.

Step 4: Come together

- The class comes together to compare and share words.
- Write the words on the board, and research the Chinese versions.

Step 5: Create a new list

- Select the most useful (common) words and compile a new list.

Note:

If the class can be held in a computer lab, it is recommended that students type the word lists with a Chinese word processor.

Follow-up: Homework

- Make a good vocabulary list.
- Memorize the vocabulary.

• Prepare for a vocabulary quiz.

Elaboration:

This activity can be also used for learning other vocabulary, such as rooms, furniture, etc.

Activity 2　Where Do We Go from Here?　上哪儿去？

Language task: Giving directions: Tell us where to go

Functions: Using vocabulary and sentence patterns needed to give directions

Use: Class activity, homework assignment, assessment

这个活动对学习指路比较有效。

准备：

• 与指路有关的词语和句式。

（预备部分可以作为家庭作业事先准备）

执行：

• 每个学生写出十个指令。

• 分组。

• 按一人的指令行动。

• 轮流给指令。

后续：

• 还可让学生把单句的指令连成串，说成、写成一个活动的描述。例如：去中国城。

Preparation for the activity:

Vocabulary and sentence patterns related to given directions.

Procedure:

Step 1: Create a list of ten commands, such us "往前走两步从这下楼"

Step 2: Walk out the door

• A direction giver is chosen.

- The whole class follows the given directions.

Step 3：New leader

- After the first move is completed，a second leader is chosen to give a new order.

Step 4：Continuation

- The game continues until the whole class returns to the classroom.

Follow-up：

- Homework

  Give directions to a place：Chinatown?

  Students may search online to help with directions.

- For a later project

  Directions to your house?

Activity 3　　My House　我家的房子

Language task：Draw a blueprint of your house and explain the layout

Functions：Writing，speaking，and listening

Use：Class activity，homework assignment，assessment

画一幅你家房子的蓝图。描述房子的结构、摆设、居家活动。也可以相互问答、总结。

Pre-activity：

- Vocabulary related to rooms and layout of a house or apartment
- Position words and sentence patterns indicating positions

Procedure：

Step 1：Draw a blueprint of your house

- Ask students to draw the layout of a house.

Step 2：Describe it

- Ask students to use these sentence patterns in writing：

  这是我家。我家有……层（楼），有……个房间。

  客厅在……客厅和卧室的中间有……

  我的卧室的右边是……

Step 3：Explain it

- Have students explain the drawing of the house room by room using the above sentences.

Elaboration：

Have students interact with one another giving questions and answers.

Follow-up：

- The results can be the foundation for a more comprehensive project.
- Don't throw the work away！Revise it and expand on it for later use.

Activity 4 An Invitation to a Party at My House 请来我家做客
Language task：Write an invitation to your house with directions
Functions：Writing
Use：Class activity，homework assignment，assessment

写一张邀请，请朋友来你家做客。交代时间、地点、活动，并给出路线图。

Pre-activity：

- Vocabulary relating to positions and transportations
- Sentence patterns used for given directions.

Writing：

- Create an invitation for a celebration at your house：
  Purpose/Time/Location
- Directions to your house：
  Driving，using public transportations，on foot（northbound，southbound）
- Requirements：
  Must use all discussed sentence patterns.

Follow-up：

- This result lays a foundation for a more comprehensive project.
- Don't throw the work away！Revise it and expand on it for later use.

Activity 5　Group Project: A Guide Book for Chicago Tourists
芝加哥旅游景点介绍
Language task: Make a guide book for visitors to Chicago
Functions: Integrated language use
Connect language learning with learning about culture
Research, cooperative learning
Use: Class activity, homework assignment, assessment

The class is going to make a tourist guide as a book or a brochure.

这是一个合作项目：全班做一个旅游大全或旅游须知。每个小组选一个景点，调查研究，收集资料，做一个景点介绍手册，包括：地区简介、背景介绍、周围的设施、旅游须知、交通图等。

Procedure:

Step 1: Form teams
- Divide the class into teams of three to four.

Step 2: Divide tasks
- Each team selects a tourist attraction in the Greater Chicago Area. (Note: Teacher, please prepare a list of suggestions in advance)

Step 3: Take a role
Each team member must take two roles:
- A leadership role: A manager, a resource organizer or a recorder
- A writing role: Write one section

Step 4: Gather information
Information must include but is not limited to:
- Brief introduction to Chicago
- Brief introduction to the selected attraction
- Description of the neighborhood and its facilities
- Visiting times
- Detailed directions

Step 5: Drafting and editing
- Schedule due dates: First draft, peer editing, final revision.

Step 6：Putting it together

- Team Presentation

Elaboration：

- The final presentation may require formal attire or historical costume for dramatic effect.
- A competition may be organized to elect the best project（rubric needed）.

Caution：

- Don't forget to cite the sources correctly.
- Plagiarism is using other people's work without proper acknowledgement.
- Plagiarism is also cheating.

Critical Thinking and Comparative Study 评判和比较

Activity 6 Guessing Game — Winning Bonus 猜猜看：有奖游戏

Activity 7 Discovering Rules 找出规律

（See Unit One，Activity 6 and Activity 7）

（请参照第一教学单元活动 6 和活动 7）

Don't forget to constantly use these activities in class.

Suggested Assignment Focus 建议作业的重点

- Speaking with fluency 增强说话的流利程度
- Reading with increasing number of Chinese characters 阅读加大汉字数量
- Writing in sentences and paragraphs，using an increasing number of Chinese characters，and using a Chinese word processor 用汉字写作，写作加大汉字量，会用中文处理软件
- Developing all four language skills 发展听、说、读、写技能
- Completing basic language tasks in Chinese 用目的语完成语言任务
- Asking questions and exchanging information 提问并交换信息
- Using authentic materials 使用真实语言材料

- Integrating information technology and research methods　查阅资料

Suggested Assignments　建议作业

- Assign listening materials: Listening.
- Copy words or characters: Reading and writing.
- Memorize some language materials, and prepare to perform during the next class: Reading and speaking.
- Produce language materials as instructed, and prepare to perform during the next class: Writing and speaking; open-ended tasks.
- Writing on topic: Speaking and writing and task-based presentation.
- Peer editing and writing: Cooperative learning, interactive learning and discourse development.
- Create projects using oral and written presentations: All language skills.
- 听力练习。
- 读写练习。
- 记忆语言材料，准备测试：读说。
- 创造性地运用语言材料，预备课上展示：说写，语言实践任务。
- 有题目的写作：说写，语言实践任务。
- 同伴互相编辑写作：合作学习，学习交流，成段表达。
- 创作口语和书面报告：综合训练。

Suggested Assessment Focus　建议评估重点

Listening comprehension　听力理解

- Comprehension of short passages with pre-activity clues　在有预听活动的情况下听懂成段叙述
- Comprehension of questions　听懂提问
- Comprehension of interpersonal exchanges　听懂人际交流与对话

Speaking　说

- Emphasizing speaking in discourse　承前启后的叙述表达

- Emphasizing fluency　表达流利
- Emphasizing ability to initiate and respond properly to interactions　发问并回答

Reading　阅读

- Reading passages in Chinese characters　阅读理解汉字书写的段落
- Reading texts that have unfamiliar words　阅读理解有生词的文章
- Guessing meaning with common sense and contextual clues　根据背景知识和上下文猜断语义

Writing　写

- Using correct spelling of *pinyin* and selecting the correct characters when using a Chinese word processor　用电脑输入时能用拼音正确拼写并选择正确的汉字
- Handwriting Chinese characters correctly　正确手书汉字
- Developing writing skills with correct use of patterns and with logic　写作有逻辑性，语法错误较少
- Writing in paragraphs　成段写作表达
- Creating texts with known characters and using a Chinese word processor　用汉字写作会用中文处理软件

Suggested Assessment　建议测试评估形式

See page 90.

见 90 页。

Rubrics for Assessment　测试标准

Make a clear rubric to specify expectations and the required elements according to the content coverage of the day or lesson.

根据每日课堂的学习进度，制定明确、清晰的测试评分标准，以申明期待和要求。

Sample Unit Project　教学单元综合项目测试例案

Unit Eight Group Project: A Tourist Guide

第八教学单元群体项目：旅游手册

My Kind of Town Chicago Is　芝加哥：我心中的城市

(See Unit Eight, Activity 6 above for details)

这是一个合作项目：全班做一个旅游大全或旅游须知。每个小组选一个景点，调查研究，收集资料，做一个景点介绍手册。包括：地区简介、背景介绍、周围的设施、旅游须知、交通图等。

Format:

Oral and written presentation

- A printed brochure, PowerPoint presentation or video production

Topic:

A tourist guide: My kind of town Chicago is

Content:

- A brief introduction of Chicago
- Brief introduction to the selected attraction
- Description of the neighborhood
- Description of neighborhood facilities
- Best season to visit
- Visiting times, schedule
- Detailed directions
- Positive and negative forms of all sentence patterns
- Complex sentences
- Questions and answers
- Three questions for listening comprehension

Evaluation:

- Group:

  Originality in design

  Artistic design

  Coordination and organization

  Completed on schedule
- Individual:

Content knowledge:
  Linguistic components
  Functional use of the language
  Mechanics (grammatical and technical errors)
Delivery:
  Pronunciation, tones and fluency
  Organization of information
  Presentation
  Reference
Contribution to the group

Writing Sample 范文

Sears Tower (Part)

外地人觉得芝加哥怎么样？外地人爱芝加哥！外地人在芝加哥喜欢做什么？外地人喜欢去芝加哥的Sears Tower。不但外地人想要看看Sears Tower，而且芝加哥很多人也喜欢去那儿。

每天从早到晚许许多多游人和芝加哥人跟朋友和家人来到Sears Tower。

Sears Tower的特色一言难尽。这是美国的最高的大楼。Sears Tower有一百零三层，可是，要是你很懒不想上楼梯，你就坐电梯。每天来的人越来越多。有的人去工作，有的人去宴会，还有的人去观景台。游人常常喜欢在观景台上看看芝加哥。很多游人往往拿著照相机去Sears Tower。因为他们要摄很多像，芝加哥人常常讨厌他们。

如果你对这个问题感兴趣，要是你想看芝加哥全景可是又没有空去那儿看看，可以用电脑上网看。

(By Alina N. and Team, Northside College Preparatory High School, Chinese 3)

Unit Eight Individual Project: Come to My House

第八教学单元个体项目：请到我家来

写一张请柬，请朋友来你家做客。交代时间、地点、活动，并给出路线图。

Format:

Oral and written presentation

- A PowerPoint presentation or a printed invitation

Topic:

Come to my house: An invitation with directions

Content:

- Introduction to your house and your neighborhood
  Your neighborhood, your house, a favorite room
- Create an invitation for a celebration at your house
  Purpose, time, location
- Directions to your house:
  Driving, using public transportations, on foot (northbound, southbound)
- Writing requirements:
  Must use all discussed sentence patterns
  Positive and negative forms of all sentence patterns
  Complex sentences
  Questions and answers
- Three questions for listening comprehension

Evaluation:

- Content knowledge:
  Linguistic components
  Functional use of the language
  Mechanics (grammatical and technical errors)
- Creativity in presentation:
  Overall design
  Visual aids or artistic expressions
- Delivery:
  Pronunciation, tones and fluency
  Organization of information
  Presentation
  Reference
- Effort

Writing Samples　范文

My House　我家

我家住在芝加哥。芝加哥在美国的中西部。芝加哥是美国中西部的一个大城市。我家在芝加哥的北部，在 Harlem 和 Devon 的附近。我家的房子是个老房子。这个房子有两层楼。一共有十一个房间和四个厕所。我房子的外边有院子、花园、车库、栅栏和凉台。花园在后院的中部，花园里有很多花。车库在后院的后部。我家的车在车库的里边。栅栏在后院的左边和右边。凉台在后院的前边。后院有很多树。我的房间在我家的房子的前部。我的房间有两个门和三个窗户和四个灯。我不喜欢我的房间，因为我弟弟跟我住在一起。我的卧室里放着两个书桌、两张床、四个衣橱、一张桌子、一个大书架、一个录像机、一个电话、一个电视和一个电脑。我的卧室不大也不小。

（By Sean K.，Northside College Preparatory High School，Chinese 2）

A Favorite Room　一个我最喜欢的房间

我们的厨房是我的家的最有用的房间。墙上没有画，墙上挂着很多的架子，架上放着食谱和餐具。我爸爸在烤炉旁边站着，他高兴地做饭。我妈妈站在洗碗机旁边，她笑着。我姐姐坐在我父母旁边，她在桌子上做功课。我们有冰箱、水池和微波炉，这些都摆在餐桌上。我喜欢我家的厨房。

（By Simon S.，Northside College Preparatory High School，Chinese 2）

Unit Nine：My Favorite Dish：Eating in Chicago
第九教学单元：我最爱吃的菜：吃在芝加哥

Theme　主题

My Favorite Dish：Eating in Chicago　我最爱吃的菜：吃在芝加哥

Topics　交谈要点与话题

- Food　食物
- Drinks　饮料
- Vegetables　蔬菜
- Animals　动物
- Cooking　做饭
- Dining Experience　在饭馆吃饭

Content of Teaching and Learning　教学内容

Linguistic Functions　语用

- Asking and giving instructions　指令
- Introducing　介绍
- Commenting　评论
- Talking about specific events　谈已发生的事件
- Relating actions with location, means and manner
  明确行为与地点、方式
- Narrating in paragraph-length passages　成段表述
- Asking about and exchanging information in interactions　问答对话
- Listening with comprehension to passages of increasing length
  听力理解
- Reading passages with comprehension　段落的阅读理解
- Using a Chinese word processor　使用中文处理软件

- Writing in paragraphs 写作

Grammatical Patterns and Vocabulary 语法点与词汇

(Refer to *Functional and Grammatical Walk Through*)

(《什么篇：语用与语法走廊》(索引：B/7/8/12/13/21/22))

Vocabulary 词汇	Grammatical Points 语法点
Food 食物 (22) Drinks 饮料 (22) Vegetables 蔬菜 (22) Animals 动物 (22) Cooking 做饭 (22)	Dual objects 双宾语 (7) "把" sentence (22) Resultative complements 结果补语 (21) Potential complements 可能补语 (21) Modal verbs 情态动词 (8) Complex sentences 复句 (12) Use of "了" (13) Chinese characters 汉字 (B)

Cultural Studies and Connections 文化及跨学科联系

- Cultural appreciation through food 文化鉴赏：食物
- Chinese holidays and festivities 中国传统的节庆假日
- Community 社区
- Consumers and consumption 消费者与消费
- Family budget 家庭预算

Variations of Unit Nine 第九单元的变量设置

The instructor can customize this unit design according to the needs of the class, curriculum at large, the available instructional hours and course schedule.

教学单元应根据课堂教学的需求、课程设置的全局情况及课时的限制酌情加减。

Variables that can be taken into consideration are:

- Number of grammatical patterns involved,
- Extensiveness of vocabulary,

- Depth of communication tasks, and
- Proficiency of language skills.

应考虑的变量如下：

- 语法点的数量，
- 词汇的覆盖面，
- 语用实践活动的深度，
- 语言技巧的水平。

Suggested Variations of the Unit by Topic　建议参考如下

Variation A:　**The unit can be easily divided into three sub-units. Each unit can include an expandable, related vocabulary list.**

方案 A:　**这个单元可以分成三个教学单位。每个教学单位的词汇表可增减。**

Sub-Unit One: Food and Cooking　教学单位一：做饭		
Vocabulary 词汇	**Grammatical Points 语法点**	**Linguistic Functions 语用**
Food　食物（22） Drinks　饮料（22） Vegetables　蔬菜（22） Animals　动物(22) Cooking　做饭(22)	Dual objects 双宾语（7） "把" sentence(22)	Asking and giving instructions 指令

Sub-Unit Two: Leisure in Chicago　教学单位二：芝加哥的休闲生活		
Vocabulary 词汇	**Grammatical Points 语法点**	**Linguistic Functions 语用**
Food　食物（22） Drinks　饮料（22）	Resultative complements 结果补语（21） Potential complements 可能补语（21） Complex sentences　复句(12)	Introducing　介绍 Commenting　评论

Sub-Unit Three：Restaurant Review 教学单位三：评论饭馆		
Vocabulary 词汇	Grammatical Points 语法点	Linguistic Functions 语用
Food 食物（22） Drinks 饮料（22）	Modal verbs 情态动词（8） Complex sentences 复句（12） Use of “了”（13）	Discuss specific events 谈已发生的事件 Function use of the language 融会贯通地使用

Variation B： **The unit can simply keep the first two sub-units of Variation A.**

Map vocabulary and grammatical patterns according to language use；and

Keep vocabulary and grammatical patterns to a functional minimum.

方案 B： **保留方案 A 的前两个教学单位。控制词汇、语法点的难度和量。**

Sub-Unit One：Food and Cooking 教学单位一：做饭		
Vocabulary 词汇	Grammatical Points 语法点	Linguistic Functions 语用
Food 食物（22） Drinks 饮料（22） Vegetables 蔬菜（22） Animals 动物（22） Cooking 做饭（22）	Dual objects 双宾语（7） “把” sentence（22）	Asking and giving instructions 指令

Sub-Unit Two: Leisure in Chicago　教学单位二：芝加哥的休闲生活		
Vocabulary 词汇	**Grammatical Points 语法点**	**Linguistic Functions 语用**
Food　食物（22） Drinks　饮料（22）	Resultative complements 结果补语（21） Potential complements 可能补语（21） Complex sentences　复句（12）	Introducing　介绍 Commenting　评论

Variation C:　**The unit has smaller and simpler sub-units.**

Map vocabulary and grammar according to functional language use; and

Keep vocabulary and sentence patterns to a functional minimum.

方案 C：　**分四个简单的小教学单位。控制词汇、语法点的难度和量至最基本。**

Sub-Unit One: Food　教学单位一：食物		
Vocabulary 词汇	**Grammatical Points 语法点**	**Linguistic Functions 语用**
Food　食物（22） Drinks　饮料（22） Vegetables　蔬菜（22） Animals　动物(22)	Modal verbs　情态动词（8） Complex sentences 复句（12）	Preferences and choice 表述喜好和选择

Sub-Unit Two: Cooking　教学单位二：做饭		
Vocabulary 词汇	**Grammatical Points 语法点**	**Linguistic Functions 语用**
Cooking 做饭(22)	Dual objects　双宾语（7） “把” sentence(22)	Asking and giving instructions 指令

Sub-Unit Three: Dining out 教学单位三：出去吃饭		
Vocabulary 词汇	Grammatical Points 语法点	Linguistic Functions 语用
Food 食物（22） Drinks 饮料（22） Services 服务（22）	Use of "了"（13）	Discussing specific events 谈已发生的事件

Sub-Unit Four: Leisure in Chicago 教学单位四：芝加哥的休闲生活	
Grammatical Points 语法点	Linguistic Functions 语用
Complex sentences 复句（12）	Introducing 介绍 Commenting 评论

Instructional Tips 教学指导策略提示

Tip 1:

Talking about food is, for the most part, about vocabulary. The vocabulary can be overwhelming. Teach vocabulary by topic. Ask students to select the vocabulary they want to use.

谈食物要学很多词汇，按话题展开词汇的学习。让学生选择最想说、最想做的能提高学习兴趣。

Tip 2:

Connect vocabulary to sentence patterns naturally by using a variety of topics: Talking about preferences, daily necessities, special diets and recipes.

用话题引出句型和词汇的学习。这样的话题很多：喜好的食物、每天必吃的东西或特别的饮食需要和菜谱等。

Tip 3:

There are many ways to spice up this topic. Talking about food by using rhymes or songs. Make it fun!

教这个题目能有不少有意思的活动：有关食物、动物的歌谣，歌曲等。

Tip 4:

This theme provides a good chance to review verbs, time expressions and the conditions of other general activities while learning new ones.

这也是一次反复运用动词和时间等活动条件的机会。

Tip 5:

Discuss Chinese holidays. What Chinese people eat and do. It is also a good topic for practicing cultural comparisons and making connections.

谈中国的节日和文化习俗。中国人吃什么、做什么。这样的话题涉及文化比较和联系。

Tip 6:

Don't be afraid to let students bring in a variety of food experiences. The purpose includes — but also goes beyond — learning about Chinese food and food culture. Encourage intercultural comparison and exchange by allowing students to use Chinese language to explore other cultures through food.

让学生把与自己有关的生活经验带入课堂的讨论。课堂的语言的学习不应局限于中国的东西或特别的饮食需要和菜谱等。

Tip 7:

There are also many authentic materials available concerning this theme and related topics. Use them.

有很多活教材，真实语言素材可用。

Tip 8:

"Reach a person's heart through his or her stomach." Learn through eating. Bringing food to class or taking a food related field trip is always a good idea.

把好吃的东西带到课堂上来或带学生去吃饭，让真实的生活经验与语用的实际结合起来。

Tip 9：

Use authentic materials and concrete teaching and learning tools. Use visual aids. Connect language, especially characters, with images and live objects. Things that can be used as instructional materials include posters and cards. Use large character posters or cards. If you don't have visual aids available, mobilize students to make them in class or as homework assignment.

使用真实语言材料和实物做教具，使用形象的教具。让语言，特别是汉字、图像和实物挂钩。可用的教具还包括挂表、挂图与卡片，挂图和卡片上的汉字要大，若没有这样的教具，发动学生动手制作。

Suggested Activities 建议教学活动

Activity 1　Nursery Rhyme 童谣
Language task：Sing and memorize rhymes
Functions：Learning vocabulary
Writing, reading, listening and speaking
Use：Class activity, homework assignment, assessment

学童谣，或把要学的词汇编成歌谣。这样的学习朗朗上口，便于记忆。

还可以让学生按照所教的歌谣形式，自己填词，创作一个自己喜欢的新歌谣。活学活用，要求会说、会背、会写。

Preparation for the activity：

List of vocabulary (*Functional and Grammatical Walk Through* (22))

Procedure：

Step 1：The Rhyme

- Find an easy nursery rhyme and adapt it to learn food vocabulary.
- Example：The one we use in class was adapted from old and fond memories：

一二三四五六七，
七六五四三二一，
七个朋友来摘果，
七个篮子手中提，
七个果子摘七样：
苹果、香蕉、橘子、葡萄、李子、栗子、梨。

Step 2: Practice

- Teacher models and students follow.
- The class sings the rhyme with the teacher until memorized.

Step 3: Create own versions

- Ask students to select their own preferred fruits to end the rhyme.

Step 4: Prepare for presentation

- Students practice and memorize their own versions.

Step 5: Competition

- Students recite their own version.
- See who the most fluent presenter is!

Follow-up: Homework

- Write down your own rhyme in Chinese characters.
- Share with others as a reading.

Activity 2　Weekly Grocery Shopping List　本周采购清单
Language task: Record your family's weekly grocery list
Functions: Learning vocabulary
Writing
Potential for reading, listening and speaking
Use: Class activity, homework assignment, assessment

这是一个活学活用新词汇的活动。

让学生跟家长采购本周食物时，把在超级市场看到的和所买的东西分类记下来。

按照食物清单，写出购买经历。在课上讲自己的采购故事。

Preparation for the activity：

List of vocabulary（*Functional and Grammatical Walk Through*（22））

Procedure：

Step 1：Go shopping

- Ask students to help their parents with grocery shopping.

Step 2：Record the items

- Ask students to write down the groceries purchased，or what they see in the stores' sections.

Step 3：Elaboration

- Ask students to write about their shopping experience in sentences that list the items.

Step 4：Prepare for presentation

- Students practice and memorize their own versions.

Step 5：Presentation

- Students share their own shopping stories.

Activity 3　　Sharing Stories　分享你的故事

Language task： Peer editing，telling and retelling a story

Functions： Cooperative learning：Assisted writing and speaking

Reading，listening and speaking

Use： Class activity

This activity is a follow-up of Activity 2 above.

这个活动是在前一活动的基础上开展的合作学习活动。

做法：

- 同伴相互修改作文：要先阅读同伴的文章；找出好句子，指出错误；提出修改建议。
- 分成3～4人小组，讲述自己的故事。
- 每人用2～3句话总结另一人的故事。

Preparation for the activity：

Complete stories for peer editing and presentation.

Procedure:

Step 1: Pair up students to do a peer editing

- Read your partner's writing to identify good sentences and mistakes.
- Make suggestions for revision.

Step 2: Form teams

- Divide class into groups of three to four.
- Designate a group leader.
- Make instructions and expectations clear.

Step 3: Share stories

- Each student tells a story prepared as homework assignment and edited in class.

Step 4: Group summary

- Each gives a brief (two to three sentences) account of another's story.

Activity 4　Timed Speeches　计时快说

(Please see Example 8 in Part Ⅰ "Timed Speeches" for more details.)

(请参照上篇课堂活动案例 8 "计时快说")

Activity 5　Share a Recipe, Share Cooking　分享你的菜谱和厨艺

Language task: Find a recipe, learn it and teach how to cook it

Functions: "把" sentence

Cultural learning and sharing

Listening and speaking, reading and writing

Use: Class activity, homework assignment, assessment

This activity consists of three independent, but associated parts. It can be used as progressive classroom learning or a comprehensive project for cumulative assessment.

这个活动分三个独立但又相关的部分。

执行：

第一部分：介绍一个菜

- 学生找一个特殊的或最喜欢的菜谱。
- 用汉语写下来，并在课上展示。

第二部分：做菜品尝评论

- 学生自己按菜谱把菜做出来，带到课堂，大家分享。（会做饭也是上大学必备的技能之一）
- 全班点评。

第三部分：展示：介绍菜的做法

- 写出菜谱用料，操作步骤（用“把”字句），并列出词汇。
- 报告展示。
- 准备当场问答。
- 有条件，最好加与菜有关的文化背景知识或文化习俗方面的介绍和讨论。

Procedure:

Part 1: Find and Introduce a Recipe

Step 1: Students are to research a special or favourite recipe.

Step 2: Write it down in Chinese.

Step 3: Present it to class.

Part 2: "Taste of the Class"

Step 1: The class sets a date for sharing the students' cooking.

Step 2: Students bring in the food they have cooked. (Please have the students cook it themselves. Cooking is part of college survival, and this is a college preparatory course.)

Step 3: The class enjoys and also critiques the dishes in turn.

Part 3: Teach Cooking

Step 1: Prepare a PowerPoint presentation

- List all ingredients.
- Give step by step cooking instructions.
- List vocabulary.

Step 2: Presentation

- Give a presentation on how to cook your favourite dish.
- Allow questions.

Elaboration:

If time allows, include a cultural introduction to the dish.

Activity 6　Test Your Memory　考考你的记忆力
Language task: Retell as much as possible of another's favorites
Functions: Listening and speaking
Use: Class activity, homework assignment, assessment

This game originated from the ideas of Dr. Yvonne Lau, a professor of Sociology at DePaul University. There are two versions of this game.

这个活动有两个版本。

简本：

- 一个学生说一个句子"我最喜欢（吃/喝）……"
- 下一个学生用同样的句子说自己的情况还要加上重复上一人说的句子。
- 第三人如此说三句，第四人四句……依次类推。看谁说得最多。
- 还可以加或改用不同的句子。

繁本：

- 分两队。
- 同上，但说错者退出比赛。
- 每一轮换一个句子。
- 最后看哪队剩下的人最多。

Game 1:

My Favorite (food, fruit, drink, animal, etc.) 我的最爱

The students take turns to speak and gradually build up the number of sentences used.

Student 1 says a sentence:

我最喜欢（吃/喝）……

Student 2 says his or her own sentence as the above but repeats what the Student 1 said：

Student 1 最喜欢（吃/喝）……

我最喜欢（吃/喝）……

Student 3 adds one more sentence to his or her speech：

Student 1 最喜欢（吃/喝）……

Student 2 最喜欢（吃/喝）……

我最喜欢（吃/喝）……

As more students participate, the number of sentences builds up.

The winner is the one who remembers and says the most correct sentences.

Elaboration：

Complexity can be introduced by using or adding sentences like：

我想……/我要……/etc.

Note：

You may also restrict the number of sentences to seven, and then start a new round.

Game 2：

Divide the class into two teams.

Round 1：

- Players of Team 1 each make a statement：

  我最喜欢（吃/喝）……

- Players of Team 2 each retell what all of Team 1 said until all members have had a turn.
- A player who makes a mistake is out.
- Switch：Repeat the above by reversing roles.

Round 2：

- Same as Round 1 but change the sentence patterns and vocabulary.

Winners：

- After a few rounds, the team with the most number of players remaining wins the game.

Activity 7　Project:(See the sample assessment projects below for ideas.)
综合项目（见下教学单元综合项目测试标准例案）

Language task: Create and assemble an oral and written presentation

Functions: Integrated language use
Connect language learning with cultural learning
Research

Use: Class activity, homework assignment, assessment

综合项目的发展步骤包括:

- 选题;
- 复习本单元所学的知识及技能;
- 收集资料并起草初稿;
- 修改，定稿;
- 补充或设计其他视觉艺术内容;
- 记忆;
- 展示。

可用来做教学活动或教学评估手段。

Procedure:

Step 1: Select a topic and gather information

Step 2: Review and draft a writing

- Pull all previous work as resources.
  (Class materials and finished homework)
- Teacher provides list of required elements to be included in the project.

Step 3: Edit and revise

- Edit drafts and finalize the writing.

Step 4: Visual and artistic support

- Design a display with artworks or graphics.

Step 5: Memorize your materials

- Prepare for an oral presentation to go with the display.

Follow-up:

- Present it to class.
- Can be used as a quarterly or term assessment.

Caution:

- Don't forget to cite other's work.
- Plagiarism is using other people's work without proper acknowledgement.
- Plagiarism is also cheating.

Critical Thinking and Comparative Study 评判和比较

Activity 8 Guessing Game — Winning Bonus 猜猜看：有奖游戏

Activity 9 Discovering Rules 找出规律

(See Unit One, Activity 6 and Activity 7)

（请参照第一教学单元活动 6 和活动 7）

Don't forget to constantly use these activities in class.

Suggested Assignment Focus 建议作业的重点

• Speaking with fluency	增强说话的流利程度
• Reading with increasing number of Chinese characters	阅读加大汉字数量
• Writing in sentences and paragraphs, using an increasing number of Chinese characters, and using a Chinese word processor	用汉字写作,写作加大汉字量，会用中文处理软件
• Developing all four language skills	发展听、说、读、写技能
• Completing basic language tasks in Chinese	用目的语完成语言任务
• Asking questions and exchanging information	提问并交换信息
• Using authentic materials	使用真实语言材料
• Integrating information technology and research methods	查阅资料

Suggested Assignments 建议作业

- Assign listening materials: Listening.
- Copy words or characters: Reading and writing.
- Memorize some language materials, and prepare to perform during the next class: Reading and speaking.
- Produce language materials as instructed, and prepare to perform during the next class: Writing and speaking; open-ended tasks.
- Writing on topic: Speaking and writing and task-based presentation.
- Peer editing and writing: Cooperative learning, interactive learning and discourse development.
- Create projects using oral and written presentations: All language skills.
- 听力练习。
- 读写练习。
- 记忆语言材料，准备测试：读说。
- 创造性地运用语言材料，预备课上展示：说写，语言实践任务。
- 有题目地写作：说写，语言实践任务。
- 同伴互相编辑写作：合作学习，学习交流，成段表达。
- 创作口语和书面报告：综合训练。

Suggested Assessment Focus 建议评估重点

Listening comprehension 听力理解

- Comprehension of short passages with pre-activity clues 在有预听活动的情况下听懂成段叙述
- Comprehension of questions 听懂提问
- Comprehension of interpersonal exchanges 听懂人际交流与对话

Speaking 说

- Emphasizing speaking in discourse 承前启后的叙述表达
- Emphasizing fluency 表达流利
- Emphasizing ability to initiate and respond properly to interactions 发问并回答

Reading 阅读

• Reading passages in Chinese characters	阅读理解汉字书写的段落
• Reading texts that have unfamiliar words	阅读理解有生词的文章
• Guessing meaning with common sense and contextual clues	根据背景知识和上下文猜断语义

Writing 写

• Using correct spelling of *pinyin* and selecting the correct characters when using a Chinese word processor	用电脑输入时能用拼音正确拼写并选择正确的汉字
• Handwriting Chinese characters correctly	正确手书汉字
• Developing writing skills with correct use of patterns and with logic	写作有逻辑性,语法错误较少
• Writing in paragraphs	成段写作表达
• Creating texts with known characters and using a Chinese word processor	用汉字写作,会用中文处理软件

Suggested Assessment 建议测试评估形式

See page 90.

见 90 页。

Rubrics for Assessment 测试标准

Make a clear rubric specifying expectations and the required elements according to the content coverage of the day or lesson.

根据每日课堂的学习进度，制定明确、清晰的测试评分标准，以申明期待和要求。

Sample Unit Project　教学单元综合项目测试例案

Unit Nine Project A: My Best Recipe

第九教学单元综合项目（一）：我的拿手好菜

介绍一个喜爱并会做的菜。

Format:

Oral and written presentation

- With a PowerPoint presentation or artistic displays

Topic:

- My Best Recipe

Content:

- A brief self-introduction
- Your favorite food in general
- Reasons you are representing this recipe
- Your favorite recipe
  Ingredients, cooking instructions
- Positive and negative forms of all sentence patterns
- Complex sentences
- Questions and answers
- Three questions for listening comprehension

Evaluation:

- Content knowledge:
  Linguistic components
  Functional use of the language
  Mechanics (grammatical and technical errors)
- Creativity in presentation:
  Overall design
  Visual aids or artistic expressions
- Delivery:
  Pronunciation, tones and fluency
  Organization of information
  Presentation
  Reference
- Effort

Unit Nine Project B: Dining Experience

第九教学单元综合项目（二）：去餐馆吃饭

介绍一个饭馆并讲述去饭馆吃饭的详细经历。

Format:

Oral and written presentation

- A story book or a PowerPoint presentation

Topic:

A Meal in a restaurant

Content:

- A brief self-introduction
- A brief introduction to the restaurant
  Reputation, location, business hours, parking, etc.
- Dining in a restaurant
  Occasion, ordering, services, quality of the meal, etc.
  Payment, conclusion and comments
- Directions to the restaurant
- Positive and negative forms of all sentence patterns
- Complex sentences
- Questions and answers
- Three questions for listening comprehension

Evaluation:

- Content knowledge:
  Linguistic components
  Functional use of the language
  Mechanics (grammatical and technical errors)
- Creativity in presentation:
  Overall design
  Visual aids or artistic expressions
- Delivery:
  Pronunciation, tones and fluency
  Organization of information

Presentation

Reference

• Effort

Unit Nine Project C: A Good Restaurant

第九教学单元综合项目（三）：我常去的一家好饭馆

用对话的形式具体介绍一家饭馆，包括概况、设施、有名的菜、路线图等。

Format:

Oral and written presentation

• A dialogue, a narration, a PowerPoint presentation or artistic display.

Topic:

My favorite restaurant

Content:

• A brief self-introduction

• Introduction to the restaurant

Reputation, location, size, business hours, parking, services, etc.

• Specialties

Famous dishes or a recipe

• Directions to the restaurant

Invite your friends to the restaurant

Detailed directions for driving

Detailed directions using public transportation

• Positive and negative forms of all sentence patterns

• Complex sentences

• Questions and answers

• Three questions for listening comprehension

Evaluation:

• Content knowledge:

Linguistic components

Functional use of the language

Mechanics (grammatical and technical errors)

- Creativity in presentation：
  Overall design
  Visual aids or artistic expressions
- Delivery：
  Pronunciation，tones and fluency
  Organization of information
  Presentation
  Reference
- Effort

Writing Sample 范文

我的拿手好戏：沙杯布丁

用料：

两杯：	冷牛奶
一包：	布丁混合料
八盎司：	奶油，解冻
二盎司：	香草精饼干，压碎
八个：	塑料杯
两包：	软糖卷
一包：	少年熊饼干渣
一包：	鱼软糖
一包：	小玩具伞

做法：

把冷牛奶加在一个大碗里。把布丁混合料加进去。拌差不多一分钟。把碗放在一边放五分钟。把奶油加进去。把六盎司的压碎的香草精饼干加进去。把布丁混合料倒进八个杯子里。把软糖卷、少年熊饼干渣和鱼软糖加上去就做成了。再把小伞插上作装饰。

一个餐馆的故事——介绍我爱的饭馆

我最喜欢的餐馆是“七个兄弟”。七个兄弟在芝加哥的北部，七个兄弟是一个美国餐馆。我喜欢吃美国饭。每月，我家和我爷爷和奶奶去那里吃早饭。我们去过那里很多次。上次我们去那里是上星期六。我们是八点开车去的。我们走进去后，在餐馆的里边，一个服务员招待了我们。他把我们带到一个桌子那里。他问我们：“你们要点什么菜?”

我弟弟点了一个法国三明治。我妈妈点了一个鱼三明治。我爸爸点了一个羊肉。我爷爷和奶奶点了两个鸡肉和面条沙拉。我点了炒蛋和排骨。饭菜来到以前，我们都一边吃面包一边喝水。饭菜来到以后，我们一起吃。我的饭很好吃。点完了菜，不一会儿，服务员问我：“你们要点甜点吗?”我告诉他不用。因为我们吃饱了也喝足了。

吃完了，我们都很满意。我们的服务员很热情，他把账单给了我爸爸。我爸爸去付钱了。我们一共吃了差不多四十块钱。一会儿，我们一起回家了。我们回了我爷爷和奶奶的家。

我喜欢七个兄弟，因为那里离我家不太远，以希腊饭闻名。那里的饭菜又便宜又好吃。那里是世界上最好的。其实那个声明不对，可是那里仍旧太好了。没问题。

七个兄弟在芝加哥的北部。周围有很多的商店。前边是停车场和车库。后边有很多的房子。左边是麦当劳和加油站。右边是银行和餐馆。

餐馆的其他服务：

七个兄弟是一个美国餐馆，是一个有名的饭馆，以希腊饭闻名。那里有停车场，停车场就在前边。那里的营业时间是八时至十时——早上八点开门晚上十点关门。

去七个兄弟很方便：

1. 从芝加哥的北部沿着 Waukegan 街往南走，走到 Beckwith 街然后再往右拐就到了。
2. 从芝加哥的南部沿着 Waukegan 街往北走，走到 Beckwitt 街然后再往左拐就到了。

3. 从芝加哥的东边沿着 Beckwith 街往西走。

4. 从芝加哥的西边沿着 Beckwith 街往东走。

（By Andrew M.，Nothside College Preparatory High School，Chinese 3）

Unit Ten：My Past and Present：Body and Health
第十教学单元：我的过去与现状：身体与健康

Theme　主题

My Past and Present：Body and Health　我的过去与现状：身体与健康

Topics　交谈要点与话题

- Body　身体部位
- Physical Health　身体状况
- Illness　疾病
- Visiting a Doctor　看病
- History and Past Experience　过去的经历

Content of Teaching and Learning　教学内容

Linguistic Functions　语用功能

- Describing body parts and functions　描述身体部位与情况
- Exchanging information　交换信息情报
- Talking about history and past experience　谈过去的经历
- Narrating in paragraph-length passages　成段表述
- Asking questions and providing answers in dialogue　问答对话
- Listening with comprehension to passages of increasing length 听力理解
- Reading passages with comprehension　段落的阅读理解
- Using a Chinese word processor　使用中文处理软件
- Writing in paragraphs　写作

Grammatical Patterns and Vocabulary　语法点与词汇

(Refer to *Functional and Grammatical Walk Through*)

（《什么篇：语用与语法走廊》（索引：B/1/2/6/9/13/24））

Vocabulary 词汇	Grammatical Points 语法点
Body 身体部位（24） Adjectives 形容词（9） Physical health 身体状况（24） Illness 疾病（24） Visiting a doctor 看病（24）	"过" indicates past experience（24） Ordinal numbers 序数（1/24） Measure words for actions 动量词（24） Adjectives as predicate 形容词谓语句（2/9） "了" indicates completion of specific events（13） Duration 时间段（6） Wh-questions 特殊疑问句 什么时候/多长时间/哪/怎么/怎么样/ 多少/为什么/是……的？（13） Chinese characters 汉字（B）

Cultural Studies and connections 文化及跨学科联系

- Medical expressions 医用术语
- Basic medical knowledge 医用常识
- Traditional Chinese medicine and Western medicine 中医与西医

Variations of Unit Ten 第十单元的变量设置

The instructor can customize this unit design according to the needs of the class, curriculum at large, the available instructional hours and course schedule.

教学单元应根据课堂教学的需求、课程设置的全局情况及课时的限制酌情加减。

Variables that can be taken into consideration are:

- Number of grammatical patterns involved,
- Extensiveness of vocabulary,
- Depth of communication tasks , and
- Proficiency of language skills.

应考虑的变量如下：

- 语法点的数量，

- 词汇的覆盖面，
- 语用实践活动的深度，
- 语言技巧的水平。

Suggested Variations of the Unit by Topic　建议参考如下

Variation A： **The unit can be easily divided into three sub-units. Each unit can include an expandable, related vocabulary list.**

方案 A： **这个教学单元可以分成三个教学单位。**

Sub-Unit One: The Body　教学单位一：身体部位		
Vocabulary **词汇**	**Grammatical Points** **语法点**	**Linguistic Functions** **语用**
The Body　身体部位（24） Adjectives　形容词(9) Physical health　身体状况(24)	Adjectives as predicate 形容词谓语句(2/9)	Describe physical attributes 描述体征

Sub-Unit Two: Past Experiences　教学单位二：过去的经历		
Vocabulary **词汇**	**Grammatical Points** **语法点**	**Linguistic Functions** **语用**
Illness　疾病(24)	“过”indicates past experience(24) Ordinal numbers　序数（1/24） Measure words for actions 动量词（24）	History and past experience 谈过去的经历

Sub-Unit Three：Visiting a Doctor 教学单位三：看病		
Vocabulary 词汇	Grammatical Points 语法点	Linguistic Functions 语用
Illness、疾病（24） Visiting a Doctor 看病（24） Duration 时间段（6）	“了” indicates completion of specific events （13） Duration 时间段（6） Wh-questions 特殊疑问句 什么时候/多长时间/哪/怎么/怎么样/多少/为什么/是……的？（13）	Visiting a doctor 看病 History and past experience 过去的经历

Variation B： **The unit has two sub-units.**

Map vocabulary and sentence patterns according to language use；and

Keep vocabulary and grammatical patterns to a functional minimum.

方案B： **这个教学单元有两个教学单位。适量减少词汇和语法点。**

Sub-Unit One：The Body 教学单位一：身体部位		
Vocabulary 词汇	Grammatical Points 语法点	Linguistic Functions 语用
The Body 身体部位（24） Adjectives 形容词(9) Physical health 身体状况(24)	Adjectives as predicate 形容词谓语句（2/9）	Describe physical attributes 描述体征

Sub-Unit Two：Past Experiences 教学单位二：过去的经历		
Vocabulary 词汇	Grammatical Points 语法点	Linguistic Functions 语用
Illness 疾病（24） Visiting a doctor 看病（24）	“过” indicates past experience（24） Ordinal numbers 序数（1/24） Measure words for actions 动量词（24）	History and past experience 谈过去的经历 Visiting a doctor 看病

Variation C: **The unit is the simplified version of Variation A.**
Map vocabulary and grammar according to functional language use; and
Keep vocabulary and sentence patterns to a functional minimum.

方案 C: **化简方案 A。把词汇和语法控制在最基本的使用上。**

Instructional Tips　教学指导策略提示

Tip 1:

Use visual aids and physical activities to teach body parts.

教身体部位建议用视觉辅助教材或肢体活动。

Tip 2:

Make it personal.

把教学活动个体化。用学生自己的例子和经验。

Tip 3:

Discussing physical attributes may also lead to talking about personalities and characteristics. Prepare a vocabulary list to expand learning for advanced learners. Especially when a class has multiple levels, it is important to provide more advanced students with extra topics and related sentence patterns and vocabulary for learning expansion.

谈体征外形也可以延伸到谈性格和特长。为需要的学生提供可用的词汇表。特别是当班里的学生程度参差不齐时，应为程度高的学生提供条件扩展学习内容。

Tip 4:

Discussing past experiences opens up many possible topics such as travel, food, entertainment, sporting events, etc. Be flexible.

谈过去的经历可引出很多话题：旅行、餐饮、娱乐、运动等，灵活掌握。

Tip 5:

Individualized learning requires respecting and creating opportunities for different learning styles. It is a way to incorporate differentiated learning. Give different topics from which students may choose so that they may have the opportunity to express themselves with creativity and enthusiasm.

个体化的学习是尊重不同的学习风格并为不同学习提供施展的机会。个体化的学习就是兼容性的学习。给学生不同的题目，让他们自由选择发挥就是形式之一。

Tip 6:

Memorization in language learning should not be a taboo. Memorization is one method to learn language. It is best used at an early stage of learning. Memorization can be done meaningfully and tastefully. Perform from memory, then expand. Encourage students to add creativity and original use to memorized language materials and make the language become their own.

记忆（背诵）不应该是语言学习的禁忌。记忆是学习语言的方法之一，是语言学习的最初阶段。记忆可以通过有意义的、有趣的方式取得。根据记忆展示并发挥。鼓励学生创造性地、有独到之处的运用记忆的语言材料，使之成为他们自己的语言。

Suggested Activities 建议教学活动

Activity 1 Simon Says 赛门说
Language task: Do what Simon says: Point at body parts
Functions: Learning vocabulary, listening and speaking
Use: Class activity or assessment

This is based on a traditional children's game. Instead of "Simon," we may choose a Chinese name.

这个游戏差不多每个学生都听说过或玩过。谁都可以当"赛门"，"赛门"说什么，大家跟着做。不想用"赛门"这个名字，就用个中国名字。

可以用来复习身体部位名词或练习与之有关的动作。

Rules:

- Simon usually speaks and points at the same time. Players follow what he instructs and demonstrates.
- If Simon's words and actions do not match, players should not follow.
- Each of Simon's instructions must begin with the pattern: "Simon says."
  If Simon gives an order without this phrase, players must not follow.

Procedure:

Round 1:

- Teacher is "Simon."
- Do what Simon says: Quickly point at the body part.
- Simon says "眼睛", students all point at their eyes.

Round 2:

- Let students be "Simon" in turn.

Activity 2　Students teach two words to the class　请你当老师
Language task: Select two words to teach the class
Functions: Learn vocabulary and characters
Listening and speaking, reading and writing
Use: Class activity

This activity can be used for learning vocabulary. Depending on the number of vocabulary words or characters involved, each student can teach one or two.

学习词汇可以用这个小活动。发下词汇表。让学生当老师：每人选两个词，想办法教给大家，让全班能生动地记忆词汇。若有选择上的冲突，老师可以与学生核实选择。

Materials: A list of vocabulary

- (For body parts or vegetables, etc. we also use visual charts to demonstrate.
- These charts can be made by students from previous levels or purchased)

Preparation for the activity:

- Ask students to select two words each (if they pair up, then double the number of words).
- As homework, ask the students to find ways to make the words they have chosen memorable.

In class:

Ask the students to introduce the words in turn.

Note:

Sometimes, there will be duplicates. Teacher may let it be or prevent duplication by confirming the students' selections.

Activity 3	Make a Personal Medical Record 个人体检表
Language task:	Describe your physical condition and medical history
Functions:	For individual learners: Writing and speaking, For others learners in class: Listening and reading
Use:	Class activity, homework assignment, assessment

让学生描述自己的身体状况，可在听说的基础上写作，也可以加性格爱好等描写。

下次上课时报告。如学了看病，还可加谈病史、家族史等。

Writing assignment:

- Use all learned vocabulary to describe:

  Personal information: Name, age, address, etc.

  Physical condition: Height, weight, heart rate, blood pressure, etc.
- Elaboration:

  Medical history

Speaking Assignment:

Be prepared to discuss the above without notes.

Follow-up:

Use for Activity 4.

Activity 4　Peer Editing, Telling and Retelling a Story　讲故事

Language task: Peer editing, telling and retelling a story

Functions: Cooperative learning: Assisted writing and speaking
Reading, listening and speaking

Use: Class activity

This activity is a follow-up of Activity 3 above.

这个活动是上面活动的延续。

做法:

- 学生互读或就所写的身体状况展开对话，并相互建议修改文章。
- 分 3 ~4 人小组。每人讲自己的故事。
- 用 2 ~3 句话概要地总结别人的故事。

Preparation for the activity:

Finished stories for peer editing and presentation

Procedure:

Step 1: Pair up

Pair up students to do a peer editing:

- Read your partner's writing.
- Look for mistakes.
- Make suggestions for revision.

Step 2: Team up

- Divide class into groups of three or four.
- Designate a group leader, and make instructions and expectations clear.

Step 3: Share stories

- Each student tells a story prepared as homework and edited in class.

Step 4: Group summary

- Each gives two to three sentences brief account of another's story.

Activity 5　　Quiz Show：Have You Been to. . . ?
　　　　　　　　智力游戏：你曾经……？

Language task：Answer questions on the spot

Functions：Quiz knowledge and vocabulary

Use：Class activity，homework assignment，assessment

This activity uses a more elaborate version of the game. This game consists of a preparation part and an execution part. It is recommended to divide the parts into separate class periods.

这个游戏分“准备”和“执行”两部分，可在不同课时完成。

准备：

- 分 3 ~4 人小组，做卡片，写问题，如：

  你去过……吗？

  你吃过……饭没有？

  你知道……在哪儿？

  ……人说什么语？

执行：

- 检查卡片对错。逐队当主持人。
- 选一队挨个抽卡，念卡上问题并回答。
- 一次一分。
- 三分钟一轮。
- 得分多的队获胜。

Preparation：

- Index cards
- Reference may also include *Functional and Grammatical Walk Through* (4)：Glossary of countries，languages and continents.

Procedure：

Step 1：Team up

- Divide the class into teams of three to four.
- Clearly specify instructions and expectations.

Step 2: Prepare for a quiz show (can be a homework)

- Each group is given a number of cities.
- Team writes a set of questions on index cards:

  你去过……吗?

  你吃过……饭没有?

  你知道……在哪儿?

  ……人说什么语?

Step 3: Double-check questions

- Team meets to make sure all questions are correct.

Step 4: Quiz begins!

- One team goes on stage at a time as hosts.
- Hosts take turns to give questions.
- Select other teams to answer questions.
- One player answers one question at a time.

Scoring:

- Each round lasts three minutes.
- The team that answers the most questions within the time frame wins.

Activity 6 Personal Story: I Have Been... 个人故事：我曾经……

Language task: Write a personal story

Functions: Talking about a past experience or a specific event

Use: Class activity, homework assignment, assessment

用这个活动讲述过去的经历。

以问答形式开始，问题见下。对话进行完毕，可总结叙述，再阅读小故事，然后把自己的故事加工整理成文。

Procedure:

Step 1: Questions and answers

- Talk about a personal past experience guided by questions:

  过去的经历:

  你去过什么地方? 你吃过什么饭? 你得过什么病?

你第一次/最近的一次的经历……
那是什么时候？你做什么了？

Step 2：Reading samples

- Read a couple of essays.
- Check for comprehension with similar questions as above.

Step 3：Homework

- Write your own story similar to in-class oral practice and sample works.

Follow-up：

- The result can be a part of a later project.
- The result can be used in combination with Activity 4 above or Activity 8 below.

Activity 7	Project：(See the sample assessment projects below for ideas.) 综合项目（见下教学单元综合项目测试标准例案）
Language task：	Create and assemble oral and written presentations
Functions：	Integrated language use Connect language learning with cultural learning, research
Use：	Class activity, homework assignment, assessment

综合项目的发展步骤包括：

- 选题；
- 复习本单元所学的知识及技能；
- 收集资料并起稿；
- 修改、定稿，补充或设计其他视觉艺术内容；
- 记忆；
- 展示。

可用来做教学活动或教学评估手段。

Procedure：

Step 1：Select a topic and gather information

Step 2: Review and draft a writing

- Pull all previous work as resources (class materials and finished homework).
- Teacher provides list of required elements to be included in the project.

Step 3: Edit and revise

- Edit drafts and finalize the writing.

Step 4: Visual and artistic support

- Design a display with artworks or graphics.

Step 5: Memorize your materials

- Prepare for an oral presentation to go with the display.

Follow-up:

- Present it to class.
- Can be used as a quarterly or term assessment

Caution:

- Don't forget to cite other's work.
- Plagiarism is using other people's work without proper acknowledgement.
- Plagiarism is also cheating.

Activity 8　Timed Speeches　计时快说

(Please see Example 8 in Part Ⅰ "Timed Speeches" for more details.)

(请参照上篇课堂活动案例 8 "计时快说")

Critical Thinking and Comparative Study　评判和比较

Activity 9　Guessing Game — Winning Bonus　猜猜看：有奖游戏

Activity 10　Discovering Rules　找出规律

(See Unit One, Activity 6 and Activity 7)

(请参照第一教学单元活动 6 和活动 7)

Don't forget to constantly use these activities in class.

Suggested Assignment Focus　建议作业的重点

• Speaking with fluency	增强说话的流利程度
• Reading with increasing number of Chinese characters	阅读加大汉字数量
• Writing in sentences and paragraphs, using an increasing number of Chinese characters, and using a Chinese word processor	用汉字写作，写作加大汉字量，会用中文处理软件
• Developing all four language skills	发展听、说、读、写技能
• Completing basic language tasks in Chinese	用目的语完成语言任务
• Asking questions and exchanging information	提问并交换信息
• Using authentic materials	使用真实语言材料
• Integrating information technology and research methods	查阅资料

Suggested Assignments　建议作业

- Assign listening materials: Listening.
- Copy words or characters: Reading and writing.
- Memorize some language materials, and prepare to perform during the next class: Reading and speaking.
- Produce language materials as instructed, and prepare to perform during the next class: Writing and speaking; open-ended tasks.
- Writing on topic: Speaking and writing and task-based presentation.
- Peer editing and writing: Cooperative learning, interactive learning and discourse development.
- Create projects using oral and written presentations: All language skills.
- 听力练习。
- 读写练习。
- 记忆语言材料，准备测试：读说。
- 创造性地运用语言材料，预备课上展示：说写，语言实践任务。
- 有题目的写作：说写，语言实践任务。

- 同伴互相编辑写作：合作学习，学习交流，成段表达。
- 创作口语和书面报告：综合训练。

Suggested Assessment Focus　建议评估重点

Listening comprehension　听力理解

• Comprehension of short passages with pre-activity clues	在有预听活动的情况下听懂成段叙述
• Comprehension of questions	听懂提问
• Comprehension of interpersonal exchanges	听懂人际交流与对话

Speaking　说

• Emphasizing speaking in discourse	承前启后的叙述表达
• Emphasizing fluency	表达流利
• Emphasizing ability to initiate and respond properly to interactions	发问并回答

Reading　阅读

• Reading passages in Chinese characters	阅读理解汉字书写的段落
• Reading texts that have unfamiliar words	阅读理解有生词的文章
• Guessing meaning with common sense and contextual clues	根据背景知识和上下文猜断语义

Writing　写

• Using correct spelling of *pinyin* and selecting the correct characters when using a Chinese word processor	用电脑输入时能用拼音正确拼写并选择正确的汉字
• Handwriting Chinese characters correctly	正确手书汉字
• Developing writing skills with correct use of patterns and with logic	写作有逻辑性,语法错误较少
• Writing in paragraphs	成段写作表达
• Creating texts with known characters and using	用汉字写作，会用中文

a Chinese word processor 处理软件

Suggested Assessment 建议测试评估形式

See page 90.

见 90 页。

Rubrics for Assessment 测试标准

Make a clear rubric to specify expectations and the required elements according to the content coverage of the day or lesson.

根据每日课堂的学习进度，制定明确、清晰的测试评分标准，以申明期待和要求。

Sample Unit Project 教学单元综合项目测试例案

Unit Ten Project A：My Medical History

第十教学单元综合项目（一）：我的健康史

描述身体状况和病史及一次具体的得病经过。

Format：

Oral and written presentation

- With a PowerPoint presentation or artistic displays

Topic：

Physical attributes and medical records

Content：

- General self-introduction
  Name, age, address, hobbies, etc.
- Physical condition
  Height, weight, heart rate, blood pressure, body temperature, etc.
- Medical history
  Personal medical history
  Family medical history
- An incident of illness and treatment

Cause and symptoms

Visiting a doctor

Current situation

- Positive and negative forms of all sentence patterns
- Complex sentences
- Questions and answers
- Three questions for listening comprehension

Evaluation:

- Content knowledge:

  Linguistic components

  Functional use of the language

  Mechanics (grammatical and technical errors)

- Creativity in presentation:

  Overall design

  Visual aids or artistic expressions

- Delivery:

  Pronunciation, tones and fluency

  Organization of information

  Presentation

  Reference

- Effort

Unit Ten Project B: I Have Been...

第十教学单元综合项目（二）：我曾经……

描述经历，具体发生的时间、地点、方式和经过。

Format:

Oral and written presentation

- A story book or a PowerPoint presentation

Topic:

Past experience and stories

Content:

- A brief self-introduction

- Past experiences
  What, How many times?
- Specific events
  What, when, where, how
- Conclusion and comments
- Positive and negative forms of all sentence patterns
- Complex sentences
- Questions and answers
- Three questions for listening comprehension

Evaluation:

- Content knowledge:
  Linguistic components
  Functional use of the language
  Mechanics (grammatical and technical errors)
- Creativity in presentation:
  Overall design
  Visual aids or artistic expressions
- Delivery:
  Pronunciation, tones and fluency
  Organization of information
  Presentation
  Reference
- Effort

Unit Ten Project C: Hospital Visit
第十教学单元综合项目（三）：看病

描述个人身体状况、病史、一次看病的经历和结果以及与大夫的对话。

Format:

Oral and written presentation

- A dialogue, a narration and a PowerPoint presentation or other artistic displays

Topic:

Visiting a doctor

Content:

- Narration:
  - General self-introduction:
    - Name, age, address, hobbies, etc.
  - Physical condition:
    - Height, weight, heart beat, blood pressure, body temperature, etc.
  - Medical history:
    - Personal medical history
    - Family medical history
  - An incident of illness and treatment:
    - Cause, sympotoms, visit a doctor, current situation
- Dialogue:
  - Doctor's questions and advice
  - Patient's questions and answers to the doctor
- Positive and negative forms of all sentence patterns
- Complex sentences
- Questions and answers
- Three questions for listening comprehension

Evaluation:

- Content knowledge:
  - Linguistic components
  - Functional use of the language
  - Mechanics (grammatical and technical errors)
- Creativity in presentation:
  - Overall design
  - Visual aids or artistic expressions
- Delivery:
  - Pronunciation, tones and fluency
  - Organization of information
  - Presentation
  - Reference
- Effort

Writing Sample 1　范文（一）

Visiting a Doctor Ⅰ　看病Ⅰ

病人

- 我的名字叫岚岚。我 17 岁。我住在 M 街 123 号。
- 我的身高是 1.59 米。我的体重是 61 公斤。我的心跳每分钟 73 次。

病史

- 我伤过两次脚。我得过眼睛疼。
- 我哥哥得过过敏。我爷爷和妈妈有关节炎。我爸爸有高血压。

我脚疼

我脚疼。我在 Diversions 玩电动的时候。我摔了所以伤了脚。脚疼了一个星期了。以前我没伤过脚。以前我伤过手，我没伤过别的身体部位。这是第一次我伤了我的脚。

因为我的脚很疼所以我不高兴。因为我不能走路所以我生气。因为我不能跑步，所以我的体育课的老师发怒了。我告诉妈妈我脚疼。我妈妈和我去看病了。我妈妈是开车带我去医院的。我听说爸爸说我是装的。

我来到医院，我问大夫我怎么了？大夫给我吃药，可是药不管用。大夫问了另一个大夫。另一个大夫给我透了视。我伤了脚。我吃了止疼片。一天两次，一次一片。现在我好多了。我不着急了。

(By Heleina C. , Northside College Preparatory High School, Chinese 3)

Writing Sample 2　范文（二）

Visiting a Doctor Ⅱ　看病Ⅱ

我跟大夫的对话

大夫：你好吗？

病人：我不好！

大夫：你怎么了？

病人：我有病了。

大夫：你哪儿不舒服?

病人：我后背疼极了！

大夫：你后背疼了多长时间了?

病人：疼了一天了。

大夫：我给你检查检查。

继续谈话

大夫：你还有哪儿不舒服?

病人：我尿不出来。我小便的时候，我疼。

大夫：我想你得了肾炎。你以前疼过吗?

病人：我没有得过肾炎。

大夫：我给你开抗菌素和激素。抗菌素一天吃三次，一次一片。激素一天一 次，一次一片。要多喝水，好好休息。

(By Merisa B. , Northside College Preparatory High School, Chinese 3)

Reference

建议参考资料

This series focuses on concrete examples and practical tips for classroom teaching and learning. For teachers who are interested in current research, theoretical frameworks and further guidance and tools, we provide a topical list of references.

这套书主要是为初高中学汉语课堂教与学提供操作实例和具体技巧。都是经验之谈。对相关教学研究、教学理论或纲要及工具有兴趣的老师,可参阅下列书目和网址。参考资料也是按题目排列的。

Adolescent Psychology

Rice, F. Philip. *The Adolescent — Development, Relationships, and Culture.* Needham Height, MA: Allyn & Bacon, 1999.

Assessment and Rubric

Bachman, L. F. & A. S. Palmer. *Language Testing in Practice.* Oxford: Oxford University Press, 1996.

Pearson Education Development Group. *Authentic Assessment Overview.* Retrieved from http://teachervision. fen. com/teaching-methods/educational-testing/4911. html

Chicago Public Schools. *The Rubric Bank.* Retrieved from http://www. cps. k12. il. us

The Web Portal for Educators! At http://www. teach-nology. com

Oral Language Assessment — *Oral Proficiency Interview (OPI)* and Written Language Assessment — *Written Proficiency Test* (*WPT*). Retrieved from http://www.languagetesting.com

Hancock, Charles R. *Alternative Assessment and Second Language.* ERIC Clearinghouse on Languages and Linguistics Washington D. C., 1994.

Baker, E. L., O'Neill, H. F., Jr., & Linn, R. L. (1993). Policy and validity prospects for performance-based assessments. *American Psychologist*, *48*, 1210 – 1218.

U. S. Congress, Office of Technology Assessment. (1992, February). *Testing in American schools: Asking the right questions.* (OTA-SET-519). Washington, D. C.: U. S. Government Printing Office.

Bloom's Taxonomy

Bloom, Benjamin S. *Taxonomy of Educational Objectives.* Boston MA: Allyn & Bacon, 1984.

Differentiated Instruction

Tomlinson, C. *How to Differentiate Instruction in Mixed-ability Classrooms.* Alexandria, VA: ASCD, 1995.

Tomlinson, C. *The Differentiated Classroom: Responding to the Needs of All Learners.* Alexandria, VA: ASCD, 1999.

Wiggins, G. & McTighe, J. *Understanding by Design.* Alexandria, VA: ASCD, 1998.

Chinese Grammar

黎锦熙,刘世儒.《汉语语法十八课》. 北京:商务印书馆,1964.

李德津,程美珍.《外国人实用汉语语法》. 北京:华语教学出版社,1988.

Cooperative Learning

Silver , Strong, & Perini. *So Each May Learn*, *Alexandria.* VA: Association for

Supervision and Curriculum Development, 2000.

David & Roger Johnson. *Learning Together and Alone.* NJ: Prentice Hall, 1999.

Foreign Language Teaching and Learning Standards

ACTFL Foreign Language Learning Standards. Retrieved from http://www.actfl.org

ACTFL Performance Guidelines for K-12 Learners. Yonkers, NY: The American Council on the Teaching of Foreign Languages, 1998.

Language Learning

Curtain, H. & Carol Ann Dahlberg. *Language and Children — Making the Match.* Boston: Pearson Education, Inc., 2004.

Learning

Sousa, David A. *How the Brain Learns.* NASSP, VA: Corwin Press, 2000.

Multiple Intelligences

Gardner, Howard. *Frames of Mind: The Theory of Multiple Intelligences.* New York: Basic, 1983.

Gardner, Howard. *Multiple Intelligences: The Theory in Practice.* New York: Basic, 1993.

Gardner, Howard. *Intelligence Reframed: Multiple Intelligences for the 21st Century.* New York: Basic, 2000

Armstrong, Thomas. *Multiple Intelligences in the Classroom.* Alexandria, VA: Association for Supervision and Curriculum Development, 1994.

Problem Solving

Stanovich, Keith E. *Progress in Understanding Reading: Scientific Foundations and New Frontiers.* New York: Gilford Press, 2000.

Woll, Stanley. *Everyday Thinking: Memory, Reasoning, and Judgment in the Real World.* Mahwah NJ: Lawrence Erlbaum Associates, Inc., 2001.

Reading

Koda, Keiko Koda. *Insights into Second Language Reading.* Cambridge: Cambridge University Press, 2005.

Alderson, C. *Assessing Reading.* New York: Cambridge University Press, 2000.

Day, R. R. & Bamford, J. *Extensive Reading in the Second Language Classroom.* New York: Cambridge University Press, 1998.

Grabe, W. & Stoller, F. *Teaching and Researching Reading: Applied Linguistics in Action.* New York: Longman, 2002.

Pressley, M. *Reading Instruction that Works.* New York: Guilford, 1998.

Reading Critically. Reading Guide. Retrieved from http://writing.colostate.edu/guides/reading/critread/pop4b.cfm

Student-Centered Learning

Aaronsohn, Elizabeth. *Going Against the Grain: Supporting the Student-Centered Teacher.* Thousand Oaks: Corwin Press. 1996.

Benson, P. & Voller, P. *Autonomy and Independence in Language Learning.* London: Longman, 1996.

Tudor, I. *Learner-Centeredness as Language Education.* Cambridge: Cambridge University Press, 1996.

Task-based Learning

Krashen, S. D. *Principles and Practices in Second Language Acquisition.* New York: Prentice Hall, 1987.

Willis, J. A *Framework for Tasked-Based Learning.* London: Longman, 1996.

Thematic Instruction

Bruning, R. H., Schraw, G. J., & Ronning, R. R. *Cognitive Psychology and Instruction*. Englewood Cliffs, NJ: Merrill, 1999.

Vogt, M. (1997). *Cross-Curricular Thematic Instruction*. Retrieved from http://www.eduplace.com/rdg/res/vogt.html

National Standards in Foreign Language Education Project. (1996). Retrieved from http://www.actfl.org

TPR

Seely & Elizabeth Kuizenga Romijn. *TPR is More Than Commands — At All Levels*. Berkeley California, 1995.

US Department of Education — Teacher to Teacher Initiative Workshops on Chinese Language Teaching. (2006). Retrieved from http://www.t2tweb.us/Workshops/Sessions.asp

Bibliography
参考书目

ACTFL Foreign Language Learning Standards. Retrieved from http://www.actfl.org

Bachman, L. F. & A. S. Palmer. *Language Testing in Practice.* Oxford: Oxford University Press, 1996.

Bloom, Benjamin S. *Taxonomy of Educational Objectives.* Boston MA: Allyn & Bacon, 1984.

Chicago Public Schools. *The Rubric Bank.* Retrieved from http://www.cps.k12.il.us

Curtain, H. & Carol Ann Dahlberg. *Language and Children — Making the Match.* Boston: Pearson Education, Inc., 2004.

Krashen, S. D. *Principles and Practices in Second Language Acquisition.* New York: Prentice Hall, 1987.

黎锦熙,刘世儒.《汉语语法十八课》.北京:商务印书馆,1964.

Rice, F. Philip. *The Adolescent — Development, Relationships, and Culture.* Needham Height, MA: Allyn & Bacon, 1999.

Silver , Strong, & Perini. *So Each May Learn.* Alexandria, VA: Association for Supervision and Curriculum Development, 2000.

The Web Portal for Educators! At http://www.teach-nology.com

US Department of Education — Teacher to Teacher Initiative Workshops on Chinese Language Teaching. (2006). Retrieved from http://www.t2tweb.us/Workshops/Sessions.asp